FROM MAUMEE TO THAMES AND TIBER

BY THE SAME AUTHOR
Testimonium Animae, 1908
Annals of Caesar, 1911
Cicero of Arpinum, 1914
Hellenic Civilization (with G. W. Botsford), 1915
From Augustus to Augustine, 1923

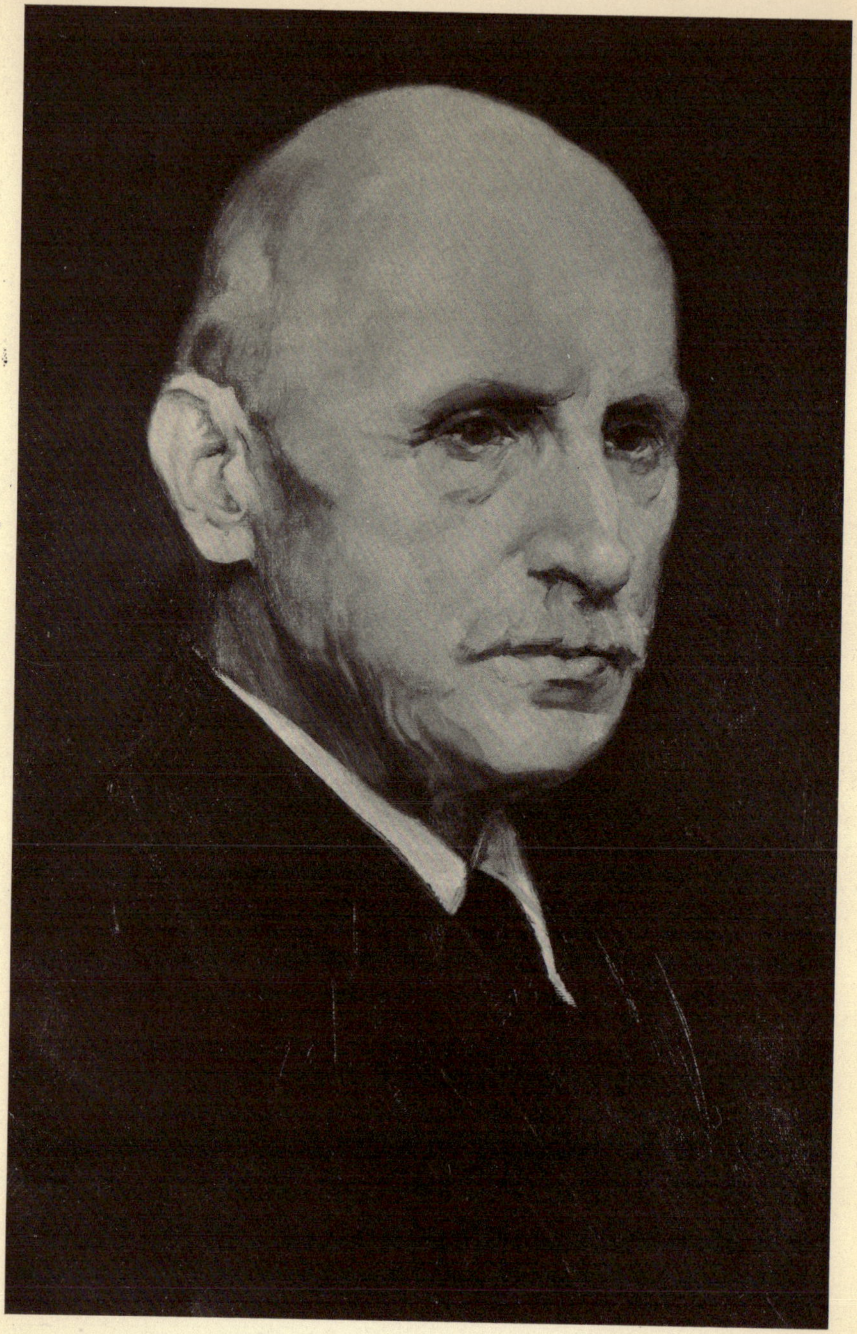

FROM MAUMEE TO THAMES AND TIBER

The Life-Story of an American Classical Scholar

"*And gladly wolde he lerne and gladly teche*"

By

ERNEST G. SIHLER

Ph.D., *Johns Hopkins, 1878*; Hon. Litt.D., *Lafayette, 1915*
Professor Emeritus of the Latin Language and Literature
New York University

THE NEW YORK UNIVERSITY PRESS
WASHINGTON SQUARE EAST, NEW YORK CITY
1930

COPYRIGHT 1930 BY NEW YORK UNIVERSITY

THE NEW YORK UNIVERSITY PRESS
Arthur Huntington Nason, Ph.D., Director

PRINTED IN THE UNITED STATES OF AMERICA
PRINTING HOUSE OF WILLIAM EDWIN RUDGE
MOUNT VERNON, N. Y.

TO NEW YORK UNIVERSITY

PAST, PRESENT, AND FUTURE

AND TO THE CLASSICAL TEACHERS OF AMERICA

THIS BIOGRAPHY IS INSCRIBED

BY

ERNEST G. SIHLER

PREFACE

Since completing three-score years and ten, I have been urged by many scholars of our land, among them many former pupils, and also by one very eminent classicist of Europe, to write the story of my life. Now a scholar's life, if viewed from the conventional distance, and labeled in advance, does seem to be far from adventure, romance, or struggles—a peaceful passing through existence amid books, students, and lectures. Mine was not. The "purely human" elements, with many an outlook into contemporary history, will be given fully. The obstacles and trials will be told, the sombre and severe stages in my journey, as well as many apparently "little things," out of which, after all, so much of life is woven together on the loom of many years. It is a long span of time from the first election of Abraham Lincoln to the last year of Calvin Coolidge. In my early life, I read history with passionate fondness and was an honest Carlylean hero-worshipper; in the maturer years, I became a critical student of great historians from Herodotus to Leopold von Ranke.

I trust that I may deserve for my story, which embraces two continents, the attention and good-will of my fellow workers in the academic life of America. Perhaps some British and German classicists may read this volume, and learn that even in America there are some lives not set upon the accumulation of wealth or the gaining of political honors, indifferent to the changing breezes of the *popularis aura*.

E. G. S.

New York University,
Spring, 1929.

CONTENTS

CHAPTER		PAGE
I.	My Forebears	3
II.	The Parsonage of St. Paul's and Primeval Fort Wayne, 1853–69	13
III.	The Concordia Gymnasium at Fort Wayne, 1862–69	29
IV.	The Divinity School at St. Louis, 1869–72	43
V.	Berlin, 1872–74	53
VI.	The University of Leipzig and my Return to the Maumee, 1874–75	73
VII.	A Stern Beginning of Teaching and a Good Ending, 1875–76	85
VIII.	The Beginnings of Johns Hopkins, 1876–79	95
IX.	Hopes Deferred. The Greek Club of New York, 1879–91	117
X.	A Prelude in Wisconsin, 1891–92	139
XI.	Vita Nova. Washington Square and University Heights, 1892–1923	147
XII.	Undergraduate Teaching and Graduate Lectures, 1892–1923	167
XIII.	My First Visit to Italy and Farther, 1897	183
XIV.	The Happiness of my Seminar-Room, 1900–1923	203
XV.	From Homer to Augustine: The Chief Themes of my Pen, 1908–23	217
XVI.	De Senectute	249
	Index	261

FROM MAUMEE TO THAMES AND TIBER

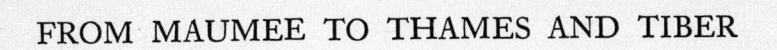

I

MY FOREBEARS

Honour thy father and thy mother.—Exodus, 20, 12.

My family name, *Sihler*, is derived from a Swiss river, the *Sihl*, an affluent of the Limmat; both enter the lake of Zurich. An entire quarter of that noted city of German Switzerland is called *Aussersihl*. There are also in Zurich a *Sihlquai* and a *Sihlhofstrasse*. Some twelve miles south is the station *Sihlbrugg* on the *Sihlthal* railway. Clearly my ancestors were farmers or herdsmen living on that stream, but the name itself seems to be defunct, as I ascertained on a visit in 1909. One of the Sihlers emigrated to Württemberg and settled in Blaubeuren, a small town west of Ulm. Here my paternal grandfather, Christian George Sihler, was born in 1752, but he did not remain there. After growing up, he enlisted in a cavalry regiment of Prussia, during the later reign of Frederick the Great. It was the regiment called Ploetz Hussars. Here my grandfather ultimately reached the rank of Lieutenant, rising from the ranks, a rare achievement in those days. He had three sons, all Prussians by birth. The eldest, Frederick, born in 1778, also became a Prussian officer; but after the family had been knighted by royal patent in 1804, he married a lady of an old Silesian family, a Fräulein von Heydebrand, on February 5, 1805, the lady's dower being an extensive manor, or *Rittergut*, in Eastern Silesia, hard by what is now again the Polish frontier. I saw the urn on his grave and that of his wife on a visit in August, 1927. The manor covers some three thousand acres; great flocks of wild

FROM MAUMEE TO THAMES AND TIBER

ducks flew up from the river Bartsch as the laird, George von Heydebrand, drove me about the estate. The grave of my grandfather is not far from the manor house or *Schloss;* he died in 1828. The second of his sons, Gotthold von Sihler, served under Bülow von Dennewitz in 1813, when Prussia took the lead in throwing off the yoke of the Corsican usurper Napoleon, sometimes miscalled "the Great," as were Tamerlane and Genghis Khan.[1] Gotthold von Sihler took part in the battle of Leipzig, October 16–19, 1813, after which he followed Bülow into Holland when the French were driven out of it; but he perished in the siege of Breda, leaving no issue.

My father, Wilhelm Sihler, was a late and unexpected child, born November 12, 1801, at Bernstadt near Oels, Silesia, where his father was in garrison service. Although much spoiled in infancy and early childhood, as he often told us, in the end, I believe, he proved to be the most energetic and most gifted of all his kin. Later his father lived at Schweidnitz—in the civil service, as royal *Salzfactor*, salt then being a government monopoly in Prussia. After the battle of Jena, October, 1806, and the swift collapse of Prussia, Silesia too was soon overrun by the French; and Schweidnitz was besieged by the youngest of Napoleon's brothers, Jerome, in the latter part of the year 1806. My father, a little boy of just five, frequenting a dame-school, once observed a spent ball slowly rolling over the pavement of the marketplace; at another time he was knocked over by the horse of a hussar, but the horse leaped over the child without injuring him.

The fearful hardships and privations which the Peace of Tilsit (1807) imposed on the stricken kingdom, the bright little lad was bound to notice in his further boyhood, when the utmost frugality and Spartan simplicity

---

[1] George Washington once, when asked about imperial expansion, said: No: because it could not be maintained without two things: Force and Fear.

4

dominated court and people alike in what was left of the kingdom by the ruthless Corsican. Softness and luxury were bound to disappear.

At Schweidnitz, too, Wilhelm von Sihler attended the gymnasium. In the first little volume of his autobiography (St. Louis, 1879), he has sketched the various instructors and the Rector or headmaster. He seems to have been fully two or three years younger than his classmates, for he was graduated from *Prima* before completing his sixteenth year. He was enraptured by Homer and the gods of Greece; but mathematics were poorly taught. From a native Frenchman who lived at Schweidnitz he received private lessons in French; but, although he mastered the language quickly enough, it gave him no satisfaction, partly because his robust German feeling had an instinctive aversion to French *esprit* and partly because Napoleon's oppression lay heavily upon Prussia, and because he as a patriotic boy entertained supreme hatred for the rule of the stranger.[2] Further on, my father took hold of athletics in many forms and with a kind of Spartan devotion: skating, swimming, running, high and broad jump, also excursions and foot-tours in the environs of Schweidnitz such as the famous solitary mountain peak, the Zobten, on whose slopes he was wont to pick wild strawberries in season, or to stretch out on his back amid the wildflowers and watch the white clouds drifting in the blue. Most of the juvenile reading available in those years—apart from Robinson Crusoe—he condemned in his maturer years, especially the stories of knights and robbers.

In 1817 his father was pensioned with what was then a generous allowance, and moved to the capital of Silesia, Breslau. William, not quite sixteen, was neither ready nor willing to enter the University, but determined to enter

[2] The reader may profitably consult Gustav Freytag's historical novel *Aus einer Kleinen Stadt*.

FROM MAUMEE TO THAMES AND TIBER

the army as *avantageur*. This meant that he began as a common soldier, and later on, having had a liberal education, took the examinations, first for ensign (*Fähnrich*) and later for second lieutenant. His first superior was Major Keller, who had captured Napoleon's carriage in the rout after Waterloo, June 18, 1815. So efficient were the youth's conduct and work, as well as in his studies in the *Divisionsschule*, that at eighteen he became a second lieutenant and joined the 22nd Infantry at Neisse. Here he became an intimate friend of Lieutenant Pochhammer, whose son, many years later, in the Staff-college of Berlin, became a teacher of Strategy for men like Hindenburg, the victor of Tannenberg in August, 1914. I need not add that my father chose as friends always men of kindred aims, of serious ideals in conduct and cultural aspirations. Thus too he came to attend the Staff-college in Berlin from 1823 to 1826. Here they studied topography, tactics, history of war (with Clausewitz), fortifications, and strategy. The famous expert on geography, Carl von Ritter, who taught geography at the University, was his teacher in that branch and became his personal friend. Moltke was a classmate of my father's; also Roon. Of the former, he says in his autobiography:

> Among those who entered with me was Lieutenant von Moltke, my senior by one year, now [1879] as the world knows, a famous and historical personage. Although no personal intimacy of friendship resulted, I perfectly recall his countenance and his entire manner of appearance. . . . I was greatly impressed with the pensive seriousness evinced in Moltke's countenance, wherein he, who moreover was more pale and wan, very positively differed from the commonplace countenance of other young officers with their red cheeks and well-fed appearance.[3]

But after graduation William Sihler decided to abandon the military career and to study philosophy and philology at the University. His petition for an honor-

[3] Vol. I, p. 35.

MY FOREBEARS

able discharge addressed to Frederick William III, was granted; and this document was signed by Neidhardt von Gneisenau himself. In the summer of 1900, long after my father's death, I found this document among his papers at Fort Wayne. My father's general aim was to qualify himself to lecture on Modern Literature. So he took up Dante, Cervantes, and Shakespeare, exchanging lessons with a Mr. Montague attached to the British Embassy at Berlin. The impression of English letters then gained by him is still noteworthy: "For a German who knows Latin and has a real gift for languages, it is not difficult to master the English tongue in a short time to the point of understanding the classic works of English historians, who by their sober objectivity, often lacking to German historians, made a great impression on me, for we Germans have an inclination to intertwine our own reflections and philosophical contemplations with the course of historical happenings and so to interfere with the matter-of-fact distinctness of the same and their connection." In 1828 his father Christian G. von Sihler died in Silesia, and the paternal allowance came to a sudden end. Private pupils often provided by Carl von Ritter and other University professors provided a precarious subsistence. Still his marvelous energy found vent in a volume of essays (*Arabesken*), 1828, and in a notable work, *Symbolik des Antlitzes*, 1829, for which the University of Jena gave him the Ph.D. degree.

In 1830 came an incisive event in his life. He became an instructor or *Erzieher* in the Blochmann's Institute at Dresden. Blochmann had observed the methods and principles of the famous pedagogical genius Pestalozzi at Iverdun in Switzerland where he was a pupil, and subsequently opened a preparatory school, from *Quarta* to *Prima*, at Dresden, largely a boarding-school which soon gained a European reputation. Here my father became one of the assistant masters, who not only shared the meals of the pupils, but also in a certain routine of duties slept among them. In the long vacations, foot-tours, under guidance of one of the tutors, were often undertaken, even as far as the Rhine, the Erzgebirge, "Saxon Switzerland," and the like. Of course the treasures of the Dresden Gallery were a resource of exceptional excellence, while the music of Beethoven and Bach could often be enjoyed. The home of Tieck, the translator of Shakespeare, was open to Dr. Sihler.

It was during this preceptorial period that he experienced an epochal, a spiritual change, which determined, more or less, all his coming years: in a word, he determined to make his ultimate vocation that of a Lutheran pastor. He sought and found association with other earnest Christians, many of whom had conquered the world and the vanities ever bound up with it. Further, too, Dr. Sihler more and more became hostile to the principles and certain phenomena inherent in a state-church and hostile too to the so-called Union superimposed on Lutherans and Reformed, since 1817, by the Prussian Government.

In 1838, Dr. Sihler resigned his position at Dresden and assumed service as a domestic tutor in the Baltic provinces of Russia, especially at Riga. Associating now in many ways with positively Christian people, he devoted himself systematically to the study of Christian doctrine and often shared in the stated conferences of Lutheran clergymen on the Baltic. For a while he looked forward to ordination at their hands. But in the spring of 1843 he chanced upon a pamphlet calling in strong appeal for Lutheran Missionaries to serve the German settlers in the West of the United States, in what we now call the Middle West. He determined suddenly but irrevocably to enter that service. Political sympathies had nothing whatever to do with that resolution. He was fully aware that

MY FOREBEARS

privation and hardship would be his lot if he went. Both the Lutheran Missionary Society of Riga and that of Dresden — of which he was a member — furnished his equipment to sail to the Western World, into a field absolutely unknown and a career devoid of all worldly prospects. He owed much in this period of preparation to an eminent Lutheran scholar, Dr. Rudelbach of Glauchau, Saxony, who in a measure had guided Dr. Sihler's theological studies. Before embarking at Bremen, the expectant Lutheran Missionary visited the noted Christian leader, Reverend W. Löhe, in Franconia, near Erlangen, who had been vigorously supporting the spiritual concerns of Lutherans emigrating to America, some of whom had already settled in Ohio. A few years later, Löhe furnished in great part the means for the establishment of a theological seminary in the little frontier town of Fort Wayne, in 1846, under Dr. Sihler's direction. From Dresden to Brunswick, Dr. Sihler could avail himself of the new railway; the rest of the journey to Hanover and Bremen, the post-coach still had to serve. The ship in which he sailed from Bremerhaven to New York on September 17, 1843, was the *Caroline*, Captain Volkmann, who repeatedly invited the new missionary to preach on deck. Dr. Sihler also gave lessons to the children of the emigrants. On November 1, 1843, he landed in New York. Almost forty-two years of great and ever-widening service lay before him, more than four decades of devoted spiritual labor; but he never returned, or cared to return, to his ancestral land, closing his life eventually in his modest little chamber in St. Paul's parsonage, Fort Wayne, on October 27, 1885. His first charge, largely among coal-miners, was at Pomeroy, Ohio, from January 1, 1844, to July, 1845. He then accepted a call to Fort Wayne, having declined vocations to many more notable places.[4]

[4] Such as Boston, Milwaukee, Chicago, Allegheny City, and Dayton.

FROM MAUMEE TO THAMES AND TIBER

That place then was a small town of barely four thousand inhabitants, but also a missionary post for work among German immigrants, notable through the labors of Pastor Wyneken, the Hanoverian pioneer whose Macedonian call had drawn William Sihler across the Atlantic— Wyneken, whom, when a little boy, I was wont to call "Uncle Wyneken."

In 1845-46 Sihler joined hands with the Saxon immigrants of St. Louis, and on Jubilate Sunday, 1847, at Chicago, helped to found and organize the Evangelical Lutheran Synod of Missouri, Ohio, and other States, which to-day has grown into a body of some three thousand pastors and congregations, extending from coast to coast, and from Alberta to the Rio Grande, doing more for spiritual ends and for sound education than I have here space to tell; its missions have gone into Brazil, Argentina, and Australia. To Chicago, on that important occasion, Dr. Sihler travelled on horseback, then a distance of one hundred and eighty miles, because the Kankakee swamps necessitated a wide detour—a journey of four days. To-day the fast trains of the Pennsylvania make the one hundred and forty-eight miles in three hours.

In June, 1846, the Reverend Dr. Sihler visited a settlement of Lutheran immigrants, Franconian farmers, some twenty-five miles northwest of Columbus, Ohio, and married Miss Susanna Kern. Her father in 1837 had bought there in Union County a farm of one hundred and twenty acres, near Marysville, for ten dollars an acre, but in gold, which, in that year of national panic, 1837, was very rare indeed. My mother, in the memories of her aging years, wrote that the former owner carried away his $1200.00 gold in his hat, rejoicing. Little Susan, then eight, went at the English language energetically, reading an English and German Bible jointly, in company with her older sister Margaret. Labor then was rare: Susanna

MY FOREBEARS

in 1838, at nine years of age, with a sickle helped in the cutting of the first wheat crop. Their dwelling for the first eight years was a log cabin; but in 1845 the energy of her parents had a kiln erected, and had bricks burned from their own clay, and built a commodious brick house, the first one in the settlement. Also of course they procured their own maple-syrup and maple-sugar from their own "sugar-camp," and the spinning-wheel whirled in the winter evenings. Those were hard times: apples in 1838 brought about five cents a bushel, and peaches twenty-five cents. One could still hear the panther screaming at night in the forests. Susanna rode on horseback, in 1844, to her confirmation lessons; also, often to the country store at Marysville to exchange butter and eggs for groceries. She told us of the comet of 1843. She made a pet of a young deer that came into the barnyard, and which became so tame that it even accompanied her to the district school. Finally, however, it disappeared in the forest, and perished from a hunter's gun, deeply grieving Susanna's tender heart. In that red schoolhouse, Susanna acquired English speech without any flaw in pronunciation. Even then her gentle and finer soul laid hold of nobler things always: thus she learned by heart that American idyl of the home-farm and the fond memories of childhood, the classic poem of

> The old oaken bucket,
> The ironbound bucket,
> The moss-covered bucket
> That hung in the well.

This farmer's daughter my father married in the brick house already mentioned, on June 8, 1846, the bride being seventeen and the groom forty-four.

She often told us of the Election of 1840, log cabin and hard cider: "Tippecanoe and Tyler too." Never was a bride more admirably fitted to become the helpmate of a

FROM MAUMEE TO THAMES AND TIBER

missionary and Christian organizer, in those pioneer times, than Susanna Kern. One of her sweetest spiritual traits which I like to recall was this: Apart from her incessant and wisely planned domestic industry in which she was a daily model, preaching to our young souls sermons without words, she had a winning way of teaching her rapidly growing flock contentment. She would point to many people whose living and daily resources were even more slender and precarious than our own in the parsonage of St. Paul's. She would describe the ocean voyage of 1837 in a sailing vessel, when even the water in time became almost unfit to drink. Any utterance of complaint or impatience with the *res angusta domi* in the parsonage of St. Paul's, where I was born, I do not recall.

II

THE PARSONAGE OF ST. PAUL'S AND PRIMEVAL FORT WAYNE

The child is father of the man.—Wordsworth.

As I am here entering upon the simple and still curious annals of my childhood, I pause for a general observation. *Environment*, that much quoted convenience in the zoölogical philosophy of these later times, environment, I say, had little if anything to do with those early years, and even less with the turn and direction which, I am now sure, my course of life did take at that time.

I was born on January 2, 1853, in the last months of Millard Fillmore's administration, in St. Paul's parsonage, about half a mile south of the Maumee river and the quondam site of the Fort, and was rocked in the same cradle as all of my eight brothers and sisters. To-day Anthony Wayne is officially much more honored than in my childhood, when the urgent need of daily bread left little time for historical retrospect. When I was born, the little town had barely five thousand inhabitants, whereas to-day it has attained more than one hundred thousand. I must limit myself in antiquarian matters: the Miami Indians had been the chief tribe along the Maumee. They must have in their day advanced somewhat beyond the Hunters' stage, because they planted and harvested a great deal of what we still call Indian corn: I did not know in my childhood that in England 'corn' means wheat. The Maumee itself was one of the chief delights of my childhood. Its two sources are the St. Joseph from

FROM MAUMEE TO THAMES AND TIBER

the north and the St. Marys from the southeast. Most probably French *voyageurs*, even in the eighteenth century, gave these names to the two streams, before the English wrested the continental supremacy of North America from the French: we need merely name Montcalm, Wolfe, Quebec, and the Plains of Abraham. Some of the oldest families in little old Fort Wayne were French, such as La Salle, whose fine old home in the south end I distinctly recall, and an old lawyer, "Squire" Du Bois, who still was fond of talking French, and Comparet, whose mill and warehouse were hard by the Wabash and Erie Canal, on a basin where the "packets" landed their passengers. To return to the very beginnings, in Washington's second term: the first two generals sent by Washington to cope with the troublesome Indians on the Maumee were Harmer and St. Clair, who preceded the energetic and intrepid Wayne; they failed, but both are commemorated in modern Fort Wayne by streets that bear their names. The original plotting of the town as a town was carried out by two men with Scottish names, Barr and McCorkle. They purchased a tract of land from the federal government and laid out the original 148 lots in about 1825, some twenty years before Dr. Sihler came to St. Paul's. Barr himself is curiously commemorated: both St. Paul's Lutheran church (the oldest Lutheran church in the State of Indiana) and the adjacent parsonage are on Barr Street. The chief streets of our neighborhood perfectly mark the times of 1825 or thereabouts: Washington, Jefferson, Madison, Clinton, Harrison, Columbia, Clay, Lafayette, Calhoun, Wayne. Columbia, contiguous to and parallel with the canal, was the main shopping street in my childhood, generally known as "store street": here too was the bookstore where I was fond of gazing at engravings in the show-window, such as *Evangeline* or *Daniel Boone* in the wilds of Kentucky. Later, as the

THE PARSONAGE OF ST. PAUL'S

Pittsburgh and Wabash railways were built, Calhoun Street became the chief artery for retail shopping and holds that preëminence to this day. The farmers, especially on Saturdays, were the most important customers of the storekeepers. The first school was opened in 1833 by a Mr. Aughinbaugh, clearly a Pennsylvania-German, whose ancestral name was Achenbach. The first Lutheran congregation of the little town, as well as of the State of Indiana, was St. Paul's, organized in 1837 by a young Pennsylvanian, the Reverend Jesse Hoover (Huber). Services at first were held in the original County Courthouse, a plain, one-story brick building which I distinctly remember. Pastor Hoover died in 1839. On his tombstone in Concordia cemetery, close by my father's grave, one may still read the first stanza of a noted Christian hymn, "Mir nach, spricht Christus, unser Held," a fit memorial of the brief labors of the young missionary. As time went on, both the town of Fort Wayne as well as the county of Allen, and Adams to the south, and Noble and De Kalb to the north, were largely settled, and brought into a high degree of cultivation by German immigrants. The words *settler* and *settlement* were household words in St. Paul's parsonage in my childhood. No one said: "I am going to the *country*." The term was *bush*. I was always happy when I could go "to the bush," "Lange's bush."

I now cite from the *History of Fort Wayne*, by Wallace A. Brice, published in 1868:

Many of the German settlers have now been here between thirty and forty years, some of them poling their way at the period of their coming to this point, up the Maumee in pirogues [flatboats] to the then village of Fort Wayne—all quite poor in means, but able of hand and willing of heart, to *work*—to till the soil and build themselves homes. Such are the Germans of Fort Wayne; and may their better sense of frugality, perseverance, integrity and general spirit of industry and philanthropic liberality ever serve as worthy examples of emulation and regard for the generations to come.[1]

[1] *Op. cit.*, appendix, pp. 29–30.

FROM MAUMEE TO THAMES AND TIBER

I now return to my own memories. Although the bulk of the German settlers came from Westphalia and Hanover, *every* part of Germany was represented, from East Prussia to the Rhine, from Bremen to the Black Forest; so that as a young boy I became familiar with the dialects of Mecklenburg and Pomerania, of Bremen and Minden— the latter a veritable hive of ever more newcomers—of Bavaria and with the guttural articulation of the Swiss. All this was especially notable on market days, particularly on Saturdays, when the seasons in their order presented their gifts: watercress, dairy products, the various berries and currants, "roasting ears," cauliflower and every form of vegetables, apples, plums, peaches, pears, grapes, and melons late in October. Many of the farmers were also florists; and everything was fairly within the purse of all: a market-basket belonged to the equipment of every household.

My father aided the newcomers in every way, advising them as to the various settlements, while he himself organized Lutheran congregations in all directions and installed pastors trained in the Theological Seminary under his guidance, as noted before, visiting, counselling, encouraging: apostolic work in the best sense of the word. Often he made long tours, sometimes in his buggy, sometimes in the saddle, raising funds also for the new Seminary property a mile east of St. Paul's, purchased from the miller Wines in the later forties. My mother, an expert in English, was present when the deeds were passed, and told me later.

To-day Fort Wayne has more than 100,000 inhabitants, 65,000 of German stock, and, of the remaining 35,000, the bulk are of Irish race. Still the assimilative process of two generations has fully Americanized them; Italians and Slavs being few and far between. Still ancestral self-respect is a mighty force. I will urge one fact, often for-

THE PARSONAGE OF ST. PAUL'S

gotten. Fairly one half of the "Middle West," rating it from Western Ohio to Nebraska, has been turned into garden and granary, from primeval forest or virgin prairie, largely by German and Scandinavian immigrants. Of my childhood days, I remember a solitary Indian, who had a farm on the St. Marys: I think he was called "Godfrey." It was said that, when he brought cordwood to town, the money was soon spent for "firewater."

To-day one may walk about Fort Wayne and rarely hear any utterance but English, but the physiognomies are largely Teutonic. Taking almost any German name of my childhood days and consulting the current directories, in 1925, I made a curious observation. The leading and ruling families, the "First Families" of that distant past, have moved elsewhere or have left no descendants. In my childhood days they ruled town and county. I will name some of the aristocrats of my childhood: Edgerton, Hamilton, Williams, Breckenridge, Hanna, Edsall, Olds, Fleming, Bass,[2] Hoagland, Colerick, and especially McCulloch.[3] On the other hand, with a recent directory before me, I readily identify scores of names of sixty-five to seventy years ago: those ending on *meyer*, a sure sign of Westphalian origin—Ahlersmeyer, Kammeyer, Kahmeyer, Seemeyer, Homeyer; plain Meyer, Meier, or Myer and Myers, more than one hundred appear. In my childhood there was one Rodenbeck family; now I find twenty-eight; Walda two, now fourteen. Similar are the data of families like Lepper, Korte, Kramer, Mensing, Krause, Krudop, Baade, Hilker, Goeglein, Goebel, Prange, Franke, Foellinger, Lauer. The Dutch *Vans* are well represented, also the Scottish *Macs*.

As a young boy, say in February or March when forests are leafless, when standing at the intersection of

---
[2] Famous for his car-wheel factory.
[3] Hon. Hugh McCulloch was Secretary of the Treasury under Andrew Johnson.

FROM MAUMEE TO THAMES AND TIBER

Washington and Barr Streets, scanning the horizon in all the four directions, I found my vision limited by forests. It was all "bush." My mother's kinsfolk all followed her from Union County, Ohio, to Allen County, Indiana. I remember distinctly the arrival of my Uncle Jacob in a huge moving-wagon covered with canvas, a so-called "Prairie Schooner." As a rule they began as "renters," giving one third of their crops to the owners of the farm; but in time they all became landed proprietors in their own right, leaving extensive farms and good homesteads to their offspring. My favorite visits, when going into the "bush," were made to Uncle Jacob and Aunt Margaret. At first, as "renters," they lived in a log cabin: the well nearby held water of sulphurous taste, with a moss-covered bucket. I fought shy of the water, preferring the dairy products which were there in great abundance, or the "light-cakes." The radishes in the garden and the dahlias I have not forgotten, or bringing the horses from the pasture, while riding on them and crossing a creek without any bridge. From later July onward I rejoiced in the gifts of Pomona. I have rarely known a more excellent apple orchard: "Early Harvests," "Seek no Furthers," "Roman Knights," "Bell Flower" (Belle Fleur), "Maiden Blushes," "Pippins," "Russets," "Rhode Island Greenings," "Pound Sweets" (which I disliked, they were so insipid), "Rambos," and many others. In the attic there was a spinning-wheel brought from Ohio.

In the parsonage at home, living of course was plain, an economic necessity, as my mother's allowance was slender. Except Sundays, she baked cornbread every morning, of an excellence that I have rarely met again: the boys got the *corner pieces* on Mondays, Wednesdays, and Fridays; the girls, on the three other days. My dear mother practiced all the domestic economies which she had learned on the farm in Ohio. Our kitchen was so built as to cover the

THE PARSONAGE OF ST. PAUL'S

cistern, and was contiguous to a regular oven of goodly dimensions; and on Saturdays when her wheat-loaves were browning, a sweet and wholesome fragrance filled kitchen and dining-room. We had a kitchen garden which produced cabbage, carrots, turnips, and currants, largely turned to currant wine, the preparation of which was a rare holiday. Mother made her own sauerkraut, her own laundry-soap, using lye gained through the ash-barrel near the kitchen—wood-ashes of course. She even made the Christmas candles by melting wax and pouring it into moulds, wax candles adorning the Christmas tree, that made the very parlor fragrant. We always had a cow; also, for many years, a sty for pigs at the rear of the garden. The slaughtering-day generally came in February. Soon after breakfast appeared Mr. H., a member of St. Paul's, with his keen tools: the screams of the dying swine always stirred my horror and pity. In the evening there was sausage-making in the kitchen, at which we children gladly assisted. We also had a "smoke-house." Of course father in his study was not disturbed. In the cellar there were spacious boxes and barrels, for apples, potatoes, turnips, cabbages, and other winter stores.

One day in summer of 1858—during Buchanan's administration—my father called me from my playing, took me on his lap, and opened a spelling-book. In a very short time I learned to spell and to read—the whole to me was a delightful diversion. I was proud and happy. There began my real living. In the autumn of that year, I was enrolled in the elementary class of St. Paul's Christian day-school. I was eager and ambitious, determined to excel. There were then three classes, of two years each, called the "Little School," "Middle School," and "Big School." The masters of the first and third class were apt and devoted pedagogues. Johann Georg Wolf, my first teacher (1858–1860), was a man of great spiritual earnestness and a pattern of Christian virtues: with him, lying or any form of insincerity or weak excuses were impossible. By his example he taught me more than primers or elementary arithmetic or Bible story. He passed away in a smallpox epidemic in the spring of 1862. I bless his memory with deep reverence. In the "Middle School," Easter 1860 to Easter 1862, I had a curious experience. When the little folk often stood up and held out their hands to the switch ever ready over Mr. Wilde's desk, I quietly read and reread my copy of Wackernagel's *Lesebuch* (reader), first volume. That book I have honored ever since, and so too the great Germanist who chose and arranged the materials presented in that exquisite anthology of prose and verse. It is meant for young readers and still it harbors nothing childish, presents nothing but what is pure and noble, stimulating, suggestive, and faultless—a youth's classic. I must beg leave here to dwell on this particular book, for, looking back on a long life, I now see in Wackernagel the first and enduring influence that really marked an epoch in my life and growth, although I could not then know it. Of course I readily admit, there must be some affinity between a young mind and the nurture on which a young mind feeds. My English primer in comparison was infantile. I remember a poem:

> I had a little pony, his name was Dapple Gray,
> I lent him to a lady, to ride a mile away.
> She whipped him, she lashed him, she rode him through the mire,
> I never would my pony lend for all the lady's hire.

But to return to Wackernagel: I received a noble standard which made me immune, later on, to dime novels and kindred fodder. Things vicious and vile or mere sawdust pretending to be food touched me but slightly or not at all. Somehow, through Wackernagel, I gained an instinctive and true feeling for what was noble and wholesome, even when it was not so fascinating as *Robinson Crusoe*. This

THE PARSONAGE OF ST. PAUL'S

came into my life on the Christmas table in an abbreviated German form enriched with excellent woodcuts, where even the dress of Defoe's age was perfectly drawn. The rapture in my soul when finally Friday came into that solitary life, cannot be described. But to return to my Wackernagel: it was and is indeed a Golden Treasury more comprehensive than Palgrave's famous collection. Here there passed into permanent possession not only some of the exquisite fairy tales gathered by the greatest of Germanists, Jacob and Wilhelm Grimm, but veritable pearls of German letters from the Nibelungen onward: Luther, Gellert, Schubert, Hans Sachs, Goethe, Schiller's ballads, Uhlands ballads and lyrics, Hebel, Chamisso, Bürger, Claudius, Pestalozzi, Novalis, W. Müller (*Griechenlieder*), and many others. My young soul was purely receptive and untroubled by critical analysis. Matrons sometimes preserve the dolls of their childhood, but these noble selections, on the whole, please me as much now when I am old, as they did then, in the long ago, at the beginning of the Civil War. I cannot, in glancing at those distant and happy years, forego citing a few stanzas from Rückert's *Aus der Jugendzeit:*

> Aus der Jugendzeit, aus der Jugendzeit
> Klingt ein Lied mir immerdar;
> O wie liegt so weit, o wie liegt so weit
> Was mein einst war!
>
> O du Heimatflur, o du Heimatflur,
> Lass zu deinem heiligen Raum
> Mich noch einmal nur, mich noch einmal nur,
> Entfliehn im Traum!

Now Melpomene did not bend over my cradle, while Kleio did; but I too, in mature life, wrote a short lyric on the sweet and fleet memories of childhood:

> Fair and fairy time of childhood's distant day—
> Day of bliss and beauty, must you pass away?

FROM MAUMEE TO THAMES AND TIBER

> Fragrance fainting from the air,
> Dulcet timbrels ring no more:
> Closed for me and closed forever—but in dreams—
> That distant door.

But there was another element in Wackernagel that engaged my liveliest sympathies: the patriotic verse of Prussia, especially of the uprising against Napoleon's cruel oppression, and the years of delivery, 1813–1815, whereby the names of Blücher, Scharnhorst, Gneisenau, and others were hallowed and enshrined in my young soul. So deeply did the martial lyrics by Körner, Eichendorff, Schenkendorf, and especially by the German Tyrtaeus, Ernst Moritz Arndt, impress those early years that I know many of them by heart even now.

From these secular poems there is but one step to hymnology: in domestic prayers, in the parsonage, my father had a way, after scripture reading, of having us sing the great chorals of Luther, Paul Gerhardt, and many others, in consonance with the church year, long before I even knew the name of Johann Sebastian Bach. In time I was privileged to accompany these matutinal and vesper singings on a modest little melodeon, and so, without being aware of it, I gained a practical mastery of harmony, which in time embellished my own domestic life when I myself became a housefather. Of course I must not omit here the intense anticipatory happiness of the Christmas season, how I would count the days from the first Sunday in Advent to Christmas eve, when my oldest brother rang the bell, and we, speechless with joy, filed into the parlor, ordinarily reserved as guest-chamber for the many clerical visitors of my father, and grouped ourselves around the festal pine tree with its garlands and sweets, and intoned Martin Luther's Christmas hymn

> Gelobet seist Du, Jesus Christ,
> Dass du Mensch geboren bist.

THE PARSONAGE OF ST. PAUL'S

On the eve of the three great holidays of the Christian year, Christmas, Easter, and Pentecost, there was a beautiful custom at St. Paul's to "ring in" these festivals. St. Paul's had three noble bells cast for the congregation. All three bells were rung together, *three times*; and all three bells *once* every Saturday evening, to ring in the Sunday. My youngest sister, Mrs. Lily Sihler Bowerfind, in 1906 wrote a poem which she called "Memories," which at this point of my own memories may find a place of almost ideal fitness:

> Often in the strife of living,
> Faith assailed and heart depressed,
> There come gently o'er me stealing
> Thoughts of home that bring me rest.
> Suddenly there comes a ringing,
> Swinging, until I believe
> That I hear the rhythmic chiming
> Of those bells on Sabbath eve.
>
> With their glad yet solemn measure,
> How those bells did swing and ring!
> Telling of that heavenly treasure,
> Christ in manger, yet a king.
> And my heart goes upward swinging
> With the bells and I receive
> In my heart the soothing comfort
> Of those chimes on Sabbath eve.
>
> Blessed thoughts of childhood thronging,
> Let them, Lord, be not in vain;
> Come and still that untold longing;
> Let me be a child again.
> Let my thoughts go upward winging,
> Saying: "Lord I do believe,"
> Till I hear the angels singing
> On that last great Sabbath eve.

The most notable and most frequented service at St. Paul's[4] during the entire church-year was, and still is, "die

---

[4] Now a noble Gothic edifice seating some 1600 worshippers.

Christmette" (Christmas matins) at six o'clock in the morning of the birthday of the Christ-child, the singing largely done by the children specially trained in classes; and at the end of that unique service the teachers were remembered with Christmas presents. "Vom Himmel hoch da komm ich her" and many other golden hymns of Luther's church have been done into English with exquisite felicity by an Englishwoman, Catherine Winkworth. I bless her memory. Still the best of versions must limp behind the idiomatic power of the original. This matter I felt more strongly later on when I strove to become a classical scholar; and since my Berlin days (1872), I have consistently avoided all translations, especially with my students: it is like buying photographs of landscapes, instead of traversing them oneself on foot, or like buying busts when one may directly converse with the minds represented by the busts, and receive from them the best of their lives and achievement.

To mention Luther, the greatest, I think, of all Germans, is to return to my father's study, where the works of the great reformer were much turned over. The study was always a commodious and well-appointed room even in those pioneer times; and I rarely dared to enter without first knocking. In winter, when I often got wet feet in the slush or when storming a fort made from pressed cubes of snow, I was apt to suffer from certain complaints brought on by these winter sports—rubbers being then unknown to me—which kept me from school. In such emergencies I was made free of my father's sofa; and, while his restless and energetic pen drove across the pages of his sermons or correspondence, my eyes would wander about the pattern of the wall-paper to the engravings of the leaders at Wittenberg which adorned the study: Luther, Melanchthon, Bugenhagen, Justus Jonas, the Saxon Elector who sheltered the Reformation, Philip of Hesse, and others. Par-

THE PARSONAGE OF ST. PAUL'S

ticularly was there one picture, where Luther, still in his monastic habit, is preaching at Möhra, a village near his birthplace; his audience plain folk under the village trees, peasants and miners, with women and children, especially an old grandame, she alone sitting, while her little grandson stands by her, holding her crutch.

In summer-time my father was wont to bathe and swim in the Maumee, as in his youth he had done in the Oder. He drove in his buggy very early before breakfast across Clay Street bridge and then along the farmer's road skirting the river, then turned aside and hitched the horse to some elm or sycamore. I watched his powerful strokes with envious admiration. Never did I see an amateur swimmer cover more distance with fewer strokes. In time I strove to imitate him, but I never attained his forceful speed. Later I swam across the Mississippi, the Rhine, the Tiber.

In serious matters of discipline my father did not indeed spare the rod, but he used it wisely and rarely, not in anger and only after repeated monition. I am convinced that he had predetermined the number of strokes. These were applied with either his green or brown cowhide, his riding whips, which stood in a wooden box at the foot of one of his bookcases, a box that also held some German pipes. He was a moderate smoker, and only at ministerial conferences cigars of more than very moderate quality were provided.

He was very fond of riding, and often on horseback visited his ministerial brethren in their country charges. I liked to see him in the saddle, for he was a masterful and graceful rider. His sons in succession acted as stablegrooms. In springtime, when the country roads were very soft and miry—"gravel-roads" came later—the work of currying the faithful steed was often laborious and took much time, but, like other domestic tasks, had to be performed satisfactorily. The hayloft was above the stalls of cow and horse: when the new hay came, we had to lend a hand with the pitchfork. Often I reposed in the new hay, musing on many things. In our yard there were several good apple-trees, Rambos, and the harvesting of these in the autumn was always a pleasant family festival. One tree, near the church, bore the so-called "grindstones," which became mellow and eatable only by the following Easter.

I now come to my first contact with the political history of our wide land, the Know-Nothing Movement and the Presidential campaign of 1860. As to the first: but rarely was I sent forth on domestic errands in the latter fifties, being too small; but whenever I did sally forth, it was not a rare experience that boys on the street hooted after me, "Damned Dutchman! Damned Dutchman!" It was very much later that I began to understand the deeper source of this bitterness. Soon came the Civil War, when hundreds of thousands of German-Americans helped to preserve the Union, and the "American" Party passed into history.

Next, with much more detailed remembrance, I come to the autumn of 1860, when I was not quite eight years old. It was a Douglas rally, and the "Little Giant" himself had come to town to speak on the Fair-Grounds in his canvass against the "Railsplitter of the Sangamon." Great numbers of farmers came in—Fort Wayne was still a farmer town. Business was at a standstill. Douglas was one of the great political figures of the day; it was a great occasion for young and old. First there was a parade and procession, so-called "floats" (often drawn by four horses), on which men were pursuing their various trades: carpenters, blacksmiths, tailors, cobblers, etc. On one of the floats there was a bevy of young girls dressed in the national colors, one for each state. But one float was unique: small

THE PARSONAGE OF ST. PAUL'S

fence-rails forming a pyramid in which there crouched a black boy, making curious grimaces at the public. It was "the nigger in the woodpile," and was meant to be a challenge or defiance of the "Black Republicans." Quite near us, on Jefferson Street, was the residence of Mr. S., an architect, who had just completed the new courthouse. When the political float arrived before the house, it halted, because Mrs. S. was reported in town to be a rabid abolitionist. Most unwisely the good lady came out upon the porch and with angry words raised her fist against this provocation. Early in the afternoon, young and old wended their way westward out Main Street to the Fair-Grounds. I too, under care of my brother Christian, went with the crowd. Now in the official procession on that afternoon there was a huge sawlog drawn by six oxen; on it astraddle sat a straw figure wearing a broad straw hat. This was to represent Abraham Lincoln; and when they reached a point close to St. Marys river, the oxen were stopped and Lincoln was flung down into the stream. Of the speech of Senator Douglas, of course, I could not follow the points; but I still recall the little man with the black ringlets of long hair framing his countenance. We came home, but at sunset there was a hue and a cry: "Everybody to the Courthouse!" Again a straw figure: Abraham Lincoln was hanged in effigy. That autumn we little boys, in our primer age, at our marbles were wont to say to one another: "If the railsplitter of the Sangamon is elected President, there will be Civil War." I must not leave unrecorded the custom of that autumn called "pole-raising." Some long hickory trunk to which with iron bands a slender top-piece had been fitted, was "raised" before the house of some citizen, the higher the pole the better. At the top there floated a pennant proclaiming the ticket preferred. Quite near us was the home of a neighbor, a furniture-maker, and a member of St. Paul's. The pennant bore the names of the "Union ticket, Bell and Everett," Bell of Tennessee, Everett of Massachusetts.

Thus contemporary history, no matter how imperfectly understood, was deeply graven in the curious and questioning mind of the lad.

Of course games figured in my young life. At marbles I generally lost, and so stopped playing "for keeps." Generally I played within the spacious limits of the churchyard and the adjoining gravelled yard of the school, and in the "alley" in the rear. The favorite game in season was "Hide and Seek," or, as we called it, "Hide and Coop," and we resorted to the most difficult hiding-places, as under the old St. Paul's frame church, a dark and dusty spot. One of our devices was to exchange caps and jackets and peek around the corner of the church, to deceive the seeker. Then there were the counting-out rhymes. I will set down two:

> Monkey, monkey, barley beer,
> How many monkeys are there here?
> One, two, three,
> Out goes he!

The other one, much more used, was this:

> One ye, ury, ichory, Ann,
> Fillerson, falleson, Nicklas, John,
> Queeby, quaby, English snaby
> Stinklam, stanklam, buck! [5]

The first book that I ever read through was a juvenile, a birthday gift on my sixth birthday, January 2, 1859, *Die Nacht im Walde* (of a woodman's boy, lost in the forest and taken in by a hermit). About 10 A.M. I knocked at my father's study, and entering, I said: "Father, you may examine me about the story." Even then ambition ruled my young life.

[5] In summer 1873, when studying at the University of Berlin, I became acquainted with the Reverend John Paton, then director of the Congregational Institute at Nottingham, England, a native of Scotland. He told me that in his boyhood, in Scotland, apart from a word or two, they used the identical rhyme.

III

THE CONCORDIA GYMNASIUM AT FORT WAYNE

THE Concordia Gymnasium, now officially known as "Concordia College," grew from a very humble germ. In 1839 in Perry County, Missouri, a log cabin was built by three candidates of divinity, former students at the University of Leipzig. Their names are: Brohm, Buenger, and Fürbringer, and they were members of the Saxon Lutheran emigrant body that, in five sailing vessels specially chartered, had left Bremerhaven for New Orleans not many months before. These emigrants had this in common with the Pilgrim Fathers of Plymouth Rock, 1620: they sought religious freedom from control or interference by a state church. Furthermore, these Saxons were devoted to the Lutheran articles of faith as gathered in the "Formula of Concord," hence their fondness for the term "Concordia," as Presbyterians cherish the term "Westminster." I am not now writing a chapter of the history of Lutheranism in America, but I must set down one important fact: the founders referred to, and others who became my preceptors in the classics, were scholarly men, not half-baked products of the crude educational beginnings of the West. They had been trained at German gymnasia and subsequently studied at German universities such as Berlin, Göttingen, Leipzig, Erlangen. The Missouri Concordia had soon been transferred from Perry County to St. Louis, in organic relation and as a feeder to the Theological Seminary there established, until the Civil War in 1861 suggested a change; the classical gymnasium was transferred to Fort Wayne, while the "Practical Theological Seminary" organized by my father in 1846 was transferred from the Maumee to the Mississippi. It was the Fort Wayne Concordia which I may truthfully call the cradle spot of my intellectual life. Whether one holds in honor the Augsburg Confession, the Prayerbook of the Anglican Church, or the Westminster Catechism of Scotland, all the higher things in America have come from Europe; and the only truly indigenous and full-blooded American is the red Indian.

The Concordia of Fort Wayne, then, conforming to its German prototype, had six classes: Prima, Secunda, Tertia, Quarta, Quinta, and Sexta; but the ages of course differed greatly from the German standard. As a rule, the boys had completed their fourteenth year when they entered in September, while the "Primaners" on graduation were between twenty and twenty-one. But I was not even quite ten when my father had me join the Sexta of 1862. He was convinced that I lacked exertion and stimulus in the limitations of the elementary St. Paul's schools; to my good mother this early transfer to Latin seemed a bold educational experiment.

In February, 1862, I had my first Latin lesson at the hands of my older brother Christian. Starting with the declension of *mensa*, he, with inborn analytical trend, strove earnestly to have me grasp the following: that *mensa* had six cases and case-functions, but only three distinct forms. I could not make anything out of this—to me —tenuous and delicate differentiation, and was grieved. It was so much easier to learn rhymed rules like this one:

> Die Männer, Völker, Flüsse, Wind'
> und Monat' Masculina sind.

I was really happy and proud that I was permitted to go into Latin so early. When, in September, 1862, I joined the

THE CONCORDIA GYMNASIUM

regular Sexta, the fact of my tender years and of my relative immaturity—for one thing, in physical prowess—was ever before me and around me, never left my consciousness; it really dominated my life from 1862 to 1872. I knew, of course, that my classmates surpassed me in bodily strength and so in all games; but I was deeply determined to earn something more than their condescending tolerance, nay to compel their respect, in the work of the classroom. For seven years, from 1862 to 1869, I walked out to the college, in all seasons and all weathers. The last half-mile was then called the "Commons." In these daily walks I learned to interpret the signs of the weather. An overcoat I never had, and I became truly hardened like a Spartan. Winter often brought in its train very cold days, but not once did I stay at home on such account. There were no street-cars in that primitive age, in the town. Of course I envied the bulk of my fellow students who lived at the college. I had my dinner in the first year at the private table of the steward, a Mr. Reinke, and his energetic and resourceful spouse. In subsequent years, I sat down at noon in the general dining hall, a simple brick structure of one story, extended northward as the institution grew.

Sexta and Quinta had special duties after dinner: cleaning knives, forks, and spoons. The upperclassmen had to work in the woodyard, for coal-fires or central heating then were unknown; and in sweeping, heating, bed-making, we were rigidly trained to be our own servitors. A welcome service was that connected with the apple-harvest, when, I am compelled to remark, some of the choicer fruit found its way into the desks of the upperclassmen.

It was a bilingual existence. On the playground our language was almost exclusively English, especially when baseball began. This really began at Concordia in the autumn of 1865, after the conclusion of the Civil War. Games, especially with the town clubs, often lasted four

FROM MAUMEE TO THAMES AND TIBER

hours, from two to six P.M. I recall one when the score was 85 to 35. As the pitching then really was pitching, not throwing, somewhat like British cricket, and the batter could await what he wanted—"knee-high," "waist-high," "shoulder-high"—games of course were drawn out. I remember that once I myself made eight runs in a single game. I played centre field with the Alerts, but the crack club at Concordia was the Empires. There were no gloves in those days. The Empires generally defeated the leading town club, the Kekiongas (an Indian name of early times on the Maumee). There was an oak-tree on the diamond at Concordia; many a hit was diverted by its stout trunk and could not be fielded by the eager hands of shortstop or second base.

But I must now return to the classrooms. Not all those who were heroes on the playing-field excelled equally with book and pen and mind. Our "study-hours" on the whole were faithfully utilized. Little bands of three generally worked together: one consulting the Greek or Latin lexicon, the others writing down the vocabulary and construing. In my upperclass years, I sometimes stayed overnight in such joint labors. Once I remember, when no bed was vacant—sofas were unknown in that Spartan age—I actually passed the night on a working-table with a lexicon for my pillow.

A little before Gettysburg, on June 30, 1863, I had my first promotion from Sexta to Quinta; I was very proud and happy. The books and texts we used—apart from English and English literature — almost all were published by Weidmann of Berlin or by Teubner of Leipzig; and the instruction in the Classics was rigorously exact to a fault. The Latin work began with a *Tirocinium:* later came Nepos, Caesar, Livy, Cicero, and Horace, and Latin exercises every week both written and oral. When, in September, 1864, I entered Quarta, Greek was begun under the admirable guidance of the Director, Alexander Saxer, a Hanoverian, who, after passing through one of the best gymnasia of Berlin, had studied at Göttingen. I was then not quite twelve, while my classmates were sixteen to seventeen. I was too young to master the phonetic laws which clarify the inflection of the Greek verb. I learned my tables by rote. I could not understand why the liquid verbs have no Sigma in Future and Aorist; it was difficult too to grasp the difference between Middle and Passive, or to understand why the oblique moods of the Aorist had no past-tense meaning, but expressed merely a single act. But I was determined to succeed.

Later came the famous Greek syntax of Krüger, whose keen and laconic definitions often were beyond us. Madvig, the great Danish scholar, was my veritable daily companion for three or four years. His illustrative quotations from standard Latin authors were never accompanied by translations. Thus I gained my knowledge of Latin syntax from Latin texts, by deduction, rather than from mechanical committing of the rule. With all due respect for our own distinguished grammarians such as Gildersleeve-Lodge or George Martin Lane, I hold that Madvig's method is preferable, for it puts more genuine study on the learner. The written exercises in Tisher's *Uebungsbuch* (book of exercises) loomed very large in my Fort Wayne years, say from 1866 to 1869. There were oral parts and more elaborate "connected" pieces for written translation, handed in every week, in clean copy and faultless penmanship. Here coöperation was strictly forbidden —a rule pretty regularly obeyed. It was a matter of honor to me *never* to ask an upperclassman about a difficult passage, let alone a classmate. One of the sentences, an axiom from Cicero's pen, stuck fast and deep in my young and ambitious soul: "A laudato viro laudari summa laus est" ("To be praised by a man who has been praised is the

FROM MAUMEE TO THAMES AND TIBER

highest praise"). I will say, without excuse or apology, that this sentence became a veritable beacon in my later and maturer years.

In returning our connected pieces of Latin prose, Rector Schick merely marked the mistakes with red ink; it was for us to find the emendations. Among my classmates of Secunda and Prima, two were especially preëminent: William Hattstaedt of Monroe, Mich., and August Graebner of St. Charles, Mo. They were full three years my seniors. My keenest ambition was to equal them. When their books showed two errors to my three, I could not sleep the next night. Both have long entered the Silent Land. Professor Rudolph Lange had charge of higher mathematics. He was a close thinker and a man of ever expanding culture; but I was a wretched mathematician, a field in which my older brother Christian excelled, for he had an analytical mind, while mine, as my father was wont to observe, was more intuitive. In geometry, for instance, the only matter that I really carried away was the Pythagorean theorem, where I was aided by configuration.

In Greek, the course after the first year, inclusive of the verbs on *mi*, was: Jacob's reader, Xenophon, Homer, (Herodotus was neglected); while in Prima (1868–69) we did the *Antigone* of Sophocles and a part of Thucydides I—stiff work. In that year we witnessed a curious rivalry, calling into question the supremacy, hitherto undisputed, of Rector Schick. A new man came into the faculty. It was Professor Robert Engel, then about thirty-five, a nephew of Dr. Walther, President of the Synod, a soundly trained Leipzig classicist. With him we had a course in Quintilian. Further—what to me was absorbingly interesting—he *spoke Latin* in connection with his course. I was not troubled with his Saxon pronunciation, realizing that the thing was feasible. Hebrew came in Prima, taught very efficiently by Rector Schick. I could

THE CONCORDIA GYMNASIUM

not understand how the same form could function for Imperfect and for Future. At the end of Prima, I gathered A1 in Greek and Latin. We had a course in Logic also with Professor Lange (Drobisch's manual). Music figured much. The *whole* student body was trained in singing in the four voices—the Sextaners furnishing sopranos and altos. The general choir was trained by Conrector Achenbach, that gentle soul who had come to America from the University of Giessen. On the great festivals of the Christian year the choir was heard at St. Paul's. The finest work, as I then felt, was the *Requiem* by Mozart. We had to copy our own notes.

But these memories must not pass over the Maumee and the contiguous Erie Canal both for winter and summer; fishing, skating, and swimming. The Maumee immediately above Wines's mill-dam furnished an ideal swimming place, the season beginning May 15th and ending with the close of the school year, June 30th. The right bank was sandy and sloped gently into deeper water. We Sextaners were generally content with a modest loop, swimming out a bit beyond our depth and returning for a new start. I began to reason thus: if, instead of returning, I swim straight across, the actual swimming and the exertion will not be much more. One day I went down to the canal alone; a few strokes carried me across. It was a kind of rehearsal. On the same day, in the afternoon, I got Henry Succop of the class of 1866 to swim the river at my side; sometimes I put my left hand on his right shoulder, but not often, and so crossed to the much-coveted left bank. The very next day I achieved it alone. I was then only in my eleventh year, and I was proud and happy, as, panting, I sat on that more precipitous bank. The deeper feeling was a sense of power and the following reflection ensued: I reasoned that greater tasks must and would be accomplished by steadily growing strength, especially in

FROM MAUMEE TO THAMES AND TIBER

the domain of the mind. But in one of my earlier swimming feats I came very near to death. The miller had built a bridge of planks across the mill-race, the planks lying directly on the water. Who will dive under the bridge? So I dove in, but, O horrors! I was for a moment held fast by the branches of a tree-trunk in the bottom of the mill-race. Agony: "What will my mother say when my corpse is brought home?" With desperate energy I pushed the branches asunder, and in a moment the swift current carried me to light and life. Among our feats there was one: who can stay under water longest? We tested this by holding watches on the divers. On the further side of the mill-dam there were several very deep holes, and at the bottom of these the water was very cold. The only proof accepted by us experts that the diver really had reached bottom was that he brought up one of the big stones lodged down there. This too I accomplished. In the autumn the wild grapes on the other side were ripening; harvesting these, in the simplicity of Adamic costume, we often enjoyed, human habitations being far away. Youth will ever seek to adorn its simple life with a little adventure that makes life romantic.

Winter brought skating. The canal, of course, was the main resort for speeding on the winged steel. Near the college was a large basin; the framework of a defunct whiskey distillery stood nearby: this basin was still called the "stillery." Here ice formed soonest, and our season began soon after Thanksgiving. It ended generally soon after Washington's Birthday, February 22nd, which of course was always a holiday at Concordia. The great performance was to skate backwards in a circle. I remember one of these Washington's Birthdays, in 1868 or 1869. We celebrated the forenoon of that day on the Maumee itself. There were games on skates and then a simple lunch: sandwiches and big cans of cold coffee heated by little fires

THE CONCORDIA GYMNASIUM

on the ice, the provisions having been brought down by the college team guided by "Christian" the Dane. "Christ" was so strong that he could lift a two-bushel bag of grain with his teeth. I once saw him do it. The ice at noon began to seem a bit soft and treacherous; so after lunch the students went up to their rooms in the college. Two of my comrades, however, and I returned to the Maumee with skates, because in the forenoon we had been compelled to be but onlookers. Now we hoped to have our fill. But not for long. There were treacherous "air-holes" covered with very thin ice, and suddenly I broke through to my neck and had to make my way to the bank breaking the ice before me. I hastened up to the college in my soaked garments and dried myself sitting by a hot stove. No evil befell me, but I said nothing at home.

Another incident: once, early in March when the Maumee was high and there was still ice on the canal, some of us went down to do some boating. But the boat in question had drifted across a creek tributary to the river and was found lodged on the opposite bank of the creek. To run down some distance inland and come back on the opposite bank of the creek seemed the only way to get the boat. But I said: "I will get the boat!" I stripped on the spot then and there, on that day in early March, swam across the creek, and with a few strokes brought the boat back for our use. Dressing promptly, I found that nothing happened to my health. But I was always filled with a boy's foolish confidence that nothing *could* happen to me or my health.

There was a lock in the canal near the college. The lockkeeper was an old Bavarian by the name of Motz who also sold vegetables to the canal-boat men. We often annoyed him, when he would shout at us in his Bavarian dialect: "Hat eich der Ludder wieder am Seil!" From the top of the lock we fished much in spring with so-called "dipnets," for sunfish mainly, which came up from Lake Erie. I was fishing there on Saturday morning, April 15, 1865, when one of my college friends, Albert B. of St. Louis, told me the terrible news of the assassination of President Lincoln the evening before, in Ford's theatre, Washington.

During most of the Civil War, silver disappeared, and the paper dollar sank to forty cents. Of course life at the parsonage of St. Paul's became harder: roasted rye had to serve for coffee both at home and at the college table. We had to sweep our own rooms at the college and make our own fires—all wood fires then—there was no central heating. Trees were felled on the college farm by the upperclassmen, and the corded wood was conveyed to the big woodyard of the college by "Christ" and the college team. The work of splitting was assigned to the same upperclassmen in turn; one of them was the supervisor of all these tasks.

On October 30, 1867, the three hundred and fiftieth anniversary of the Reformation was celebrated by all the Lutherans of city and county: ninety-five young women represented the Theses of the great Reformer.

The summer of 1868 was a memorable one. For six weeks the temperature rose to 92 degrees day after day. Most men wore cabbage leaves in their hats; and the farmers stood in rows in Meyer's drug store to buy quinine, then five dollars an ounce. In that summer I spent some weeks with farmer friends in De Kalb County, some thirty-five miles north of Fort Wayne. I turned in with a will and certainly earned my board, aiding in the conveyance of that year's rye crop to the barn and bringing fertilizer from the barnyard to the fields for the fall ploughing. During the evenings I devoted myself to writing out a version of Livy XXII. Never in my life did I pursue the classics in more difficult weather or circumstances. My steel pen became dull and the country store nearby had no

THE CONCORDIA GYMNASIUM

pens, so we sharpened the pen on a small grindstone, and I carried my task through in the hot summer nights by the light of a coal-oil lamp to gain the praise of Rector Schick.

When finally, on June 30, 1869, I had completed my Prima and came into my father's study with my fine report, he did not praise me. He never praised me to my face. On that occasion he quoted for me St. Paul, 1 Cor. 4, 7: "What hast thou that thou didst not receive? Now if thou didst receive it, why dost thou glory, as if thou hadst not received it?" And writing now, some fifty-nine years later, I may say with all sincerity that I never forgot that Paulinian monition.

My seven years at the Fort Wayne Concordia were pleasantly rounded out by the generous invitation of a wealthy Lutheran gentleman of Roxbury, Boston. For the first time in my life I saw real mountains, the Alleghanies, and the horseshoe curve near Altoona, Pennsylvania. The station in New York—then a smoky shed without any architectural pretensions—stood where later was erected the Madison Square Garden. My generous host in Boston also sent us north to visit Vermont. I dived in the White River, and the water was so clear that I could dive down and find a silver quarter. Also we ascended Mt. Mansfield from Stowe, Vermont, and sampled the sage-cheese unknown on the Maumee. In Boston I went up the Bunker Hill Monument and also ascended Parker Hill near Roxbury; I swam the Charles River near Cambridge, helped to catch big sea fish off Nahant, saw Gilbert Stuart's picture of Washington in the Boston Athenaeum, admired the big fish in Quincy market, gazed with historical awe on Faneuil Hall and the Old South Church, and finally came home via Albany and Buffalo. Of course everything having an historical association, every scene or human memorial forming a link with the past, was earnestly welcomed by me. The cornfields of the Maumee, the hickory forests, the cow pastures and the hopeless flatness of my native region had intensified the delight of that visit, in the summer of 1869, to the Atlantic ocean and to the purlieus of Harvard.

Before saying adieu to my native town and to Allen and Adams Counties, I must not leave unrecorded here several pertinent matters. The two great roads leading north and south from old Fort Wayne were these: the Cold Water Road to Michigan and the Piqua Road to Ohio. The Lutheran farmers of those settlements were bountiful providers for the table at Concordia: fruit, flour, vegetables, smoked hams, kept ever coming without stint into the cellars of the steward, housefather Reinke.

On the Fourth of July, great multitudes from town and country came to the campus of Concordia, especially into the "Oak Grove" hard by. Here there were games for the children, also speeches and recitations and singing, and also prizes. One of these games was curious: a child, blindfolded and then turned around several times, armed with a pole, was to break a pot under which a rooster was concealed. Three blows were permitted. There was great jubilation when at last some boy or girl broke the pot and carried off the rooster. The air was redolent with firecrackers exploding all day long. When at last we came home, late in the afternoon, tired and happy, we were regaled at supper with currant pie baked by our dear mother who shunned noise and crowds and gossip.

Among the earliest and most widely honored settlers in Allen County, who had been preëminent in clearing the primeval forests and who became veritable patriarchs of the countryside, two names stand out: Trier and Bleke. Their descendants in the second and third generation, I am glad to know, are, in the main, still farmers. To-day, indeed, the forests are gone; and as one speeds through Allen or Adams County in a farmer's automobile, the

THE CONCORDIA GYMNASIUM

outlook everywhere is on a veritable land of Goshen. Names like Hessen Cassel, Friedheim, Bingen, commemorate the regions where the forefathers and primeval settlers now sleep.

IV
THE DIVINITY SCHOOL AT ST. LOUIS

IN September, 1869, for the first time, I left the paternal roof to continue my studies elsewhere, viz., at St. Louis on the Mississippi. I did indeed periodically return to Fort Wayne, but I never became a definite inmate of St. Paul's parsonage—a bird of academic passage until I made my own nest, in 1881, on the Hudson.

There had been important sessions of the General Synod at St. Paul's, Fort Wayne; and our train westward was so packed that I stood about all the time, and from a cold acquired a most masculine basso for several days. I was, on this tiresome journey, really a person of standing. Never before or since did I realize so keenly the gnawing pangs of homesickness as then: home, the dearest ties, the associations of life from the cradle onward, all seemed gone. In a way they were gone.

The Lutheran Saxons who had come to St. Louis from Bremen and New Orleans in 1839–40 were germ and leaven for the spread of Luther's church, not only throughout the Mississippi valley but ultimately to California and Oregon. They were the very substance and atmosphere in which the Concordia Seminary in the southern suburbs had its being. Trinity Church, now the mother church of thousands of others, was often called "the Saxon church"; and the flour mill on Lombard Street, established by two members of Trinity, was formerly called "Saxony Mills."

In those distant days, the great stream, veritable main artery of the great republic, was not yet passable by a bridge: ferries afforded all the transportation. St. Louis itself then had some 250,000 inhabitants, and there was still some rivalry with Chicago. The climate in June and September was much warmer than at Fort Wayne. Persimmons and pecan-nuts were new to me, as well as the adage that "the longest pole fetches the most persimmons." Grapes and peaches were much more plentiful than at Fort Wayne, and sweet potatoes were as cheap and common as "Irish" potatoes.

In St. Louis proper there were then four Lutheran churches: Holy Cross, Trinity, Emmanuel's, and Zion in the north end. Going out farther, there were "Bremen" and "Bielefeld": the earlier settlers there came from those sections of Germany. The grape flourished, and wine-making was the chief industry, I believe. All students at the Concordia Seminary had their laundry done in Lutheran families and were also made welcome at Sunday dinner by the same families, a consistent form of Christian giving which could not but wholesomely react upon the students' outlook and pastoral service later on.

It is no part of this biography to present any outline of the history of the Lutheran Church in America or to tell of the struggles and controversies occurring in that history—felt more, it is true, in that center of Lutheranism, St. Louis, than anywhere else in America. Still I cannot suppress a certain conviction formed in the course of a long life. *Odium theologicum* is a term current and familiar. But there is also an *odium philosophicum* and *odium philologicum* sometimes revolving around microscopic objects. The indifferentist, of course, will look down upon many controversies with lofty contempt, because he is spiritually unconcerned, quite willing often himself *iurare in verba magistri:* academic youth from the times of Pythagoras onward is inclined to rely on the *ipse dixit* of its favorite professor.

Now it must be said of the eminent theologian of St. Louis, Dr. C. F. W. Walther, that he was free from per-

THE DIVINITY SCHOOL AT ST. LOUIS

sonal academic ambition. His consistent aim was to fortify his own theses and paragraphs not so much by his own definitions and deductions as by the greater authorities from Luther himself downward. In Systematic Theology, the course covered the second and third year of the *Triennium*, Seniors and Middlers attending together. We used Baier's *Compendium*, a work written in Latin. The task of copying the proof-texts from the Scriptures directly, of course consumed much time and mechanical labor; likewise there was much dictation—much of it, after my time, done away with by the church printing-press. Professor Walther was also an excellent organist; his speaking voice was a baritone of rare power and dignity, which for his young hearers added much to the impressiveness of his lectures. Of course, in Divinity, the soul-history of the lecturer cannot mechanically be reproduced in his hearers—an echo involves no spiritual experience; still the spoken word reaches much farther than the printed page. There was a "Luther reading" on Friday nights. Dr. Walther himself did the reading, and, with admirable current comments, brought his students to the living and burning issues of the Reformation.

Professor Brauer, among other things, presented the Symbolical books of the Lutheran Church; but his most efficient service, I believe, was in the pulpit. He had studied at Göttingen. Dr. Edward Preuss, who emigrated from Berlin in 1868, assumed the chair of Church History in the autumn of 1869. He spoke German with the peculiar dialect of his native East Prussia and her famous University of Königsberg. He was about thirty-six when I first sat under him; and he had had by far the best classical training of all the men who taught me from 1862 to 1872. Great scholars like Lehrs and Lobeck had been his teachers at Kant's University. Under his care and guidance, I began the study of the Apostolic Fathers in the original Greek.

I recall here a toilsome experience: the text that he lent me was printed in the older (Erasmian?) type; a considerable part I first copied out into the current Greek script. As to his lectures on Church History, his presentation of Constantine's victory over Maxentius at the Mulvian bridge at Rome, in 312 A.D., was, as all his teaching, impressive and lucid. His whole didactic manner was often dazzling and brilliant. But I fear he was at bottom not sincere: he soon chose a more profitable vocation, leaving both his chair and his faith behind.

I need not urge that those times were pioneer times: where now (1928) fully a dozen or more chairs are occupied in the same Concordia on the Mississippi, *then* four men had to carry the whole burden, literally consuming themselves in the service. A more unworldly band of Christian teachers it is impossible to conceive. As an old alumnus I may perhaps be permitted to stress just one point. Not this, that the majority—except Dr. Preuss—could be designated as *autodidacts*; James Russell Lowell somewhere says that every genuine scholar at bottom is that. No, it was something else. Never, I think, did we students come to read the Greek Testament *con amore*. Most of us, I know, never conceived the earnest desire to read it over and over again, to gain a textual and spiritual intimacy with it. We were not brought to master the characteristic difference of the Hellenistic (or Alexandrine) from Attic Greek. The classic foundation which we had brought from Fort Wayne was not adequate.

The students as a whole were a curious and somewhat incongruous conglomerate. On the "practical" side, we had many who had been sent to America after some preparation in Germany, to be further trained at St. Louis and fitted for the Christian ministry. Some came from Pastor Brunn at Steeden, Nassau; still others had sojourned at Hermannsburg in Hanover, guided by that eminent and

THE DIVINITY SCHOOL AT ST. LOUIS

zealous divine, Louis Harms. These, throughout, seemed to me to excel in general maturity and spiritual earnestness. It is undeniable, that we, the alumni of that Fort Wayne Concordia, being native Americans, looked at these emigrant disciples of Luther with a bit of condescension: of course they were not yet masters of English, and had much to learn of the native customs of America.

But we too, the "theoretical" (classically trained) students, had some German colleagues in our own class, that of 1872. One of these, D., had gone through the gymnasium at Celle, Hanover. He was a great wit and full of nonsense, and we gladly adopted some of his current utterances and proverbs. Another of our "green" classmates, E., came from Lemgo, Westphalia. Still another, Sch., was a native of Hesse. His desperate eagerness to acquire English at once, over night almost, together with odd performances in his pronunciation, contributed much to our hilarity. We, the natives from Fort Wayne Concordia, represented many parts of the United States: Fort Wayne, Indianapolis, Belleville, Ill., Cumberland, Md., Baltimore, Buffalo, Columbus, O., Monroe, Mich., St. Charles, Mo. Our Scandinavian classmates came, of course, from Wisconsin, Iowa, Minnesota. The most prominent and scholarly among them was Hans Gerhard Stub, leader of all the Norwegians in the Seminary. Another was Lars Reque, whose athletic feats we all admired but none could equal. Their glee-club was exquisite: the perfect harmony and the lyrical tenderness of the Norse songs still dwell in my memory.

Prayers both morning and evening brought us all together in the "Large Lecture Hall," under the guidance of Professor August Crämer. In 1845, he had led a small company of Franconian emigrants to their settlements in the Saginaw country of Michigan. Here for more than eighty years, names like Frankenlust, Frankenmuth, and

FROM MAUMEE TO THAMES AND TIBER

Frankentrost have commemorated the ancestral origin of these primeval settlers, who there, for some time, supported missions among the Indians near by.

Andacht, or Prayers, in winter especially, was a bit early; and the rising bell was often tolled for some fifteen minutes, and toilets were often made in desperate hurry. The washroom in the basement was bitter cold. We had to sweep our own rooms, fetch the soft coal from the general pile, and be our own servitors generally. It was, taking it for all in all, a hard life; but it also hardened muscle and sinew of the soul for coming trials. The modern successors at the new Concordia (1926) on which millions have been spent, with their comforts, dormitories, library, dining hall, gymnasium, and diversified courses (some elective) would shrink if suddenly thrust back into those Spartan days.

We had *some* social pleasures unknown at Fort Wayne: birthdays were celebrated more or less *sub rosa*, with the observation of certain modes of convivial tradition—never to excess—at which malt and hops figured. One of our standard chants began thus:

> O du heiliger Nepomuk, muk, muk,
> der du stehst auf der Prager bruck, bruck—

or "Gaudeamus igitur, iuvenes dum sumus," or the Horatian "Integer vitae scelerisque purus," and the like. Of course there were weaker brethren, constitutionally unfitted for the impending pastoral vocation, as always became evident, in time, with recurrent definiteness.

Dr. Walther, in addition to many other duties, had also that of chief pastor of the four local churches already named, the four pastors regularly exchanging pulpits: a most wholesome practice. The preparations of sermons, the homiletic first efforts, were also under Dr. Walther's direction. This brings me to an incisive experience of my

THE DIVINITY SCHOOL AT ST. LOUIS

young life. In the spring of 1870, I, a mere stripling in my eighteenth year, some three or four years younger than my classmates, was given this text by Dr. Walther: "But we preach Christ crucified, unto the Jews a stumbling block ($σκάνδαλον$) and unto the Greeks, foolishness ($μωρίαν$)."[1] Of course I wrote a sermon, and delivered it in Holy Cross. But, deep in my own reflections in that spring I would ask myself: "E. G. S., what do you really know of the 'Wisdom of the Greeks'? Is it not mere assurance on your part, stripling that you are, to dare to undertake such a theme and such a text? Of course you are not fitted *now*, nay, you never will be fitted to be a 'pastor' (or shepherd) of a Christian flock! This cannot prove your career in the end. Do not deceive yourself in so grave a matter. This cannot, must not, become your permanent career. Do not become something second-rate or third-rate in a profession which you never would have chosen yourself, for yourself." Thus then, more and more, in my heart of hearts and in my outlook upon manhood, I drew back from my father's profession; but this was not due to any doubting of the great verities. The Christian model of the daily life of Father and Mother at home, and the unworldly self-denial ever observable in the conduct of my teachers in divinity, all this proved for me an *Apologia pro Fide Christiana* before I ever turned the pages of Pascal, when I went to Europe to begin my real life-work as a student of classic antiquity. Of course a ministerial career should never be determined for a youth by others—of this I am deeply convinced.

The "social opportunities"—as we call them in America—in St. Louis were ample and manifold, greatly surpassing those at Fort Wayne; and the susceptibilities of youth in those vernal years did not spare me. It was the first romance in my young life, not at all hidden from the

[1] I Corinthians, I, 23.

social circles in which we students moved; the first romance, I say, but the wise veto of my father decisively snapped these slender and tender bonds. He urged, by letter, that the real making of my life was still all before me. Of the many decisive and far-reaching services of his paternal wisdom, this was one of the greatest.

A different experience that I like to recall, was in the athletic field. In May and June, we students practiced swimming in the Mississippi. Now the Missouri bank, *our* side of the great stream, was abruptly steep or muddy. So we would engage some rowboats and cross to the Illinois side, where the pebbly and sandy beach tapered gently into deeper water. One afternoon in May, 1870, two of my classmates—both long gone to rest—and I rowed across to the Illinois side. As we were making our loops, suddenly the idea shot through my head to do something extraordinary. "Bring back my clothes!" I shouted to my companions, and immediately began to strike out for the Missouri side. It was a wicked venture of juvenile audacity: many were the whirlpools (popularly known as "suckholes") and also the trees imbedded in the much changing bottom of the treacherous stream, trees whose unseen branches might not merely impede but even wound the swimmer. Moreover, a steamer was just coming up from the south, and with desperate energy I succeeded in passing west of her course. Inevitably I was carried down stream and almost a mile towards Carondelet before making my landing. Turning northward, I picked my way cautiously and slowly, in complete solitude, along the track of the Iron Mountain Railway. Finally I met my two comrades, and dressed then and there. The rumor had already spread through the Seminary that Sihler had drowned. After this foolhardy feat, few of my classmates dared to lecture about the best modes of swimming when I happened to be in the room; and my ambition was satisfied. Youth's vanity for-

THE DIVINITY SCHOOL AT ST. LOUIS

sooth, like the iridescence on the surface of soap-bubbles, assumes many forms.

The Franco-German War of 1870–1871 reverberated strongly in St. Louis, then and now largely peopled by Americans of German ancestry; Carl Schurz was then a Senator from Missouri in Washington. Immediately after Sedan, there was a parade of carriages which I saw. In the first one, with historically appropriate uniforms, sat King William of Prussia and the last of the Bonapartes. Great fairs were established, and the generous funds there gained were sent to Germany for the wounded. After the fall of Paris, January, 1871, we had a holiday in the Seminary, with speeches, declamations, and varied refreshments. For me personally with my historical retrospect of Frederick the Great, of Ziethen and Seidlitz, Blücher and Leipzig and Waterloo, those were great days. Still the name of the city and the original founders—all were French—"Laclede" and the "French Market" near our Trinity Church and Saxony Mills—all reminded me of these French origins. One of the finest residential streets then was Chouteau Avenue. On it was one of the show places of St. Louis, built by an army contractor who had become rich during the Civil War. It was popularly known as "Cracker Castle." At Christmas, fireworks were freely exploded. Was that French?

But very few of my classmates did I ever see again after I was graduated from the Seminary in June, 1872. Our land is so vast.

V
BERLIN

NEVER before in my young and eager years was I more joyfully surprised and delighted than when I came home from St. Louis and entered my father's study in the concluding days of June, 1872. He had taken steps, he told me, that I should join my brother Christian then studying medicine in Berlin; that I should sail for Bremen in September and begin in Berlin the study of Classical Philology, rooming with Christian. I could have danced for joy. Yet I marvelled how this was financially possible. My father had many friends both clerical and lay who for decades had observed his leadership and self-denial in all matters touching spiritual ends of all kinds. Contributions from such friends he carefully booked, and dealt out to me later on with the scrupulous method of monthly or quarterly remittances. Eventually, as I never served the church directly, I repaid all these funds to the donors, to the last dollar. My third year abroad was subventioned in part by my brother Christian and by my younger sister Elizabeth. These loans I repaid first.

Early in September, 1872, I saw New York for the first time—not merely passing through. I sojourned for a few days as grateful guest in a semi-rustic home near East New York belonging to a gentleman who had done much for Lutheran travellers, without money and without price. Practicing the utmost economy, I had determined to sail for Bremerhaven in the *steerage*. And so it was necessary in Hoboken to buy a mattress and some tin dishes. To be exact: this old steamer no longer had first or second class.

FROM MAUMEE TO THAMES AND TIBER

She was, after this voyage, to be converted into a freighter pure and simple, and this was the last time that she carried passengers at all. Now my material life had always been very simple. I had not been spoiled by any habits of comfort, let alone of luxury. But still, on the whole, it was a very hard experience. Moreover there were in our steerage some folk of the other sex, of whom I will preserve silence. Even my modest trunk did not remain immune from thieves. Of course marching up several times a day with our tins to the cooks of our class, was not pleasant. But my sailing days remained absolutely free from seasickness, as they always have been since. Still that first crossing of the Atlantic, in September, 1872, dwells in my memory as a drab experience. Much of the time I sat on the grate near the main smokestack, contemplating clouds and billows. Near me often sat a young fellow-American from New York, going to London. His aims of life differed greatly from my own: young as he was, he was full of great plans of becoming rich, *very* rich, some day, and that day not very far off. A common type, I dare say. At last, in some ten or eleven days, we made the Scilly Islands, skirted the south coast of Ireland, and, on a Sunday afternoon, the twelfth day of our voyage, we ran up the Solent and stopped at a pier of Southampton. What our old steamer put off or put on in the way of cargo, I have forgotten; but it was my first vision of famous Britain, and of English men, women, and children, who were abroad in great numbers in their Sunday best, spick and span. I *felt* like a pariah, banished from civilization. A curious experience was impending. On Monday morning, as we sailed eastward by the renowned Isle of Wight *(Vectis)*, I observed a rare thing. The ocean was smooth, not merely unruffled like a millpond, but really it was like glass. It remains a unique phenomenon never repeated in my numerous voyages. A little group of which I was a member determined to have some

BERLIN

variety in our diet. Accordingly, we ourselves, for ourselves, prepared some potato salad, and ate it with relish. But, after passing the chalk cliffs of historic Dover and entering the North Sea, we ran into a storm of extreme violence. It was a bad night: so furious was the sea that the sailors had to tie fast the trunks down there in that drab abode. There was little sleep on board that night: never did I have so critical a test of maritime digestion as a traveller on the deep; but I remained peacefully well. The next morning the ocean was much calmer, but only *one other* of our group could say: "I did not regret the potato salad." On Tuesday afternoon, we passed the buoys at the mouth of the Weser—the *Visurgis* of the Romans—and landed with great satisfaction at Bremerhaven. There I ordered a goodly repast; I forget the menu. As soon as I had despatched it, I repeated the order.

The journey to Dresden was slow. I had been commissioned to deliver a homiletic work of my father's which was to be published there. For the first time in my life, I ascended stone steps to the third story where the printer lived. Apart from the *Grosser Garten*, I saw but few of the *notabilia* of the Elbflorence on that first visit, but hastened on to the capital of the new German Empire on the Spree. Everything was ready for my reception. My brother Christian (M.D. of the University of Michigan, 1871) with a medical classmate from the same institution was living at No. 17 Gartenstrasse, "bei Wittwe Martens," a good mile north of the University. Of course our reunion was an occasion of great joy, and our chumming was never disturbed by the slightest disharmony. In the corner of the room there was an implement utterly strange to American eyes —a white tile stove, which in the coming winter held heat wonderfully with a minimum of coal. Every morning my brother went westward by the Karlsstrasse, to go to the Charité, the great government hospitals where most of the medical lectures were given. Once he took me along to the surgical amphitheatre of the famous Bernhard von Langenbeck, who had made a great reputation in the Franco-German War. At another time I attended the lecture of a great alienist. The patient in hand sometimes believed himself to be Jesus Christ, or again the German Emperor. It was sad, and made me ponder much on *megalomania*. Once too I attended a lecture of the famous Rudolph Virchow ('Cellular-pathologie'). At the conclusion, one of his hearers, an American, not only put on his hat before leaving the room, but actually whistled. I heard Virchow say then and there: "Natürlich, das kann nur ein Amerikaner thun."

Often, my brother, as an advanced medical student ("Practikant"), was called to an obstetric case among the poor—no fees, a regulation of the famous obstetrician Geheimrat Martin, who, in January, 1859, had assisted at the birth of Crown Princess Victoria's oldest child, later Emperor Wilhelm II. In professional circles in Berlin, it was whispered that Dr. Martin had blundered on that occasion: hence the lame arm of the future monarch, who, when I came to Berlin, was in his fourteenth year. Histology, the microscopic study of tissues and nerve-endings, was my brother's favorite pursuit, which, five years later, won for him a fellowship in Biology at the Johns Hopkins University. Of his deep trend for analysis I have spoken; it was coupled with morbid and restless self-examination, called "psychoanalysis" in these later times. The deepest problem, he told me soon after my arrival in Berlin, was this: "What is the ego?" "What is consciousness?" With this restless temperamental trait, my good brother really was never happy. In every issue and every new matter presented by the advancement of life and work, he unfailingly discovered imperfections or sinister possibilities, whereas I ever sought for and readily

BERLIN

discovered the sunny side of things, and felt quickened by every new insight to essay harder tasks, to climb steeper heights. His trend was toward melancholy, while I was sanguine, rather an optimist.

After our coffee and rolls in the morning, while he went west I went south by the Artilleriestrasse, and crossing the Ebertsbrücke passed by the Kastanienwäldchen (chestnut grove) to the University proper, Unter den Linden, where the lectures in the faculty of philosophy were then mostly delivered, as well as those in Divinity and Law. Alfred Dove, if I remember, was the Rector of the University, the "Friedrich Wilhelms Universität," but the Dean of my faculty was a scholar of world-wide and rising fame, Theodor Mommsen. I have preserved my matriculation form from that time to this hour, I am glad to say, an academic treasure of my beginnings. I copy it here:

> Virum iuvenem ornatissimum Theophilum Sihler Americanum civibus Universitatis litterariae Fridericae*Guilelmae legitime adscriptum, nomen apud facultatem philosophicam rite professum esse testamur. Berolini, a d. V mens. Oct. anni MDCCCLXXII.
> TH. MOMMSEN
> Decanus et Professores facultatis philosophicae Universitatis Friedericae Guilelmae.

I felt on that occasion, in joyful awe, as if one of the chief priests of Minerva—represented on the seal with her symbolical owl—had *in propria persona* admitted me to her sanctuary. This precious document is now yellow with age, and the paper is brittle.

As to the choice of courses, I had been advised by a distinguished classical scholar, Director Ranke (brother of Leopold von Ranke), of the Friedrich Wilhelms gymnasium. A few days before lectures opened, I was standing before *das schwarze Brett* where the personal notices of the professors were posted by the *Pedell* who also sold

---
* Thus spelled in the original.

sandwiches and photographs of professors. Here one could ascertain the particular day on which a given professor would begin: the dates on that occasion, for me, ran from October 24th to November 4th. On that particular October morning, my attention was at once riveted by a great name: "*L. von Ranke liest nicht.*"

At my side there happened to be another American seeking orientation like myself, and we speedily became acquainted. It was Milton W. Humphreys of Washington and Lee, in Virginia, who had served in the artillery on the Confederate side, now on leave of absence, destined later on to edit works of Sophocles, Aristophanes, Demosthenes, and to become the third successor of Dr. Gildersleeve at the University of Virginia, the foundation of Thomas Jefferson. We became fast friends. To many of my countrymen, whether at Berlin or later at Leipzig, I made myself serviceable in aiding them in their quest of board and lodging.

May I enumerate the courses I took in Berlin in that first semester, in October, 1872? Moritz Haupt, *The Birds* of Aristophanes; Adolph Kirchhoff, History of Greek Literature to Alexander; Emil Hübner, Tacitus' *Agricola* and the first part of the History of Roman Literature; Johann Gustave Droysen, History of Greece. I also took (i.e., paid the fee for) a Hebrew course on Job by the famous Orientalist Rödiger. But nothing came of this desire to continue my Old Testament study of St. Louis; my *Anmeldungsbuch* contains this remark by the *Quaestur* (treasurer's office): "Nicht gegeben; Honorar zurückgegeben."[1] In the same *Anmeldungsbuch*, lying at my elbow at this moment, I have, twice, the signature of those eminent scholars. Which name will outlast the others? The oldest of these scholars were Haupt and Droysen, both about 64; Mommsen was 55; Kirchhoff, 46; Hübner, the youngest, 38.

[1] Course not given; fee repaid.

BERLIN

Droysen's *Historik* (Theory of History) long ago was introduced to American students by Benjamin Andrews, at one time President of Brown University. Droysen in that course took for granted a sound knowledge of Greek history, dwelling much on the beginnings of Greek historiography, local chronicles, and the like; also the narrow limits of political geography. I readily perceived that, if Greek topography had resembled that of Illinois or Texas, the history of the Hellenic race would have been very different, not to speak of their sharp tribal and dialectic segregations, such as the Ionic and Doric races.

Haupt was equally great as classicist and Germanist, an expert on Nibelungen and medieval ballads. Of course I was interested only in his classic lectures. He remains to me, in this retrospect of more than half a century, the oddest personality, in many ways, of all the classic scholars that I have ever met or heard. Of course my direct contact was limited to *"Anmelden"* and *"Abmelden"* in the Faculty room, during the so-called academic quarter hour, all lectures being limited to 45 minutes. When I presented my book to the great man for his signature and assignment of a seat number, he glared at me as though my humble appearance had been bold intrusion. His lecture on Aristophanes was given in an auditorium once used by his eminent predecessor Carl Lachmann, still famous for his New Testament, his Lucretius. Now Haupt did not mount the *Katheder* (lecture platform) or face his hearers from that conventional elevation. No, he seated himself in the front row of the students' desks turning his back to his hearers while lecturing. Why? Because, as it was whispered, he deemed himself unworthy to sit in the chair of Lachmann.[2] Of course, Haupt's vast erudition soon made us forget the

---

[2] Haupt was extremely pugnacious. In his textual criticism he generally chose some editor or critic upon whom his philological condemnation was poured out. My friend Humphreys in one of Haupt's courses registered some eighteen terms of abuse or contempt. Was it against Heimsoeth of Bonn? I forget.

name of Lachmann. His lectures on the *Birds* of Aristophanes were given in Latin. One of my fellow-students often borrowed my lecture-notes of this course. This was the Greek Spyridon Lambros, a native of Corfu (Corcyra) and a graduate of the University of Athens, planning now to acquire also a German Ph.D. before returning to Greece. He also practiced English with me when I visited him. He seemed that winter to be economizing on heat, and generally wore a very long and heavy dressing-gown. Ultimately he gained his Ph.D. from the University of Halle, his thesis dealing with the "Honors of the Founders" (οἰκισται) of Greek colonies, written in Greek. Later on, when a professor at Athens, he made important discoveries in the monasteries on Mt. Athos. For a short time during the World War, he was Prime Minister to the late King Constantine of Greece. He too has passed away. As for Haupt's course on Aristophanes, the results for me became incisive. Not only did I resolve to read all the eleven extant plays, not only did I buy a copy of Dübner's *Scholia* (Paris, Didot, 1843), not only did I promptly set out to traverse this uncharted sea (the Scholia), red pencil in hand, but something more was the outcome. I promptly realized that I must master the contemporary history, the Peloponnesian War. Thucydides loomed up, and so I immersed myself in the combined study of these two: the stern and profound historian and the other one with his social and political persiflage and reckless invective of whatever he disliked. Of course the fragments (Meineke) came in due time: "Eupolis atque Cratinus Aristophanesque poetae." I then for all my life learned this lesson: In historical research it seems to be of supreme importance *to have more than one source*, best of all if they be contemporaries, even if one seems to overtop the rest. Thus too, while in time I read (or devoured) with rapt attention the volumes of Ernst Curtius, of Thirlwall, of Grote, and many others, I still determined, even then, to abstain from making *their* judgments and estimates my own, young though I was and not dreaming of ever climbing to such peaks, still unwilling simply *iurare in verba magistri*.

The first Greek author of eminence whom I read from cover to cover was Herodotus of Halicarnassus,[3] in the Ionic dialect, though of Doric birth,[4] who often read parts of his narrative before Greek festival assemblies. There is no stronger contrast in Greek prose letters than between him and the Attic exile, Thucydides. I felt happy when I had concluded my Herodotus, happy in this attainment as when ten years before I had for the first time, unaided, swum across the modest (and unclassical) Maumee.

I now come to Adolph Kirchhoff, the eminent Grecian who sat in the chair of August Böckh. The thing that impressed me most was his easy and intimate familiarity with Greek letters—from Homer to Plotinus, their sequence, character, and limitations—when he spoke of Aristophanes, Eupolis, and the rest, as an English scholar might speak of Swift, Thackeray, or London *Punch*. Kirchhoff had first served as a *Gymnasiallehrer*; and he said, *inter alia*, that Thucydides with his peculiar style was really unfitted for Prima. Of course I fell in love with Ottfried Müller's *History of Greek Literature*, where an idealizing presentation of those letters is curiously blended with the sunny period of that gifted scholar's life, cut short by his labors on Mt. Parnassus, 1840. His name remains one of the brightest in the annals of Göttingen. When I surveyed Kirchhoff with loving veneration—I once made a very fair sketch of his features, lost now in my lecture books—my thoughts would run thus: "You did not come from your mother's womb a finished scholar; you had to master text

---

[3] A Doric community. So was the island of Kōs, but the great physician Hippocrates, even then, published his works in Ionic likewise.

[4] Suidas s. v.

after text yourself. Supreme devotion and industry inspired you and made you one of the great scholars of Europe." And this inner voice became the *daimonion* that inspired me and led me on from nineteen to seventy and beyond. Every *Preussischer Thaler* that I could spend out of my modest allowance I invested in classical books. The *Antiquariat* of Mayer and Müller particularly furnished me many a bargain, especially in Greek books.

I now come to the youngest of the classicists whom I heard in Berlin that winter 1872–1873. Emil Hübner, but thirty-eight then, was already an *ordinarius* in Classical Philology. He was a son-in-law of Droysen. In Spain and Portugal he had spent much time in studying and copying the Roman Inscriptions of the Iberian peninsula. In Britain, I believe, he had spent even a longer time in studying the epigraphic material there preserved; and he spoke Spanish and English fluently. I presented myself at his handsome villa, 4 Ahornstrasse, in the Thiergarten section, and was very kindly received. I applied for membership in his private Seminar which met in his spacious and fine library on Friday evenings, from eight to ten. His helpfulness was most generous: he promptly realized that Latin writing was a faculty in which I needed particular practice. For this, he lent me the second edition of Madvig's Cicero *De Finibus* and made it my task to write Latin abstracts of this work, which he personally revised.[5] Hübner's every word and act betokened a man who was not merely a scholar but a gentleman in every sense of the word. I was a member of his seminar from October, 1872, to April, 1874. The work was carried on in the following way: at the beginning of the seminar, the more advanced members announced the titles of the particular pieces of

---

[5] After his death in 1901, I succeeded in having New York University purchase from his sons (none of whom were classicists) his entire classical and archaeological collection. I need not say that my graduate students and I made good use of that noble library in the last two decades of my academic service, 1903–1923.

research on which they were engaged. Then to each one was assigned a reporter or critic whose survey or critique was set down for some Friday evening in the coming semester. Further: a piece of Greek Literature was chosen for the semester. I now recall Plutarch's *Convivium Septem Sapientium* and Pseudo-Longinus *de Sublimitate* (περὶ ὕψους). Two men had the work for the given evening: a Latin translation with comments or exegesis—all in Latin. German was taboo. The amusing feature, as my memory sweeps back over more than five decades, was the endeavors of the reporter or critic to pick flaws even when there were none. The presiding professor was the court of last appeal, which ended all these Latin disputes. For the sake of biographical precision I will mention my own first douche in very cold and deep water. A member of that first seminar of mine announced as *his* theme: "The remnants of the *locative* in Plautus." Now for this particular paper Professor Hübner appointed me reporter. O horrors! I had at that time never yet read even a single play of Plautus, nor knew anything of the school of Ritschl, the greatest Plautinian since the beginning of the Renaissance. Of course I plunged into Plautus with desperate energy; and, from that beginning on, I strove earnestly, and I think successfully, to gain the good-will and approbation of Dr. Hübner. As I am now writing my biography, I should not leave unrecorded the following incident: the Crown Princess Victoria (Princess Royal of England) was seeking an English-speaking classical tutor for her sons Wilhelm and Henry. Dr. Hübner mentioned my name for this service, of course without any knowledge on my part. But the royal lady naturally preferred a tutor of British birth.

But I must now look beyond the purlieus of the University and the roots of my future there planted. Berlin in 1872–73 was only about one-eighth of her present size. Many things, such as sanitation and sewerage, in *our* sub-

FROM MAUMEE TO THAMES AND TIBER

urb certainly, were still in a primitive stage. But my ancestral feelings were mightily stirred, daily, by Rauch's Frederick the Great with Ziethen, Seidlitz, and others, in equestrian bronze on the corners; the four sides of the base being filled with eminent figures of that reign (1740–1786), all hard by the University. A little farther to the east were Scharnhorst and the fiery and intrepid Blücher, who saved the day at Waterloo and brought to an end the nightmare of the Corsican. Old Emperor William I in his palace, right across from the University, could often be seen at the corner window. Here I must mention a custom which always made a great impression on my young soul. Whenever a regiment of the large garrison returned from drill in the open country, a long file of troops drew up before that window to return the colors to the commander-in-chief, a symbolism full of meaning. The old gentleman invariably appeared at the historic window to receive the established form of military greeting. Every noon, at about one o'clock, officers representing all the regiments stationed in Berlin gathered in the "Kastanienwäldchen" (chestnut grove) hard by the University, to receive the parole for the next twenty-four hours. The officers gathered in a circle. The parole, brought by the adjutant of the Commander, passed from ear to ear, certain papers were received by the sergeants of each regiment, and then followed my daily treat: three pieces of military music by a band, changing every day. After this I turned to the north, across the Ebertsbrücke to our room, a mile away, for dinner.

The noble art of Rauch's sculpture I have already mentioned. Even then when the great world streamed in upon my young and impressionable soul, I placed Rauch on a high pedestal. His *Victory* on the column in the *Belle Alliance* Square has something of spiritual dignity. Such too is the impression made by the recumbent figure of

BERLIN

Queen Louisa in the Mausoleum at Charlottenburg. Such art indeed, defying the changes of taste and time, has in itself some of the qualities of the imperishable.

Thus then Berlin educated me in many ways, quite apart from classical philology. In the Royal Opera House I heard and saw my first operas. These were the *Zauberflöte* by Mozart and the *Freischütz* by C. M. von Weber. There were certain reserved seats for students, in the highest gallery, literally under the ceiling; and the price was very modest, some thirty-five cents in our money. There was just one drawback. Up there, in the academic heaven, one could not help realizing certain disillusionments. The "supers" of the staff, moving partly behind the scenes and acting as spooks in the *Wolfschlucht*, were not at all awe-inspiring but ridiculous. One habit I must not pass over here, a habit which I maintained both at Berlin and Leipzig. Although of course I was not indifferent to the trend of the public affairs both of Europe and at home,[6] I hardly ever, in those five semesters, bought a daily paper. I was so absorbed by the main aim of my sojourn abroad, and, besides, so close to the government of what was then the foremost state of the continent of Europe, that I often felt like an onlooker on the movement of modern history. Thus too I witnessed the state entry of Victor Emanuel of Italy and the Shah of Persia, or watched the gala coaches of ambassadors driving up before the Emperor's Palace on March 22nd, his birthday. Then, too, there were the great reviews of guard-troops on the *Tempelhofer Field*, in spring. All this to my cheerful vision at close quarters seemed to be history in the making. At one of these reviews, I observed our American envoy, George Bancroft, a *rara avis* there in broadcloth and silk hat, mounted, amid a wilderness of uniforms.

But the longer I remained abroad, the more I realized

[6] My father sometimes sent me Godkin's *New York Nation*.

an important experience. It was this: while conscious of, and well pleased with, my German and Prussian descent, and full of admiration for the monumental greatness of Martin Luther and fond of the spiritual beauty of Paul Gerhardt's hymns and with a lively sense of all German culture—with all this I felt ever more deeply that I was an American, and this not merely by the accident of birth but by ever deepening conviction. In a word, the longer I remained abroad, the better an American I became. The basic cause was this, I believe: the Jeffersonian idea, that men were equal, at least with equal right to the pursuit of happiness and freedom. The reader must not misunderstand me: I was, and am, far from considering myself the *equal* of all men. I strove for a certain *excellence* myself. I was, of course, respectful to all men and to all women. But a certain matter of *caste*, the *"Standesbewusstsein"* all about me, the very atmosphere I breathed, was something I could never make my own, nor look forward to living in it. And so I sought association whenever I could, with my American countrymen and also with a few Englishmen. For this contact there was a particular and regular opportunity. On Sunday mornings at about nine o'clock, I attended the Matthaei Kirche in the section southeast of the Thiergarten, to hear Dr. Büchsel. Here I often saw Ernst Curtius, and even royalties such as the Princess Friedrich Karl and her three daughters. From Dr. Büchsel's I generally walked — a goodly distance — to the American Chapel in the Junkerstrasse; and there I realized where I was born and where I eventually was to work. In my third semester, I became acquainted with an Englishman who was in charge of the Berlin office of the British and Foreign Bible Society. We took up for regular study in the original Greek the greatest of the four Gospels, that of St. John. I realized that I had had some growth since my St. Louis days. The text was Tischendorf's, 1873. It is at this moment within easy reach near my writing table. To return: Every day I spent a few hours at the Royal Library built by Frederick the Great with the odd inscription, "Nutrimentum Spiritus," a phrase more French than Latin. Several times I saw the great scholar Pertz, who then, I believe, was chief librarian. My card was certified by Professor Hübner. It was there that I for the first time studied Aristotle's Treatise on Poetry. The infinite condensation of the great Stagirite, the merciless analysis of all essentials and fundamentals which is his own way, all this was about as difficult as anything I had ever undertaken. The edition which I then used was one by Gottfried Hermann, in which the Leipzig Classicist actually sought a substratum derived from Kant's philosophy! I drew back at once, and learned the lesson that we must keep aloof from all extraneous matter when dealing with a given author. Strolling or wandering about the streets of that capital, I virtually never did. I had no time for that. Both my time and money were parcelled out with rigorous and systematic economy. I never attended any *Commers* of students. I considered these convivial and lyrical meetings of students silly.

In January, 1873, I passed through depths of great anxiety: my medical brother was seized by an illness that brought him to death's door. At that time surgeons knew nothing of operating for appendicitis. When at last we could issue forth once more, people almost stopped to look at us, one in blooming health, the other wan and emaciated in appearance. In the Easter vacation, we both visited ancestral Silesia and were guests at certain estates and manor-houses belonging to kin and connections of my father's early years. The energy, the social charms, the agricultural skill of the old Prussian gentry as well as their generous hospitality, we came to appreciate at close quarters. Also we stood by the grave of our paternal grandfather, who died in 1828. The journey from Breslau by a yellow postcoach via Trebnitz and the so-called *Katzengebirge* rests in my memory as an idyl.

In the summer semester, 1873, with great satisfaction I heard again Kirchhoff, Hübner, and Haupt, the latter on Aeschylus' *Persians;* this course led me more decisively into my particular life-work, for at once I realized that a comparison and critical joint survey of Herodotus and the Marathon-fighter himself would prove a good task for me. It was *Salamis* on which later, in 1877, my first publication at home centered. Salamis at once brings forward the eminent author of the *Atlas Antiquus*, Heinrich Kiepert,[7] whom I then heard on Ancient Europe. I had not then yet read Strabo; but naturally the *Atlas Antiquus* was ever on my table. Later, after my return to America, I wrote an abstract of Strabo (1878), and, in 1923, published an essay on Strabo. Kiepert always brought in huge charts, superb ones, literally his own handiwork. It was a rare privilege to listen to the foremost master in that field. His lectures evidenced absolute familiarity with all the ancient authors illumining his themes, even oriental ones. The catholicity, the wonderful sweep, of Kiepert's erudition made a great impression on me. One oddity he had: he cleared his throat with desperate energy every other minute; but after a few lectures I became quite indifferent to this interruption.

In August, 1873, through my father's personal bounty, I visited the Harz and the Rhine, and began to resume my sketching with good results: Quedlinburg, Ilsenburg, St. Apollinaris at Remagen on the Rhine. At Bonn the *Rheinisches Musikfest* was then given, specially devoted to the works of Robert Schumann; there I heard his opera *Genofeva* and also heard his widow, Clara W. Schumann, ren-

---

[7] The Puget Sound controversy between Britain and our own government, referred to William I by the contestants, was settled by Kiepert.

BERLIN

dering some of his exquisite compositions on the piano. At Rüdesheim, I hired a boatman and swam across the Rhine because my father had done it there some forty years before. I was economical: much of the Rhine from Bonn southward I did on foot.

I now come to the winter semester of 1873–1874 when I took six courses. Of course Hübner and Kirchhoff came once more, also Kiepert—on the chorography of Greece— and then at last I heard Mommsen, on the constitutional history of the Roman Republic.[8] I sat immediately under him: next to me sat a Fellow of Oxford or Cambridge. I have preserved my complete set of notes. The keen and authoritative force of Mommsen's presentation was impressive as well as his Schleswig pronunciation. I here limit myself to his introductory remark: "We must not fancy that the political sentiments of the Romans were in the slightest degree tinged with those humanistic ideas with which the moderns, with their idealization of classic antiquity, are accustomed to endow them."

A more lasting influence for all my future life were the lectures on Greek philosophy by Hermann Bonitz, unexcelled in that day as a great Aristotelian, whose concordance of Aristotle, on which he worked some twenty-five years, is a treasure house. It is true, I could have heard Eduard Zeller. But he was, for one thing, handicapped by his Suabian dialect, which he shared with the noted theologian Dorner, then also at Berlin. How important the great work of Bonitz would prove for me, decades later, in my Seminar-room at University Heights, I could not then know. The candor and modesty of that great scholar impressed me then as a veritable model. He began, of course, with Thales, but never got much beyond Plato. He was marvellously clear and fair when setting forth the

---

[8] Later, of course, at University Heights, I studied his *Staatsrecht*, *Kriminalrecht*, *Münzwesen*, and the fifth volume of his History, the *Provinzen*.

FROM MAUMEE TO THAMES AND TIBER

conflicting efforts of modern scholars in arranging the sequence or groups of Plato's dialogues. Need I say that this incentive made me read Plato with unflagging and restless enthusiasm? I used Bekker's edition with the Latin translation of Ficinus of Florence who established a Platonic Academy on the Arno under the patronage of Lorenzo de' Medici. I have since often pondered over the continuity of classic studies, so admirably surveyed in the three volumes of Sir J. E. Sandys—broken by the Sahara of the Middle Ages—from Athens, Alexandria, Rome, onward to the Arno, the Seine, the Isis and the Cam, the Spree, and finally to the Patapsco, the Hudson, and the Charles River.

To sum up: these two, Kirchhoff and Bonitz, influenced my entire life more than any other teachers. If, at this late day, I could lay a grateful wreath on their graves, I would gladly do it: here and now these poor words must suffice.

Before taking leave of the Spree and the great University of Berlin, I must make some record of an historical event. Early in September, 1873, after my return from the Harz and the Rhine, there was a celebration in Berlin of more than ordinary significance. It was the dedication of the Victory-column (*Siegessaeule*) in the west end, beyond the Brandenburg Gate. It was in commemoration of the Wars of 1866 and 1870–71. I tried to hear and see as much as possible. It was history. Prince Bismarck,[9] in his cuirassier uniform and with the gilded helmet on his head, was so near to my point of vantage that I could have touched his steed with a cane. He was perspiring.

The great collections at Berlin, especially the *Altes* and

---

[9] Here I beg leave to quote from a letter that I received from the late Viscount Bryce, dated Williams College, August 2, 1921: "Nor do I understand wherein you differ from my views of Bismarck. There was never any objection in England to the unification of Germany, but rather, I think a sympathy with the efforts of a country which had been much divided, to obtain national unity. I have often said this, and believe it to be the opinion of all English historians."

BERLIN

the *Neues Museum*, of course, I visited very often. Kaulbach's efforts to concentrate and group in a series of great tableaux epochal periods of history, such as the fall of Jerusalem, or the era of the Reformation with Luther as the central figure, caused much contemplation, reflection, and study. I was not then acquainted with Rafael's Academy of Athens in the Vatican at Rome, perhaps a model for Kaulbach's design. Although I was no archaeologist, the remnants of ancient sculpture, whether in plaster casts or in the original marble or bronze, often entertained me: Caesar's bust, the boy with the goose, the boy extracting the thorn, Agrippina, but especially the Muses with their exquisite symbolism, Kleio above them all, with tablet and stylus. I did not then know that *she* perhaps had benignly bent over my cradle not far from the cornfields of the Maumee.

I followed Ernst Curtius somewhat in his ambulatory lectures in the Museum; but I felt quite correctly that I had no means or leisure to pursue archaeology in the classic lands, while literature, history, and philosophy *could* be pursued in transatlantic places. I was then, of course, and for some decades later on, under the spell of idealization which some classicists never lose. Now in the Museum there was a cabinet which I visited again and again. In it there was a large fresco by Preller. I now quote from some reminiscences which I wrote some forty-two years later: "When I was young and often ascended the steps of the Museum at Berlin, I too often dwelled in Arcadia. There was a cabinet with a superb fresco by Preller,[10] the Apollo temple at Phigaleia, with its silent dignity and stately beauty, a consummation of architectural form, proclaiming itself a finality of taste, amid the oaks of Arcadia and the stern lines of Hellenic mountain ranges, a solitary eagle floating in the ether. Many an hour I sat

[10] The same who did the Odyssey in the Museum at Leipzig.

there and attuned my soul to ideas of majesty and beauty. *But* at the same period of my life, I entered upon the parallel study of Aristophanes and Thucydides and conceived Greece as she really was, and learned, in the balancing of such witnesses and documents so curiously illumining and illustrating one another, to apply, though with a prentice's hand, the material of historical criticism, to which, albeit on the Roman side, the later and maturer period of my life was to be devoted. Polybius, Aristotle, the Stoic system—these and many other lights reveal the later trend of the Greek spirit in a sober mood, and I think in a truer; and the pettifogging and the hopeless political incapacity of the Greeks seem to me to be the sediment in the cup of Hellenism in its later development."[11]

[11] "Confessions and Convictions of a Classicist," in *The Johns Hopkins Alumni Magazine*, June, 1916.

VI

THE UNIVERSITY OF LEIPZIG AND MY RETURN TO THE MAUMEE

Before I migrated to Leipzig, I had the good fortune to be invited to call upon Geheimrat Dr. Ludwig Wiese, Undersecretary for Education[1] in the Prussian Government of that time (1874). He was what we may call an *anima candida*. As far back as 1829, he had known my father well in Berlin, and he still recalled little traits of the Lieutenant's temperamental peculiarities. He gave me a letter of introduction to Friedrich Ritschl, the eminent Latinist at Leipzig, who at Bonn had become the ideal classicist to B. L. Gildersleeve, as I learned a few years later, when I saw a plaster cast of Ritschl's head on Professor Gildersleeve's study-table in the cradle years of the University on the Patapsco.

At first I almost regretted the shift to Leipzig. I lost all the social relations which I had enjoyed at Berlin, such as those with Colonel Pochhammer and other military gentlemen. The springtime of the Leipzig *Messe* was just in full bloom, overwhelming everything when I arrived; and for a while I had to be content with very narrow quarters. For that which I left behind on the Spree, I never gained full compensation on the Elster. On the other hand, my associations with fellow-Americans were greatly widened at Leipzig, especially with Southerners from South Carolina, Virginia, and Tennessee. I could often aid them in choosing their habitations. Many of these heard courses in Divinity: Luthardt, Kahnis, Lech-

---

[1] Bonitz became his successor. Dr. Wiese's best known work is entitled *Deutsche Briefe über Englische Erziehung.*

ler, Fricke, had many American students; and even more were drawn to the eminent Semitic scholar Franz Delitsch. Finally I found a definite domicile in the mansard story of a good modern house, 26 Humboldt Strasse, not far from the Rannstaedter Steinweg on which Napoleon escaped westward on October 19, 1813, after the great battle of Leipzig. Nor was the Rosenthal far from my rooms, the chief park of the city, crowded on Sundays. The name struck me as odd, for there were no roses but rather a great deal of leek, nor was there anything in the surface which could remind one of a *dale*.

Soon I received a chum or companion, Major Arnold, some fourteen years my senior, a Virginian, I believe. He had marched and fought under the great strategist Robert E. Lee during the Civil War. He told me of the final weeks in the spring of 1865 at Appomattox, nine years before, when they were actually almost starving, and when Major Arnold himself was sometimes so utterly spent that he marched almost asleep or nearly unconscious.

Of course I soon delivered my Berlin letter of introduction to Professor Ritschl at his house. He still seemed to nurse some feeling about his departure from Bonn—the famous feud with Otto Jahn—but he treated me with great kindness. His study-table, i.e., the particular spot where he worked, was a kind of well: books piled up on three sides, leaving only a small space where he could write. He repeatedly lent me important books from his private library. First he would consult a huge folio, a catalogue; then he would ascend a sliding ladder or steps in order to reach the desired volume. On his table also there were two Japan dishes, one filled with black cigars, the other with lump sugar. I need not say that I sampled neither. His health was suffering some impairment. He always arrived at the Bornerianum (the oldest of the lecture halls of the University) in a *droschke*, and an attend-

LEIPZIG

ant always assisted him to alight from the vehicle. But we forgot all the frailties of his aging years when he began his lectures. His manner was keen and trenchant, and the presentation of his matter was that of a master. His theme was the *Trinummus* of Plautus and a survey of Roman drama. I always felt that I was then sitting at the feet of the greatest Plautine scholar of Europe. My notes are lying before me now, some fifty-four years after they were taken. In chronology he rigorously counted *ab urbe condita*. On the Latin side of my equipment, I owed very much to Friedrich Ritschl. It may interest some of my readers to know how he ranked the comedies of the Sarsinate: he gave preëminence to *Aulularia, Mostellaria, Menaechmi, Bacchides, Pseudolus*. Georg Curtius (brother of Ernst Curtius), who combined Greek with comparative philology and phonetics, I also heard; but he sowed no seed on my soil. My Platonic studies I continued with that lovable scholar Dr. Paul Schuster. Further I heard Windelband on the history of modern philosophy. Having purchased all the three parts of *Überweg*, I had the bookbinder put on the back not *Geschichte der Philosophie*, but *Geschichte des Philosophirens* (History of Philosophizing). "Love of Wisdom" is what the Greek term originally meant. *Sophia* is wisdom. But *Sophist* and *sophism* have a bad flavour, due in part to Plato's *Dialogues* in which often he sets up the professional teachers of wisdom to be discriminated from and overthrown by his beloved master Socrates. Now I sought definite and enduring verities, as then in Windelband's lecture-room. But where are they? See Democritus of Abdera on atomism: no place for the soul there. Plato's aversion for the Abderite was profound. Nothing can bridge the chasm which separates these two. Pilate's question will recur: "What is Truth"? Pleasure, Power, and Wealth only matter. To return from the Roman praetorium in Jerusalem to Windelband's course: According to Leibnitz we live "in the best of all possible worlds." Very different is the vision of Schopenhauer. Materialism certainly leaves the questioning and aspiring soul shivering, sad, hopeless. How must I live? how die? Which of these contradictory *Weltanschauungen*,[2] must I make my own? Am I an infinite particle of the World-soul? I became deeply distrustful of the kaleidoscopic sequence of contradictory philosophies whether urged by Socrates or by the Stoics or by Kant or by Hegel. It is true that the famous thinker of Königsberg once wrote: "There are two marvelous things: *above* us the starry heaven, *within* us the voice of Conscience." And this, I was glad to know, the plain folk shared with Kant or Seneca, for that matter. The plain folk must be content with that inner guide, sovereign for us all, both learned and unlearned, to which latter class, the "Greatest of the Great"[3] devoted so much of his service and of his mission. I thought, and often think, of the Primitive Christians of Nero's time: for *metaphysical* tenets no one would give up his life.

In the autumn of 1874, Major Arnold having gone, I received a new chum in the rooms at 26 Humboldtstrasse. Again it was a Southerner, Charles Forster Smith, of Wofford College, Spartanburg, South Carolina, where many descendants of the Huguenots[4] still flourish. To anticipate a bit: on a later sojourn at Leipzig, Smith in 1881 gained his Ph.D.; served as visiting lecturer at the American School at Athens; taught Greek at Williams and at Vanderbilt; was called from Nashville to the University of Wisconsin by President Adams in 1894; and presided over the American Philological Association at Yale in 1903, being then, I believe, the foremost Thucyd-

---

[2] Cf. Lucian's *Hermotimus*.
[3] A term used by Alfred Tennyson.
[4] Dr. Gildersleeve's maternal ancestors were Huguenots.

idean scholar in America. Of course our evenings at Leipzig were full of mutual inspiration and suggestion. Very often I would conclude our dialogues with my favorite axiom: "Go to the sources"; for I held then in my springtime, as I still hold in my sunset years, that the real principle of our studies must be that of Leopold von Ranke: "Wie es denn eigentlich gewesen ist."

So too, in the University, I followed Voigt on the Roman Republic with great earnestness; but still I would say to myself: "all this, for me, is but second-hand knowledge." A world of work loomed up before me, which then was bidden to wait: Livy and Polybius, Plutarch, Dionysius, Appian, Cassius Dio, Velleius, Tacitus, Suetonius, and others. I said to myself: *Know?* As yet I know little or nothing of the real history of Rome. I also heard Ludwig Lange on Cicero. Later, at University Heights, I began to admire his work on the constitutional history of Rome: not a single statement unless fortified by the authorities—and there are blanks—but that great scholar filled out nothing by conjecture. I also heard the famous archaeologist Overbeck on the technique of ancient art, on sculpture in marble and bronze, on painting in every form: fresco, tempera (on wood), encaustic, vases, etc. I copy here a statement of the famous scholar from a lecture delivered on December 14, 1874: "The pictorial technique of the Greeks reached very great excellence and must not be placed on a level with Chinese painting." He illustrated much with Pompeian preservations, with which he had a masterful familiarity. He gave to Thorwaldsen the foremost place in approximation to the sculpture of the ancients. But, as I have intimated, archaeology is the luxury among the so-called branches of classic philology. My own study of Pausanias came much later, in America.[5]

[5] See Chapter III, "Under the Antonines," in my *From Augustus to Augustine*, Cambridge University Press, 1923.

FROM MAUMEE TO THAMES AND TIBER

In the summer of 1874, I had an experience unique in my sojourn in Germany. A Prussian nobleman, chamberlain to Emperor William I, sought a tutor for his son. He had been directed to me by Dr. Wiese of Berlin; he even came down to Leipzig for a personal conference. I was to live in England with my pupil so that both preparation for the University and thorough mastery of English might thus be combined. But my father, to whom I referred the entire matter, quite wisely judged that I should *lose* more during this period than the youth would *gain*. So nothing came of this offer, which might have given me a closer vision of Oxford or Cambridge. Nor did anything come of another opportunity. The entire educational administration of the duchy of Lauenburg had been placed in the hands of Dr. Wiese. He very kindly suggested to me that I might begin my career as a classical teacher in that province. But here, too, my American social-consciousness abruptly and sharply interposed itself. I could not entertain this offer, however kindly its motive and its manner.

I now come to October 1874. It was near the anniversary of the great battle which drove Napoleon across the Rhine, sixty-one years before. Smith and I walked well out of the city southward, stopping before various historic spots and records, stating what corps had stood or fought here or there; we especially visited Liebertwolkwitz and Probstheyda. Smith, by the way, could *jerk* a stone farther than I, an old baseball player, could *throw* it. I marvelled at this form of athletic excellence, new to me.

On Sunday afternoons there was always an American service held in the main hall of a *Bürgerschule*. The organizing spirit was Dr. Casper René Gregory of Philadelphia, a special disciple of Professor Tischendorf, the discoverer of the *Codex Sinaiticus* of the New Testament, and ultimately his successor in his chair.[6] We had sermons

[6] Dr. Gregory fell in the Great War.

LEIPZIG

by American and British clerical travellers or sojourners, sermons of varied excellence.

The ebbing of the slender financial resources from home compelled me to set my face westward in the spring of 1875. I found myself unable to fill out the number of semesters necessary for presenting myself for the degree of Ph.D. It was hard. I had as yet virtually no acquaintance with any American classicist of note, though written attestations by Ritschl and Hübner proved important later on. So, before leaving Leipzig, I printed a monograph of my own, February, 1875: *De Parodiis Comicorum Graecorum. Lipsiae, MDCCCLXXV*, fifty-five years ago. Apart from sifting Aristophanes (with a very fine sieve) as well as Meineke's fragments, apart from going through Athenaeus completely, apart from writing into Latin all of Seyffert's *Palaestra Ciceroniana*, I did something more: I wrote (in the Autumn of 1874) a Latin version of Lessing's *Laocoon*. The lucidity and limpid clearness of this famous treatise reminds one of the best prose-writers of Greece and Rome.

In the latter part of March, 1875, after having my chief possession, my books, packed with much trouble and much worry, I bade farewell to my friend Smith. In Berlin, I stayed for a few days as guest of Captain von R., who took me to the officers' mess on March 22nd, during the celebration of the Emperor's birthday. In the preceding Christmas vacation (1874–75) on my final visit to Silesia, the widow of my cousin Robert von Sihler had remembered me with a very handsome *viaticum*. This enabled me to go home via London, Edinburgh, and Glasgow.

The voyage from Hamburg to London was on a small steamer of some one thousand tons register. Violent gales in the North Sea banished almost all the passengers from the table. Only one other traveller sat down with me at breakfast. It was indeed a satisfaction to espy the coast of Britain off Yarmouth. The violent seas became gradually calmer. As we entered the mouth of the historic Thames, approaching Gravesend at eventide on Easter Sunday, we heard the bells of the parish church, a sweet and solemn peal. On the morrow, I found a room near the British Museum, in Bedford Place, not far from that mighty artery of human bustle which changes its name from West to East: Oxford Street, Holborn ("Hobbern"), Holborn Viaduct, Newgate, Cheapside, Leadenhall. I soon realized that London was indeed a trading-center of all the world. This I felt even more when I descended into the vaults of the London Docks, greatly favored by the personal guidance of a merchant to whom I had an introduction from a Scottish student at Leipzig. These Docks cover some six acres. We were fortified by a tasting order and were attended by a cooper who guided our steps by the huge vats and hogsheads, while above us there were gray garlands formed from the spirits of wine, hanging down from the ceiling of the vaults. I am temperate by habit and conviction, but I shall promptly admit that I have never before or since drunk any wines so perfect and beguiling. There were also wildernesses of ivory, of tobacco, of drugs and chemicals, some fragrant, others, like asafoetida, not so.

The Crystal Palace at Sydenham was a dream of bluish and majestic lines. Near by Captain Webb the American exhibited himself floating in his rubber garb, defying the dangers of Neptune and producing endless surprises from the tin buoy floating by his side.

My liveliest attention naturally was directed toward events in the past history of Britain now speaking to the visitor from the Nelson column on Trafalgar Square, or from the halls of Parliament, or Westminster Abbey or St. Paul's, with Paternoster Row nearby. I could not dream in those vernal days of my own life that in my sunset years one of my own works would be exposed in the windows of a book-shop in that classic lane of books and authorship. As to the English Hall of Fame, Westminster Abbey, it was curious. More than by the memorials of George Grote, Charles Dickens, and similar bearers of fame, my attention was arrested by something else: it was a memorial tablet for poor Major André, who in 1780 concerted with Benedict Arnold to secure the surrender of West Point to the British; and who was *hanged* as a spy by Washington's court-martial. The tablet in Westminster, however, as I examined it in 1875, had him *shot*, a more honorable form of death, but not historically true. I knew nothing at the time of Nathan Hale, whose statue near the City Hall in New York was erected much later. Ever more given to history than aesthetics, I copied the funeral inscription of one of the great statesmen of England, William Pitt, Earl of Chatham: "Erected by the King and Parliament as a testimony to the virtue and abilities of William Pitt, Earl of Chatham, during whose administration in the reigns of George II and George III Divine Providence exalted Great Britain to an height unknown to any former age."[7] Of Poplar, however, of Whitechapel, of Limehouse, I neither knew anything nor saw anything on that first visit.

As for Royalty in its manifold manifestations, I entertained no particular awe; tuft-hunting of all degrees I always despised, a crown prince often being chiefly an accident of primogeniture, and also often spoiled while waiting for his own succession. Every rise among mortal men should be through merit and experience alone. But such sentiments, I well know, belong to the *Pia Desideria* of our poor world.

I returned indeed to my native land a much better American than when I left it for the first time. Closer

[7] Canada and East India had been added to the British Empire.

vision destroys many idealized valuations. On the other hand, we Americans have grave faults enough; how rarely is high office bestowed upon the highest merit! Politicians we have in great abundance, but how rarely do our publicists dare to bestow the title of *statesman* on any man in our public life!

Before I leave London, I must not forget the great Christian preacher Charles Spurgeon. His Tabernacle in Southwark was packed, even in the aisles. His text on that Sunday morning in April, 1875, which I did not even jot down in my diary, never left my memory; it was, "The full soul loatheth an honeycomb; but to the hungry soul every bitter thing is sweet."[8] I marvelled then, and I still do, at the depth and the wide spiritual range of the great preacher, who was indeed a great student of the human soul and its needs. His discourse was wholly free from all the rhetorical tinsel and artifice with which we are so much regaled at home.

On my way north to Scotland, I was favored by an invitation to be the guest of Professor J. B. Paton, the Director of the Congregational Institute at Nottingham. I had made his acquaintance at Berlin, in the Harz, and at Bonn, in August, 1873. His lasting distinction is bound up with his intrepid service as Apologist of Christian Truth, as in his critique of Renan's *Vie de Jesus*. As Professor Paton has long closed his eyes, and as one of the duties of this volume is to make some grateful record of those who helped me forward in my youth, I beg to transcribe here from one of his letters: "Now may God open the way for you soon . . . let the time of waiting be one in which you are forming the purpose and temper of your whole future. Be a hero for God, using all knowledge and talent and endeavor for Him and for what is the best and the noblest in the world." In Edinburgh I was greatly impressed with

[8] Proverbs, 27, 7.

LEIPZIG

the disputative and dialectic faculty of the Scottish *ingenium*. I admired the honors shown to Scotia's greatest son, Sir Walter Scott, in the grand monument in Princess Street. Of course I tried also to retrace the chequered and tragic fates of Mary Stuart, and the minor figures in her life, Darnley, Rizzio, Bothwell. The Athens of the North seemed to have heights comparable to those of Athens on the Ilissus, the Castle and Carlton Hill reminding me of Acropolis and Museion, while Arthur's Seat furnished a parallel to Lykabettos.

The voyage from Greenock to New York was hard. The *Victoria*, Captain Hedderwick, was buffeted by headwinds almost continually. To-day one would call her a small vessel, her tonnage being about four thousand. There were only twenty-four passengers in the cabin; but, on the north coast of Ulster, we took on some two hundred emigrants, mostly earnest Presbyterians, whose hymn books and Bibles were much in evidence on the two Sundays which were included in our voyage. Near Newfoundland we passed several huge icebergs, one of them showing some two hundred feet above the surface of the ocean, and the temperature at once sank very perceptibly.

Two farmers from Illinois had some Percheron stallions on board: when at last we espied Sandy Hook, they leaped high in the air for joy. My heavy box of books also arrived safely; I had it promptly forwarded to my native city on the Maumee. There I myself arrived in May, 1875, and found all our dear ones in good health.

VII

A STERN BEGINNING OF TEACHING AND A GOOD ENDING

I CAME back a better American, as many do who had idealized what they had not known by their own vision. "Ignota semper magnifica sunt," says Tacitus. This of course had no bearing on the erudition and the solid worth of the Universities which furnished the base and the aims of all my coming life. During the absence of nearly three years, I had come to know my dear father much better. He had aided me and clarified my vision and judgment by his correspondence, as when he pointed out the preëminence of Greek literature as over against the imitative character of the Roman.

Soon after my return to the Maumee and to St. Paul's parsonage, there was at hand a great and grave decision as to all my future life. "Will you not preach in St. Paul's next Sunday?" my father said; "The gospel for that Sunday, Misericordias Domini, is that of the Good Shepherd, a simple and easy theme." At that time an assistant pastor of St. Paul's was a requisite of the near future. My father was now a septuagenarian, and the church had become very large. I was fully aware that I was then confronting the parting of the ways. Should I be a theologian or a philologian? In my heart of hearts, indeed, it had long ceased to be a question. For me it was an absolutely settled matter, not a matter of moods or of worldly computation. My father, fifty-one years my senior, received my decision quietly and kindly; but my mother, twenty-eight years her husband's junior, was bitterly grieved. She had actually named me at birth after a German theologian

FROM MAUMEE TO THAMES AND TIBER

whose hymns she dearly loved, Ernst Gottlieb Woltersdorf of Bunzlau, Silesia. There was something of Hannah and Samuel in her long cherished vision and hope. As for myself, my life-plans since eighteen had not been visionary or flighty, but clear and definite, a firm body of deep and irrevocable conviction. A classical scholar I would be, even though I had then but crossed the threshold of my real vocation.

My father sought an opening for me in the Lutheran college at Watertown, Wisconsin, and in the Luther College, a Norwegian institution, at Decorah, Iowa. There were no vacancies available in either. Now I would have been proud and happy to serve as a classical assistant in our own local Concordia, near the cornfields of the Maumee; but Rector Schick, my quondam teacher and of course no longer my ideal of learning, was not friendly to my aspirations. Naturally at that time, an enthusiast always, I was overflowing with Greek, especially in connection with the many problems of Plato's Dialogues. Now the Rector, whose habits of drill and parsing were both firmly set and limited by the practice of many years, would not have relished my assistantship at all, even though it would have been limited to the more elementary work.

How often in those anxious months of May, June, and July, 1875, a line of Hesiod reëchoed in my soul: "That perspiration must precede distinction is ordained by the gods."[1] Nor was I more successful in my application to teach Greek and Latin in the local high school on Wayne Street. The Smarts, two brothers from New England (Amherst, I believe), were not interested. My good mother said: "You will fare like Abraham: 'Get thee out of thy country and from thy kindred, and from thy father's house, unto a land that I will shew thee.'"[2] I was determined not

[1] *Opera et Dies*, 287.
[2] Genesis, 12, 1.

A STERN BEGINNING OF TEACHING

to eat my father's bread any longer. At last there came an opening, a very modest one indeed. "Aller Anfang ist schwer," says an old proverb. There was at least a prospect of earning something and repaying some of the loans incurred for my studies abroad. About twenty-seven miles north of Fort Wayne there is a small town, Kendallville, Noble County, Indiana, then of some two thousand eight hundred inhabitants. The Board of Education sought a teacher who could give instruction in German, Latin, and Greek. I went there, saw a Mr. Mitchell, the chief banker of that country town, president of the school board, and was "hired" for the ensuing school year (1875-76) with a salary of $600.00. I may say at once that of this remuneration I saved $300.00, which I repaid to those who could spare it least, i.e., to my brother Christian, then in the first years of his medical practice, and to my younger sister Elizabeth, then teaching in Bloomingdale, the northern suburb of Fort Wayne. Those eight to nine months in that little country town proved the hardest or sternest months of my life, now a long life. All the schooling in Kendallville was carried on in a single three-story building, from "high school" to A.B.C. class. My principal was a Yankee, for whom teaching was merely a mercantile pursuit. He revealed to me that, at the conclusion of the impending school-year, he was planning to open a carpet store somewhere in the East, his native section.

I devoted myself to my new work with great earnestness; but I found that certain lads in the German class simply refused to prepare their lessons, defied me to my face in the classroom, and insulted me on the streets with an extremity of provocation. So much for the German work. The Latin work was fairly successful, mostly with girls, some of whom looked forward to studying at Ann Arbor, in the University of Michigan. Even here when I insisted upon precision, I met much passive resistance. I

FROM MAUMEE TO THAMES AND TIBER

find in my diary of that winter a citation from Plato which I will give in my translation: "Of all animals the child is the hardest to handle: inasmuch as its sources of thinking are in the highest degree as yet untrained: it becomes insidious and cunning and the most insolent of animals."[3] I was, to sum it up, backed neither by the parents nor by the principal. The single student in Greek, W. D., looking towards Princeton, was faithful and of course entirely successful. I find in the same diary: "Pia Desideria," titles of books which by and by I hoped to add to my library: Anthon's *Zumpt*, Anthon's *Latin Versification*, Anthon's *Greek Prosody*. Anthon was a great name in American classicism in those days. But later on I realized that almost all his endless stream of books, two volumes per annum, were largely compilations from German learning. His successor at Columbia was Henry Drisler, destined to become one of my paternal friends in later years. Other books of that winter's list were: Bunsen's *Life of Niebuhr*, Butler's *Analogy*, Grote, 12 volumes (there was then no international copyright), H. M. Baird, *Modern Greece* (1856); I could not then foresee that I should be his colleague in the Faculty of New York University for ten years, 1892–1902. In reading a book about Joseph Smith, the founder of the Mormon cult, I made a curious observation: he taught that our Lord had five wives. I was reminded of John of Leyden and the Anabaptists at Münster in the period of the Reformation. Also I pondered much on the many slippery conceptions of "Freedom." Another entry in my diary, of October 2, 1875: "To-day for the first time in my life I received a regular salary for my work, $66.00. I have earned it at least one and a half times over."

Of the very real romance of that year of my life I will not say much, although I could write a very complete and

[3] *Leges*, vii, 808.

A STERN BEGINNING OF TEACHING

rich chapter on that bittersweet experience. It was a romance connected with a villa in South Wayne. I went so far in my devotion, as to abandon tobacco entirely, and obediently to read certain poems by Elizabeth Barrett Browning, the ideal woman for the maiden who now filled a great space in my dreams. We will call her Minerva Mayflower. She has long closed her eyes. Her aim in life seems to have been a college professor, perhaps an author even. It was she who that winter put a ring on my finger. Minerva too, almost three years my junior, analyzed my temperamental faults as calmly as a professional psychologist or phrenologist might do it. After five months she demanded the return of that sweet symbol, the ring. The prospects of a teacher in a little country town looked slender. I never shall forget that evening in May, 1876. Returning the ring wrenched my heart. She did eventually marry a professor. Her tombstone carries certain noble lines of Wordsworth, beginning thus:

> Our birth is but a sleep and a forgetting,
> The soul that rises with us, our life's star,
> Hath had elsewhere its setting,
> And cometh from afar.

I determined not to fall in love again very soon; on such vicissitudes one might quote Shelley:

> When the lamp is shattered,
> The light in the dust lies dead,
> When the cloud is scattered
> The rainbow's glory is shed.

That romance turned out merely a rainbow; but I had dreamt of a crystal bridge leading to the Isles of the Blessed. There is much bittersweet in life, especially in youth's auspicious year. But I refused to become a pessimist, let alone a cynic; I abstained from the fruitless task of picking these experiences to pieces, which in time became as unreal as the thistledown blown from one's hand in September.

Of course I wrote to many American classicists, endeavoring to introduce myself as best I could. None of them is now living. Professor Frederick D. Allen, then of the University of Cincinnati, was almost sanguine about an opening there; but local "influences" traversed his nomination.

All this winter my evenings were occupied with the elaboration of a monograph: *The Historical Aspect of Old Attic Comedy*. Once more I went through Thucydides with meticulous care, likewise through Aristophanes and all the *Fragmenta Comicorum* pertinent to my enquiry. Of this paper I also prepared an abridgment for presentation to the American Philological Association meeting in New York early in July, 1876. Professor Harkness of Brown University in his official reply bade me cordially welcome as a new member. Early in the spring of 1876, I wrote also to the eminent classicist Dr. B. L. Gildersleeve of the University of Virginia, even then chosen professor of Greek at the new foundation at Baltimore, the Johns Hopkins University. Of course I was not so silly as to aspire to his old chair. It was *he* who called my attention to the system of *fellowships* to accompany the birth of the new University. He suggested also that I submit a monograph of my own prepared for this very end. To this day I am puzzled why he was not content simply with my Leipzig study *De Parodiis Comicorum Graecorum*. But of all this, more in the next chapter.

I will now return to the Maumee, May and June, 1876. I had already actually cut my stay in that drab and doleful abode, Kendallville—a nightmare in the annals of my life —some two weeks. Did the reader ever observe a horse on a treadmill, or a squirrel in a revolving cage? My good father was not well pleased with that abrupt termination

A STERN BEGINNING OF TEACHING

at Kendallville. But it proved to be the darkness that precedes the dawn. One day in June of that Centennial year, there arrived a letter from Baltimore with "Johns Hopkins University" on the envelope as well as "President D. C. Gilman." I fairly gasped as I opened it. What was it to tell me? No declension, no rejection of my application for a Greek Fellowship. No. I was officially informed that I had been appointed Fellow in Greek, with a stipend of $500.00 for one year. Longer stay, I readily inferred, would depend on diligence, devotion, and achievement. Never yet had the leaves of the sycamores on the Maumee rustled with the whisperings of the Attic Muses. Of course the local press made prompt record of the academic distinction coming to the Hoosier town from the new and much discussed foundation in Maryland. I was vain enough promptly to order visiting-cards evidencing this distinction. I did not even go out to Concordia College to receive the felicitations of Rector Schick.

There remains one incident of a certain dramatic bearing. One afternoon as I was returning from my daily visit to the chief bookstore of Fort Wayne, on Calhoun Street, I was fairly dazed at seeing Minerva Mayflower's buggy standing before St. Paul's parsonage. Firmly and wisely, however, I kept my distance until the buggy had disappeared and returned to the villa in South Wayne; one scar was enough.

That Centennial year, 1876, I need not say was a memorable one for young and old. It was literally *rung in* at midnight December 31, 1875: all the bells of my native city rang again and again. Finally only two went on: St. Paul's on Barr Street and the bells of St. Patrick's Roman Catholic Cathedral two blocks away. St. Paul's were last. Fort Wayne has had a Roman Catholic bishop from early times, often a Westphalian—a class of immigrants very numerous both in the city and in the country.

FROM MAUMEE TO THAMES AND TIBER

Late in June, 1876, I set out for the East, stopping a bit at Cleveland and Rochester. On the day after Independence Day, I think it was, I made my bow before the American Philological Association, then seven years old. The chairman of the local committee was the Reverend Dr. Howard Crosby, one of the founders of the Association, then pastor of the Fourth Avenue Presbyterian Church in New York City and Chancellor of the "University of the City of New York," subsequently renamed New York University. In his younger years up to 1859, he had been Professor of Greek at that institution. I read my paper, not indeed before a large audience, but one that included William D. Whitney of Yale, Francis A. March of Lafayette, and B. L. Gildersleeve, now of Baltimore—for me and my future career, I need not say, the most interesting and the most important personage in the world. The first meeting then was in the Council room in the old University Building on Washington Square, and all the later meetings in a lecture-room connected with Dr. Crosby's church. The heat was intense. Many members, e.g., Professor Whitney, sat through the sessions in shirtsleeves. Professor Gildersleeve (his first attendance also) read a paper dealing with the classification of conditional sentences in Greek syntax, on some points of which he differed from Goodwin of Harvard. Both were born in 1831, and both had taken their Ph.D.'s in Göttingen. As to the preëminence of these two as ranking Grecians in America there were then probably no dissentient votes in all our land; and Gildersleeve was chosen vice-president for 1877 at this his first appearance in the Association.

On the whole, my early estimate, that of 1876, has, I believe, been justified by that acid test of worth, Time. The "Big Four" in philology in the Centennial year were these: March, Whitney, Goodwin, Gildersleeve. I name them by age.

A STERN BEGINNING OF TEACHING

On my return to Fort Wayne, I stopped at Lancaster, Pennsylvania, to visit Nathan Schaeffer, then on the faculty of Franklin and Marshall, whom I had met almost daily at Leipzig. Later he became Superintendent of Education in his native state. He too has passed away. He showed me also, on that visit, the State Normal School at Kutztown, nearby. The "Pennsylvania-Dutch" is a curious mongrel speech, and also a kind of monument in the history of American settlement and civilization, with a tenacity of survival, I believe, not paralleled by the later German settlements; I mean those in my own native section, now called the Middle West.

VIII

THE BEGINNINGS OF JOHNS HOPKINS
(1876–1879)

IN my diary, not very long before there came the welcome call to go to Baltimore as a Fellow in Greek, I find that I entered some general and impressive truths (γνῶμαι) from Pindar, not knowing that within a few years Professor Gildersleeve was to edit the Olympian and Pythian Victory odes of the great Theban lyrical poet. I will here set down a few of these "sententiae," which, like gold, defy the acid test of Time. "Time is the father of all."[1] "It is impossible to conceal one's inborn character" (τὸ συγγενὲς ἦθος). "Even wisdom becomes a bondsman to profit."[2] "Creatures of a day: who is something? who is nothing?" "A word lives a longer life than deeds." To which I may add a favorite of mine from Horace: "Whoever loves the *golden* mean, is safe from the meanness of a wretched roof."[3]

Arriving at Baltimore late in September, 1876, I was for a few days housed by the Reverend C. Frincke of St. Martin's Lutheran Church in South Baltimore, one of the two earliest theological students of my father at Fort Wayne, thirty years before. My first enquiry in the city on the Patapsco was a historical one, about the site of Fort McHenry, bombarded by the British fleet during the war of 1812, when Francis Scott Key, an American prisoner in the hold of a British man-of-war, composed *The Star Spangled Banner*.

---

[1] And also the consumer of all life. One thinks of the great symbolical group by Lorado Taft at Chicago.
[2] *Pyth.*, iii, 54.
[3] *Carmina*, II, 10, 5.

FROM MAUMEE TO THAMES AND TIBER

Soon I found a permanent lodgement at 166 Mulberry Street. No dormitories then were planned at the new University. And the housing of Johns Hopkins then was of the simplest. Two ample houses on North Howard Street, united by a party wall, immediately north of the City College, corner of Little Ross, afforded offices, faculty rooms, lecture-rooms, and professors' studies contiguous to the former, where aspirants for degrees could consult them readily. I must be cautiously conservative in these memories. I believe that in these early years I spent hundreds of hours with Dr. Gildersleeve in conferences which often meant even more than his lectures. He treated me, from the first day, as an advanced student of Greek, which indeed I was. I had a letter from Ritschl, whom, as I have mentioned, Gildersleeve placed higher than all the other teachers of his life. Another letter was from Hübner, his intimate friend at Bonn.

To sum up those initial months and years one may fairly say: Johns Hopkins began at the top. It is true that the original faculty was small, and that within the first three years President Gilman had not secured a university professor of Latin comparable to Gildersleeve in Greek. Minton Warren came after my departure. The first Ph.D. dissertation in Latin was by H. C. Elmer in 1888; there were a dozen in Greek before that year.

Two strictly new buildings had been erected against the opening in the autumn of 1876, both on the narrow side-street called Little Ross: Hopkins Hall and Remsen's Chemical Laboratory, both without architectural pretensions. On the ground floor of Hopkins Hall, there was a fairly large auditorium especially meant for academic occasions and public lectures. Above this, on the second floor, was the first Library, a general reading-room with stack-rooms adjoining. In the former were the works of reference, also the Teubner texts of the Classics, a resource for

THE BEGINNINGS OF JOHNS HOPKINS

the integration of which I worked in season and out of season. A fine large working-desk was assigned to me, at which I often spent thirteen hours daily. On the third floor of Hopkins Hall was the Biological Laboratory of Henry Newell Martin, an eminent disciple of Huxley. The latter also delivered an initial lecture, which, by the very name of Huxley and many controversial associations, stirred up much bitter feeling in Baltimore. But Dean Arthur Penrhyn Stanley was also heard in that autumn.

Two incidents of those October days are firmly lodged in my memories of that long ago. One was a general reception in the President's house on North Charles Street, not far from Monument. All the notables of the town, their wives, and also some of their daughters were present on that social and academic inaugural evening. For the first time we had the honor of meeting Mrs. Gildersleeve, whose youthful grace was such that at first I took her for a daughter of one the Trustees. I also had the honor of entertaining in conversation a younger lady who later became a munificent patroness of the University. Some of my colleagues promptly suggested later on that I should follow up such social opportunities. But I rejoined quite wisely: "What business has a penniless young scholar in the parlors or dining-rooms of the rich?"

Dr. Gilman availed himself of every possible avenue of publicity; he was on terms of intimacy with Godkin of the *New York Nation*. Gilman knew Europe well, both political and academic Europe, from Thames and Seine to Spree, Elster, Danube, and Neva. I may say at once that the new University was not grafted on any colonial beginnings or traditions, that her roots were not native at all; she was, in a word, a western offshoot of academic Europe. Her methods and ideals were derived from Cambridge, Oxford, and London; from Paris, from Bonn, Berlin, Göttingen, and Heidelberg. Agassiz the Harvard

Swiss had trained one of the new teachers of Morphology, Brooks. Some of the pillars in the new faculty counted among those who had inspired or taught them, men like Böckh, Bekker, Franz, Ritschl, Schneidewin, Helmholtz, Wöhler. Of the first Fellows, Lanman, H. B. Adams, Royce, and Sihler had enjoyed years of study at German Universities. This brings me to my special sphere and to the atmosphere and associations of those beautiful years.

The original plan had provided for ten Fellows only, but so great was the interest throughout the United States —some 145 applicants—that twenty Fellowships were established. The first holders were as follows: in Political Science, National Economy, etc., H. C. Adams of Iowa and McGregor Means of Massachusetts; in History, Herbert B. Adams of Massachusetts; in Zoölogy, S. F. Clarke (Yale) and H. J. Rice; in Chemistry, Edward Hart (Lafayette) and Malvern W. Iles (Columbia); in Mathematics, J. W. Gore (University of Virginia), Thomas Craig (Lafayette), and G. B. Halstead (Princeton); in Physics, W. W. Jacques (M. I. T.); in Engineering, D. W. Hering (Sheffield) and E. D. Preston (Cornell); in Philosophy, Josiah Royce (California) and F. B. Van Vorst (Princeton). The first five Fellows in Philology were: W. H. Page (North Carolina), Dr. Charles R. Lanman (Connecticut), A. D. Savage (Mississippi), J. H. Wheeler (Massachusetts), E. G. Sihler (Indiana). The original twenty Fellows hailed from the East, West, South. Canadians came by and by. Among the earlier Fellows was a German Russian, Constantine Fahlberg, Ph.D. Leipzig, 1873, a chemist: there came on in connection with his tenure a bitter feud about priority in the invention of saccharine. Besides Lanman the Sanscritist there was another New Englander who had already attained his Ph.D.; the universal goal after which we all strove; it was Herbert Baxter Adams, an Amherst man,

THE BEGINNINGS OF JOHNS HOPKINS

who had won his Ph.D at Heidelberg, and Bluntschli was the academic star which he particularly revered. After the latter's death, Adams secured his library for Johns Hopkins. Adams soon assumed a distinguished didactic career and trained many historians. He was greatly enamored of the dictum of E. A. Freeman: "Politics is the History of the Present; History is the Politics of the Past." In the autumn of 1877, our circle was replenished, or shall I say *redintegrated*, by the coming in of the physicist Edwin Hall, the Grecian Francis G. Allinson, the mathematician and later the publicist Fabian Franklin, the histologist Christian Sihler, M.D., (my older brother): in 1878 came the comparative philologist Maurice Bloomfield and the archaeologist Allan Marquand.

After this unavoidable bit of academic registration, I will now turn to a forenoon hour in early October, 1876. We twenty Fellows had been summoned to hear the initial address of President Gilman, who had turned forty-five and who had been nominated for his present post by the Presidents of Harvard, Yale, and the University of Michigan. The *leitmotiv* of his address was really couched in this hortatory monition: "Gentlemen, you must light your own torch." A wise and appropriate appeal, I dare say; we were indeed to be *learners*, but as independently as possible; we were as soon as possible to determine and to pursue our own tasks; we were even then to be given opportunity to *lecture* or to find pupils of our own. Soon there were launched on the Patapsco the *American Chemical Journal* (by Remsen), the *American Journal of Mathematics* (by Sylvester), some years later the *American Journal of Philology* (by Gildersleeve), the *Historical* and *Political Studies*, the *Modern Language Notes*, and so on. All these were pathfinders and pathmakers, which for the first time challenged (and earned) the attention and cordial respect of European scholars and scientific

FROM MAUMEE TO THAMES AND TIBER

men. We may fairly sum it all up in an attestation uttered twenty-five years later by President Eliot[4] of Harvard: "I want to testify, that the graduate school of Harvard University, started feebly in 1870 and 1871, did not thrive until the example of the Johns Hopkins University forced our faculty to put their strength into the development of our instruction for graduates. And what was true of Harvard was true of every other University in the land which aspired to create an advanced school of arts and sciences." And it seems undeniable that the rays of the new constellation in Maryland stirred and quickened distant souls and aspirations even *before* the average Baltimorean fully realized the work and the wide reputation of Johns Hopkins.

We twenty Fellows formed a kind of academic congregation by ourselves. At week-ends on Saturday evenings, we had our own meetings, a kind of junior academy of Letters and Sciences, and a social club at the same time. Josiah Royce, in our varied discussions, possessed then, some fifty years ago, of all of us, the most impressive faculty of what I will call sequential plausibility; and I never saw him angry or impatient or nettled. He came to us as Fellow in "Literature," but soon turned towards philosophy. On Saturday nights, then, we had our very simple and frugal symposia in the second story of a very simple hostelry, a little north of the University. Here, over a pint of beer, with some cheese and crackers and some tobacco, we discussed many kinds of questions and problems. Often I listened to Royce discoursing on the "Return to Kant" (whose *Critique of Pure Reason* I had laboriously ploughed through at Leipzig) or on Julian Schmidt whom our gentleman "from the Coast" held in high honor. Royce was not to be a compiler or an echo, one could readily see

---

[4] At the quarter-century celebration, February, 1902, at Baltimore; cf. Fabian Franklin's *Life of Daniel Gilman*, N. Y., Dodd Mead & Co., p. 389.

that. In the second winter, Fabian Franklin entered our academy, and I often heard him discourse on politics and on finance. The counting out of Tilden after November, 1876, was still a very live subject; yet we avoided all sectional rancour and bitterness.

The most eminent and most mature Fellow in philology was Dr. Charles Rockwell Lanman, a native, like President Gilman, of Norwich, Connecticut, first and last a disciple of Whitney. I see him yet, in the front room of the third story of a house in Franklin Street, registering certain data of Sanscrit syntax with stern and unflagging industry. On the shelves near him was a complete set, as then made, of the Teubner Classical texts. He was also a good Greek scholar. I felt a twinge when I surveyed his classical library, for I was too poor to own so many. I lived in a Greek atmosphere, and once coined the word "autoschediastic" which amused my phonetical friend in a lasting way.

I now come to the initial sessions of the Greek Seminar in a room in the second story of that primeval building on Howard Street, where B. L. Gildersleeve began the work so important for the development of classical scholarship in America, for which his highly dowered *ingenium* had received such enduring incentives in Berlin, Bonn, and Göttingen.

I repeat the names of the five Fellows gathered around the seminar-table: Lanman, Savage, Wheeler, Page, and Sihler. Only Savage had studied under Gildersleeve[5] before, at Charlottesville. A regular attendant and occasional critic in the Greek Seminar was Charles D'Urban Morris, one time Fellow of Oriel, Oxford, now Collegiate

[5] I must here preserve a bit from his boyhood, which came to me, in the spring of 1895 at University Heights, from the lips of the Reverend Dr. Hodges of Richmond, Virginia, an item which impressed me very much. When about eleven or twelve years of age, taught by his own father, a Presbyterian clergyman of Charleston, S. C., not only did the lad translate Horace's odes, but attempted to reproduce the original meters in English. Clearly young Gildersleeve was a *Wunderkind*.

Professor of Classics, exclusively for candidates for the A.B. degree. He was four years older than Gildersleeve, and an excellent exponent of Oxford scholarship. Gildersleeve was clearly prepared to give us much leeway—no "recitations" at all, but the elaboration of large tasks assigned in advance—the *seminarium* really being, as the very name implies, a *nursery* from which large and important growth (elsewhere) was to result, the more independent the better. The first session was not in October or November, but on December 5, 1876. The reason for this delay was as follows: at the very beginning of Johns Hopkins, President Gilman established a system of public and free lectures by eminent visitors—generally twenty lectures, with an honorarium of $1000.00. It seems proper in this place to enumerate the first ten and their themes: Gildersleeve, Greek Lyrical Poetry; Leonce Rabillon, French Literature; Simon Newcomb (the eminent astronomer of the U. S. Observatory at Washington), on the History of Astronomy; Francis Child (of Harvard), on Chaucer; James Russell Lowell, on Dante; Whitney (of Yale), on Comparative Philology; Hilgard (of Washington), on Geodetic Surveys; Judge Thomas Cooley (of Ann Arbor), on Torts; Professor Mallet (of the University of Virginia), on Waste Chemical Products. The tenth has escaped my memory. It was the course by Dr. Gildersleeve on Sappho, Alcaeus, and the minor lyrical poets of Greece, but especially on Pindar, his favorite, which delayed the opening of the seminar—which, by the by, the great Hellenist in his memories called *Seminarium*, and of which he appointed me "Senior" or Secretary. At last, then, we gathered around the academic table for the first time on December 5, 1876. In the official designation, it was called "Philological and Pedagogical Seminary." The work was to revolve around Thucydides. My official records of that first season contain this utterance of the

THE BEGINNINGS OF JOHNS HOPKINS

Director: "Teaching, being an art, can only be learned by long experience." John H. Wheeler (Harvard, A.B., 1871; A.M., 1875) read his introduction to Thucydides. Gildersleeve in his critique observed that Wheeler should have included a characterization of Herodotus, and should have begun with a survey of the primitive chroniclers of Greece, the *logographers*. Stahl's introduction was highly commended.

The first assignment, the interpretation of the initial chapters of Thucydides VI, was given to Page, the youngest and least trained of that initial band. On December 15th, E. G. Sihler read an abstract of a recent German volume: *Aristophanes und die historische Kritik*, by Müller-Strübing. In his own comments on that treatise, Gildersleeve uttered an axiom of universal bearing, especially to be heeded by young scholars: "Contempt solves no problem." To sum up briefly: We each of us felt a stimulus to put into every task, especially the self-chosen ones, the utmost devotion of which we were capable. This I know was certainly *my* experience, the more so as I had been appointed Secretary of the Seminar.

Very soon Gildersleeve began his lectures on Historical Greek Syntax, noting the usages observable in the authors from Homer downward. He now at last could bring forward a body of first-hand and most delicate observation collected or begun long before at Charlottesville, for which, hitherto, he had no students; and now, for the statistical determination of syntax, the reading of the Fellows was more and more enlisted, especially after my time.

I was given a most welcome permission to teach and lecture independently. So I gave a course of three lectures on "Attic Life and Society." Further I gave a regular course on the *Acharnians* of Aristophanes to two advanced undergraduates who had come to us from a college in Kentucky, my aim being, as always afterwards, to prepare and present my own exegesis, utilizing freely the *scholia* that I had studied in Berlin. I was very happy, especially when recalling that nightmare, Kendallville, a short year before. Soon the restless and resourceful Hellenist called into being a Philological Society, with regular meetings under his presidency where the study of language in its widest reach was cultivated by original papers read by the members: Greek, Latin, Comparative Philology (Lanman), German by H. C. G. Brandt (who after a few years returned to his alma mater, Hamilton) and by Professor Raddatz of the City College. Romance languages were first taught by A. M. Elliott (under whose guidance I made my first acquaintance with Dante) whose students in time filled many chairs in American colleges and universities. I must not pass over here the name of E. A. Fay, whose monument is his Concordance to Dante.

One of the outstanding gifts of Dr. Gildersleeve I must particularly stress in these memories. He wrote English prose with masterful skill; and his acute pen may be traced in his *Brief Mention* in the quarterly which will ever be associated with his name, launched soon after my departure from Baltimore, the *American Journal of Philology* (1880), on which more in my next chapter. I must now dwell for a moment on his *Essays and Studies, Educational and Literary*, Baltimore, 1890. My readers must not balk at the date of publication. Some of the most precious and characteristic of these monographs were written as early as 1867. *Grammar and Aesthetics* came later, but reveals much of the innermost fibre of his unique personality. These essays are written not only with grace, with an airy and easy elegance of treatment and diction, but also with a comprehensive sweep of outlook and reading. They exhibit, quite apart from the classics, great familiarity with English, French, and German letters and culture, a range perhaps never before or since shown by any American

THE BEGINNINGS OF JOHNS HOPKINS

classicist. Preëminent in this volume is the *Legend of Venus*, which ranges from Anchises of Troy to Tannhäuser, the whole quite equal to James Russell Lowell at his best. The satire and irony of Gildersleeve's pen often reminds one of Erasmus or of Lucian of Samosata. We notice the spiritual freedom with which he treats Swinburne. Gildersleeve puts his finger on the neopagan drift of that poet, but also confesses his own Christian belief with fearless candor, closing the essay thus: "for there are times when a spotless religion and a full revelation are scouted and set aside, when men leave the bread of angels for the husks that the swine do eat." Of similar excellence is his *Apollonius of Tyana*, or his essay of *Lucian*, dating back in the main to 1869, when he was thirty-eight—with the memories of the *Graeca Minora* of his Princeton youth. His wonderful early maturity is best betokened by his *Emperor Julian*, actually written in 1857, and first published in the *Southern Review*, January, 1868. The fine study of Platen again attests his extraordinary range and what I may call the polyphony of his literary sympathies.[6] It was in the Johns Hopkins Philological Society that I presented some of my earlier papers: "The Attic Oligarchs," "The Myths in Plato," "Lucian's Treatment of Greek Philosophy," and "The Attic Tribute Lists, as preserved in Attic Inscriptions." One more point about Gil-

[6] I cannot forbear transcribing from his footnotes (*op. cit.*, p. 404): "I became acquainted with Platen's poems at Bonn in 1852, having been introduced to them by my fellow student and dear friend Emil Hübner, whose friendship has known no more slackening in all these years than has his work, and what that work has been, no scholar need to be told." I may as well append at this point a few sentences from an estimate of Gildersleeve written by Gonzalez Lodge of Columbia, a short time after Gildersleeve's death (January 9, 1924), in the *Classical Weekly* of New York, February 4, 1924, (Professor Lodge entered Gildersleeve's Seminar in the autumn of 1883): "The business of the Greek Seminary was largely in the hands of the Senior Fellow, and the leonine figure at the end of the table sat as a critic, not as a helper. While uniformly patient with the halting performances of his followers, he never supplied a student with ideas or did his work for him. The student felt, immediately upon contact with him, that his work must be done by himself." To this should be added the estimates by C. W. E. Miller and by John A. Scott, in Vol. 56 of the *Proceedings* of the American Philological Association, Cornell, December, 1925.

dersleeve before I pass on. In Berlin and Leipzig I had listened to and carefully observed many classical scholars of ponderous erudition, but none whose faculty of presentation impressed me so much. I well knew that no progress of scholarship would ever endow my pen with a force and charm comparable to his own. Still I learned a lesson and it was this: that the *manner* of a scholar's presentation was almost as important as the *matter*, on which hitherto my best efforts had been concentrated.

But I must now return to the plain recital of my own life. One of the places to which I directed my steps almost daily was the Peabody Institute, at that time, even architecturally, I believe, the foremost edifice in the city. It was the library that drew me thither. Soon after my coming to Baltimore, in October-November, 1876, I was engaged in excerpting some monographs of my Berlin ideal, Professor Kirchhoff, published in the Transactions of the Prussian Academy. Most welcome then was the helpfulness of the librarian, Mr. Philip R. Uhler.[7] Not only did he give me free access to the inner library, but he did much more. As fall passed into winter, he put a rug on the marble floor before my working table and also a small portable oil stove, so that I could work in perfect comfort. The noted Peabody orchestra then was under the direction of Asger Hamerik. Under him was Sidney Lanier, veteran of the Civil War, a poet, an expert on the flute, and an expert also on the theory of English verse. He had written the cantata for the Centennial Celebration at Philadelphia. His health had been irretrievably shattered by the privations of the war, and one cannot follow the story of his last years without deep emotion. His bust, I am glad to know, is now in Gilman Hall at Homewood. Rarely in my life have I gazed upon a countenance so refined, nay spiritualized and ennobled, by much suffering.

[7] The distinguished entomologist, once a pupil of Agassiz.

THE BEGINNINGS OF JOHNS HOPKINS

My first visit to Washington, during the Christmas recess, 1876-77, had a peculiar academic occasion. President Gilman sent me to one of the specialists in the Surgeon General's Office at the capital to submit the histological studies and plates of my brother Christian, for which he received a Fellowship in Biology.

But I must hasten on. It was one day in the spring of 1877 that President Gilman detained me in the passage which connected the reading-room with the stack-rooms. Seating himself on a table there and gently swinging his legs, he asked: "Mr. Sihler, how should you like to become Reader[8] in Ancient History?" My felicity at this intimation was beyond words. A little farther on, I will explain why nothing came of it.

In July, 1877, the American Philological Association met at Johns Hopkins. I doubt whether more than thirty-five members attended, but that was the average in those early years. Some of the foremost scholars of America were there: Franklin Carter of Williams, Whitney, F. D. Allen, and Lewis Packard of Yale, and Goodwin of Harvard, Francis A. March of Lafayette; the president of that year was Haldeman of the University of Pennsylvania. I read a paper dealing with the battle of Salamis as related by Aeschylus and by Herodotus, which Goodwin commended; it was published in full in the *Transactions*. Dr. Gildersleeve was elected president for 1878 (Saratoga). The University furnished excellent luncheons for the members, enjoyed in the shade in the yard behind the original buildings on Howard Street. I had the commission of contracting with a colored caterer of good reputation: we had crabs, strawberries, raspberries, lemonade, ices, cold tea, and cigars. There was also a drive on tally-hoes around Druid Hill Park. I happened to be seated next to Professor Haldeman. I am afraid that I had been

---

[8] An academic term used at Oxford and Cambridge.

FROM MAUMEE TO THAMES AND TIBER

talking about Plato. But Haldeman said: "Mr. Sihler, why don't you rather devote your energies to the Indian languages of North America?" I considered this monition odd. But I said nothing.

I must now explain why nothing came from the rosy clouds of my becoming "Reader in Ancient History." Early in the summer of 1877, the great railways were compelled to reduce wages. There occurred a gigantic strike on the B. & O. railway at Martinsburg, Maryland. An even more terrible one, with bloody riots and vast destruction of property, came about at Pittsburgh, on the Pennsylvania Railroad, in July of that year. The shares of the B. & O., the chief asset I believe of Johns Hopkins, fell from 200 to 90. I was sobered and sad.

My vacation on the Maumee and in the parsonage of St. Paul's was, however, very happy. My brother Christian abandoned his medical practice at Cleveland and went with me to Baltimore in the autumn to assume his Fellowship in Biology. A little incident of that autumn: Page had made a vacation trip to Germany, the promised land of classical learning; I had given him some addresses in Berlin. As he came home by a Bremen-Baltimore steamer, he declared himself "strapped." So, on the first evening after his return, I yielded to him my bed and slept on the window-seat. To him it was a help in need.

In that second year of Johns Hopkins, my brother and I secured two rooms on the third floor of a new house, the *entire* rent of which in those happy times was but $25.00 a month. We made our own coffee in the mornings, with fresh rolls—sound economy.

In the second year of the Greek Seminar—there was no Latin Seminar yet—the Attic orators from Antiphon to Deinarchos were the main occupation. I suggested that Dionysius of Halicarnassus should be made an integral part of our work, and so I imported a sufficient number of copies from Leipzig, writing the pagination of Reiske's edition on our Tauchnitz margins. I also prepared an index of the technical terminology of the Greek rhetorician —which was never published. I insisted, perhaps too enthusiastically, that syntactical analysis and the study of periods would never suffice to have us realize the *power* (δεινότης) of Demosthenes. So I "got up," as the British say, during three months, the Third Olynthiac, using a morning hour daily after breakfast. In January, 1878, I spoke the speech in the original Attic, in Hopkins Hall. Allinson held the prompter's copy; and Professor Gildersleeve told me, at the end of the half-hour's delivery, that *but twice* had he to turn to the original text which he held in his hand.

In the last days of January, 1878, occurred the first examination for the Ph.D. degree in the young history of Johns Hopkins. It was held in the faculty-room on Howard Street. George Morris of Ann Arbor[9] was to be the chief examiner. The subject on this important occasion was the History of Greek Philosophy, and the examination lasted about two hours. All the full University Professors of that faculty were present, President Gilman presiding. The Collegiate Professor of Classics, C. D. Morris, was also present. The "associates" (as then constituted) were not present: Morse, Story, Austin Scott, Cross, Brandt, Elliott, Brooks. As I was waiting in the ante-room, the door opened, and President Gilman summoned me in with these words: "Here's the hour and here's the man." I had for years made myself intimately familiar with Ritter and Preller's famous collection of original source-texts, and now often answered by citing the Greek itself. I came through with flying colors; and Charles D. Morris, quondam Fellow of Oriel, as he passed by, said to me: "Sihler,

---

[9] His reputation rested largely on his being the translator of *Überweg*.

did he examine you, or did you examine him?" Of course I was very happy.

A word on the dissertation, which had been approved *before* this first oral test. I really had chosen the subject some years before: "Metaphor and Comparison in Plato." Beginning in Berlin, I had gradually written *abstracts* of all the genuine Dialogues, from Lysis to the Laws. I had convinced myself that this sort of study produced insight far superior to mere translation or excerpting: one is bound to apprehend the real design and theme, without being diverted by the peculiar charm of those dramatic conversations. I had also taken great pains to gain a first-hand acquaintance with ancient verdicts on Plato's literary manner, as preserved in Aristotle, Dionysius, Cicero, Quintilian, and Longinus, paying due attention also to modern scholars such as Ficinus, Ast, Stallbaum, Bonitz, Schleiermacher, C. F. Hermann, and Jowett of Oxford.

In March, 1878, I think it was, I faced my second oral examination before the Faculty, on the History of Greek Literature, mainly of course by Dr. Gildersleeve and Professor Morris. The hardest came last, a test unforeseen. I attended, alone, in the seminar-room, while Dr. Gildersleeve's contiguous study remained open. He gave me some sheets of paper, and my task was to write a life of Demosthenes, not in English but in *Greek*. My accents here and there were faulty, and I also confounded the Greek terms for *buying* and *selling*. Meanwhile Royce, H. C. Adams, and Craig the mathematician also had their various examinations. Adams had been given leave (after his examinations) to go to Berlin for the summer semester of 1878 to continue his study of National Economy under Wagner, while holding his fellowship in *absentia*, the University of the Spree thus collaborating with the new one on the Patapsco.

On June 13, 1878, occurred the public bestowal of our

well-earned degree of Ph.D. in Hopkins Hall. Immediately afterwards, President Gilman issued a broadsheet explaining and commemorating this academic first milestone. Two copies only seem to have survived, both preserved by me. One, framed, now hangs in Gilman Hall at Baltimore. The other remains in my keeping. It is yellow with age and somewhat brittle. It is an academic document of more than local or personal importance. The thesis of Adams was on *The History of Taxation in the United States* (i.e., the earlier decades), the chief examiner, before Adams left for Berlin, being Francis A. Walker. "The subsidiary examination was in American History. The questions on this subject, which were answered in writing, were prepared by Mr. George Bancroft of Washington." Craig in mathematics had to answer in writing questions prepared by Sylvester, Newcomb, and Associate Story. In physics, he was examined by Professor Rowland and by the visiting lecturer, Professor Mallett of the University of Virginia. The youngest and perhaps the most gifted of us four was Josiah Royce of California (and Berlin). His dissertation dealt with *The Interdependence of the Principles of Human Knowledge.* His main examination was on written questions prepared by Professor G. Morris after his return to Ann Arbor, while Associate Brandt gave him an oral examination on German Literature. In his official broadsheet, the head of the new University made a material omission: Sihler had spent five semesters in Germany, nearly three years of earnest labor, and Royce had had several semesters at Berlin.

Gildersleeve's greeting and Godspeed are also included in that official broadsheet; I will select a few passages of lasting importance: "Mindful of what the word *doctor* means, we have given them opportunity to show their power of expression as lecturers, their didactic faculty as teachers . . . We have invoked the aid of eminent men from without in making up our final decision." The concluding words of the great Hellenist, which I never forgot afterwards, should also be recorded. Turning to the graduates, he said: "Each of you gentlemen feels that the grasp of the hand which conveys the congratulation is to be returned by a grasp *which is a pledge of higher achievement.*"

All my life I treasured occurrences connecting the actual moving present with something that belonged to the historic past. Thus, in the autumn of 1876, I once observed an elderly lady on a quiet street on the north side of Baltimore, walking by herself. "That," said my companion, "is Mrs. Patterson Bonaparte (Mrs. Jerome Bonaparte) once the sister-in-law of Napoleon. Even now she still looks after many of her own business affairs."

Professor Sylvester's *Rosalind*, a poem of some two hundred or more lines, all rhyming on the queen of the piece, was recited by him to an invited audience, the élite of Baltimore, in a lower hall of the Peabody Institute: an odd piece of poetry, a *tour de force*, and still abounding in incalculable turns and graces. I remember it distinctly, because I was one of the ushers on this literary occasion. After my first oral examination, the famous mathematician invited me to accompany him to his rooms near the Maryland Club—he was a celibate—and offered me a very good cigar. Of course I deplored my ignorance in mathematics. "Mere atrophy!" he replied. I observed a Greek New Testament on his mantlepiece. Soon after this, in the reading-room in Hopkins Hall, he asked me to furnish a Greek motto for the forthcoming first number of the *American Journal of Mathematics*. I gave him a Scriptural one: "Proof of things not seen."[10]

I now come to my third and last year in Baltimore, in which, with no little satisfaction to my long nurtured as-

---

[10] πραγμάτων ἔλεγχος οὐ βλεπομένων. *Hebrews*, 11, 1.

THE BEGINNINGS OF JOHNS HOPKINS

pirations, I bore the title of *Doctor*. As I had failed to find work elsewhere,[11] I was continued as "Fellow in Greek History." At the same time I was granted authority to give a Greek course to a small class of undergraduates. Here, too, the aim and practice of the nascent Johns Hopkins University was to make the A.B. degree dependent *not* on four years somehow sat through or largely occupied with the acquisition of athletic fame, but dependent entirely upon personal energy and scholarship. I chose for my course the *Protagoras* of Plato, probably the most brilliant of that philosopher's earlier dialogues.[12] There were four men in my class: Grammer, Nichols, Richardson, Spieker. The first three became clergymen in the Protestant Episcopal Church; Spieker in time became a teacher of Greek at the University. All are now gone but the Reverend Dr. Grammer of Philadelphia. The last and, I am fond of believing, the maturest of my achievements at Baltimore was a course of ten public lectures on the History of Greece in the Fifth Century B.C. In the official announcement of these lectures I was designated as E. G. S., Ph.D., "Fellow in Greek History." The lectures came on successive Saturdays at noon in Hopkins Hall, beginning January 4, 1879.

In the official leaflet, a full survey of ancient sources and of modern books was given, *P.* standing for Peabody and *H.* for Hopkins. I see, in examining my MS.[13] of fifty years ago, that I called Niebuhr "the greatest of Classic Historians in modern times," a judgment which I believe may be still upheld, when we weigh the vast *extent* of his learning. I will limit myself to citing a passage from the introductory lecture: "I have often been impressed by many excellent people who thought that classic antiquity

---

[11] E.g., at Rutgers or at Centre College, Kentucky.
[12] Which, in 1881, I published in Harper's Classical Series, N. Y.
[13] The bound MS. of some 169 pages is now in the collection of my MSS. of some 67 volumes, in the Library of Washington Square College of New York University.

was a kind of museum containing marbles and mummies." I closed the last lecture with these words: "The ethical lessons, the political truths, which history evolves, are not subject to mould."

Among the new Fellows who came in the autumn of 1878 were two whom I came to know well. One was Louis Bevier of Rutgers, the other was Allan Marquand of Princeton, born in wealth, and so especially fitted to become a distinguished archaeologist and connoisseur of art. He lived at the St. James in comforts unknown to us frugal folk; but his mind was emancipated from devotion to fashionable garments and choice viands.

I recall the annual celebration of the University, on February 22, 1879, at the Academy of Music. Among the exercises on that occasion was the rendition of the Psalm *Non Nobis, Domine*." This was also the first appearance of the University Glee Club, in which some of us lifted up our voices; among the singers were Lanman and myself. This feature had been devised by the former Fellow of Oriel, the British scholar and gentleman, Charles D. Morris.

Not all of the original Fellows of Johns Hopkins had as smooth and straight an academic career as Lanman and Royce. Bevier, Ph.D. 1881, studied further at the German universities. Then, at his alma mater, Rutgers, he first taught French, then other modern languages, then Latin; and not until 1893 did he gain the Greek chair at New Brunswick. My own teaching career, soon to begin, was likewise slow and very far from smooth. There was no system then in America comparable to the "Privatdozenten" of Germany. These, for a while, often gain their bread as *Gymnasiallehrer* while "habilitating" themselves at a university, and so often lecture themselves into an academic reputation that permits them to drop their gymnasium-work entirely. Now, with us, "secondary" teach-

THE BEGINNINGS OF JOHNS HOPKINS

ing as a rule excludes a man entirely and definitely from the higher ranges of our common profession.

The southern colleges, during the earlier years of Johns Hopkins, still suffered from the economic aftermath of the Civil War. No door would open for me there. Finally I heard of a private school in New York City, mainly collegiate in work and aim, whose proprietor and principal, Dr. Julius Sachs (a Columbia alumnus and Ph.D. of Rostock) was seeking a well-trained classicist. So in May, I went to New York and arranged to begin there in September, 1879. Whatever my aspirations and ideals of life, the stern time had now come when my knowledge must go on the market of life, much of *vita* being *victus*. Besides there was the honorable obligation to repay the funds given my father by his friends to sustain my studies in Germany, 1872–1875. If, with Emerson, I had hitched my wagon to a star, the wheels of that wagon had to be on *terra firma*, and that too in our American Babylon, which I presumed worshipped chiefly at the shrine of Mercury, not of Minerva.

Not long before leaving Baltimore, I was sitting alone with President Gilman in his office. "You are an enthusiastic scholar," he said, "but it means a poor life." A chilling farewell, I dare say; but did anyone ever strive for true scholarship with an ultimate vision of Gold? If Mommsen had only gone in for banking and the organization of Trusts! How "successful" would he not have become!

IX

HOPES DEFERRED. THE GREEK CLUB OF NEW YORK

"We live, not as we will, but as we can."—*Menander*.

WHEN I came to live and teach in New York, in September, 1879, there were no skyscrapers; and Trinity Church, significantly facing Wall Street, was not as yet dwarfed and cramped by the financial edifices towering above her spire. Almost all the landmarks of 1879 are gone or changed. The Custom House is a private bank. There was not yet any Greater New York. To urge but one item on the present reader: the entire section west of Central Park was still free from habitations, aside from a few villas or nurseries or squatters' cabins. East of the Park, the northern extension of built-up New York fairly ended at 63rd Street. Of course building pushed northward incessantly. Yorkville was more or less detached, apart from the great continuous arteries of Madison and Third Avenues. Harlem, whose name must ever remind us of the original Dutch settlers, was really a northern suburb, with many spacious gardens flowering in May. There were but very few banks as yet in Harlem; and Mt. Morris was really a charming spot much resorted to by all Harlemites. The "Harlem Mere" was much used for boating in summer and for skating in winter.

The noisy roar and rattle of the American Babylon by day (and night) at first fairly dazed me. "How can anyone do any genuine study in this place?" I was wont to say to myself and to others. I soon found a boarding-house, and in it a rear room where I could set up my little library, on East 27th Street, between Third and Lexington Avenues; but after a few months, seeking peace, I moved one block north to a comfortable furnished room in 28th Street, opposite St. Stephen's Roman Catholic Church—a fairly quiet neighborhood then—and took my meals in a different place, on Lexington Avenue, the proprietor of which, a Captain B., had served in the Civil War. It was only fourteen years after Appomattox.

My compensation as teacher in the Collegiate Institute of Dr. Sachs was $900 in the first two years. Thereafter it rose slowly: $1200, $1350, $1500, $1600, $1650, $1800, the latter figure reached in 1887. At the very outset, I was quite sure that my occupation in this work would not last more than two or three years at the utmost, a mere stepping-stone to my real life-work in college or university. This waiting period, however, proved *twelve* years; and as September succeeded September, my heart grew heavier and heavier: hope deferred and ever deferred.

The principal, with his many financial and professional obligations, held to sound standards of teaching and attainment, and on the whole gave me a free hand to do my best in my own way. A mere taskmaster is never a good teacher. A real teacher is of incomparably greater importance than any textbook. Our country then was full of textbooks summing up chapters with an array of printed questions, making of the teacher a mere recorder or bookkeeper. But it is the personality, the tact, the initiative, the enthusiasm, the perseverance, the spiritual fidelity of the real teacher on which all depends. At that time, New York City, i.e., Manhattan Island, apart from the City College on Lexington Avenue and Twenty-third Street, founded as the "Free Academy" in 1847, had no public high schools at all.[1] Barnard College and Teachers Col-

---

[1] They began in 1894 under Mayor Strong. Brooklyn had its excellent Boys' High School and the Packer Institute for young women.

lege were still in the womb of Time. Columbia Grammar School and University Grammar School, originally feeders for the two colleges, were in 1879, I believe, in private hands. My principal's chief aim in 1879 was preparation for Harvard, much less for Columbia College; Yale and Princeton figured but slightly, if at all, in our professional outlook and pilotage.

The pupils, in the first two years of my service, were taught in a house on West 49th Street, not completely occupied by our classes. From September, 1881, onward, the Collegiate Institute was well housed in a new five-story building with a well-equipped gymnasium, designed and owned by the principal at 38 West 59th Street, opposite Central Park. The pupils were of two kinds: those who, after a general grounding by our principal, went to Packard's Business College and those destined to "go to college." The Harvard entrance examinations in the main determined our work, especially my own. Therefore, Greek, Latin, and Mathematics were the chief subjects, with an elementary survey of Physics and Chemistry. In one field, I believe, the work far excelled that done elsewhere in this preparatory stage. I mean in History. Greek, Roman, Mediaeval, and Modern History were presented in distinct courses, and this by *narrative*, and the collegiate students were trained to take notes. Often, when returning from Harvard, they talked to me about this part of their preparation with especial satisfaction.

The full Greek course in our principal's schedule covered four years, and the Latin some two years more. I always did an extra half-hour's work in the morning from 8.30 to 9.00 A.M., for special pupils and special needs. The classification of pupils—after "Primary" which concerned me not—was "Intermediate" I, II, and "Senior," several years. Certain (important) pupils had virtually private lessons. Among those who took four years of Greek

FROM MAUMEE TO THAMES AND TIBER

before going to Harvard (1879–1883) was James Loeb, who later on became a distinguished patron of the classics, i.e., of reading them with a translation on the opposite page. Among other noted pupils of mine at 38 West 59th Street may be mentioned the two sons of Carl Schurz, the brothers Jesse and Percy Straus, Mortimer Schiff, and several brothers Lehman.

I will now present the schedule of my first year as copied from my Diary of nearly fifty years ago, for the five days of the week.

8.30	Latin Ex.	Vergil, Ecl.	Aeneid	Xenophon	single pupil
9.00	Engl. Comp.	Latin I. 1	Latin I. 1	single pupil	single pupil
9.45	History I. 2	Xenophon	Greek Ex.	Greek Ex.	German I. 1
10.30	History I. 1	Ancient Hist.	German I. 1	El. German, Sr.	single pupil
11.15	El. Greek	El. German	single pupil	El. Greek	German Ex.
Recess of One Hour					
1.00	El. Latin	El. Greek	El. Latin	History I. 1	El. German
1.40	German I. 2	German I. 2	German, Sr.	Ancient Hist. Sr.	El. Latin
2.30	El. Latin I. 1	Vergil, Sr.	History I. 1	Latin I. 1	Xenophon, Sr.

A very great amount of work, and a very great variety of work indeed, in forty periods weekly. Probably not many young preceptors could have undertaken all these classes and also certain advanced individual pupils. Only very gradually I began to estimate the professional and material value of my services. In money matters I have always been rather timid.

Of course Ancient History was then as well as later on one of my chief concerns. Even then I sought living and ever widening contact with the great source-authors: Thucydides, Herodotus, Xenophon, Polybius, Plutarch. As my diary of those initial years still attests, I made much use of Carl Peter's *Zeittafeln*. It is an incomparable work. The bulk is the footnotes, where the source-texts, primarily for the teacher, are printed in full in the original Greek or Latin, and where not only the political annals thus appear, but the literary history is likewise given in an orderly

HOPES DEFERRED

way.[2] The perfect mastery of Greek, the attainment of which had been one of the chief aims of my last six academic years, now, in teaching, proved a daily joy, refreshing and sustaining me amid a mass of drudgery essential to the work that I was doing. I sometimes seemed to myself —to use a parallel of the horse-tribe—to be a hunter, but condemned to earn my oats as a dray-horse. But still, this personal and daily joy in pure scholarship, I say, was a very positive consolation in those twelve years from twenty-six to thirty-eight. There was a quasi-spiritual consolation: I strove to give to my pupils the very best that they were able to take from me, especially in their last year, before they went to Cambridge. Before that year began, many of them were not amenable to monition, were indolent or tricky or unwilling to be honestly diligent. But during the last year, when the entrance examinations were looming up before their young vision, consistent and eager study often succeeded to those faulty years of self-indulgence.

Decoration Day, May 30, 1880, proved one of the most important dates in all my life-story. With some friends I issued forth from Harlem Bridge northward; we had chosen two boats for a day's outing and picnic beyond High Bridge. We landed beyond Morris Dock where is the slope now leading to the Hall of Fame. There, looking for some early strawberries, in the company of my future wife, I somewhat suddenly declared my life-intentions to her, and, as she wrote me soon after, made her very happy. But in her making a home for me, by and by, the greater meed of praise must go to *her*: a real home, where incalculable forms of self-sacrifice, later on, were practiced by the devoted holder of her husband's name, gone from life as I

---

[2] As given in Herodotus, Thucydides, Xenophon, Diodorus, Strabo, Plutarch, Pausanias, Eusebius's *Chronicon*, Livy, Dionysius, Cicero, Velleius, Sallust, Tacitus, Nepos, Suetonius, Festus, and inscriptions.

am writing—a devoted service which proved the granite isle in the currents and gales of that uncharted ocean which men call *life*. Her maiden name was Emily Birkner. She was a native of New York, but in her teens had attended a famous boarding-school for girls at Hildesheim, Hanover. Her habits, like my own, were bilingual. Of the wedding, a little later. After she assumed my name, she never more enjoyed the ease and the measure of comforts which she had left behind in her father's house.

I now come to the Greek Club of New York. No one could gain membership by application. My entrance proved, in time, one of the most important events of my life. Both Dr. Howard Crosby, then Chancellor of the University of the City of New York, and Henry Drisler, Jay Professor of Greek in Columbia, by letter invited me to join, soon after my arrival in New York. As I learned later, both Gildersleeve and Morris at Baltimore had become sponsors for me without my knowledge. Drisler and Crosby had conceived the Club in a barber shop on December 30, 1857, twenty-two years before my entry. I believe that I was the youngest member who ever joined. The Club met on Friday evenings at the houses of members, in turn, from October to May. The first meeting that autumn was on October 17th, at the house of Professor Drisler, 48 West 46th Street. I now draw on my Diary: the reader was Howard Crosby, beginning Demosthenes *de Corona*. Other members present on that October evening in Dr. Drisler's parlor were these: Dr. Charlton T. Lewis not long before had completed his Harper's Latin Dictionary based on Freund. Mr. Overhiser had kept a private classical school in Brooklyn, had declined a call to the Greek chair at the University of Rochester, and had now turned to real estate ventures in New York, with abundant success as he told me. The Reverend Talbot W. Chambers was then the Senior Minister of the Collegiate

HOPES DEFERRED

Reformed Church of New York City, his wife being of the noted Frelinghuysen family of New Jersey. He assured me that he owed all his love for genuine scholarship to the Greek Club. James Herbert Morse, a former student of Goodwin at Harvard, an author also of occasional tasteful verse, had a private school of his own. This was also the case with an alumnus of Columbia, Duane S. Everson. The oldest member in years was Mr. Liggett, also proprietor of a classical school. Mr. Ferriss of Brooklyn, who was compelled to use a magnifying glass always, was a *rara avis;* he had studied the different forms of Greek music. A peculiar enthusiast was Frederick Cope Whitehouse, an A.B. of Columbia, even then deeply set on the project of retracing the canal (*Bar Jussuf*) which once connected Lake Mœris with the Nile. He was precisely ten years my senior. Until he went abroad on his engineering and antiquarian quest, he entertained the Club at the Brevoort House. A. D. Savage, of the Greek Seminar at Baltimore, was now a curator at the Metropolitan Museum under Cesnola the director, whose Cypriote finds were lodged at the Museum. Another member was Seth Low of Brooklyn, a Columbia man, son of the great merchant Abiel A. Low. The reading generally ceased about 10 P.M. when the Club sat down to an excellent supper, followed by cigars and general conversation—probably as good talk as could be had or met in New York at that time. For a short time Mr. Minturn was a member. He lived in a very large and fine house on Madison Avenue, if I remember rightly, and belonged, I think, to the famous firm of Grinnell & Minturn, who sent Elisha Kent Kane to the North Pole in the fifties. Soon the Club met at the house of Colonel W. P. Prentice, 9 West 16th Street. Colonel Prentice, sprung from an old Albany family, an alumnus of Williams College, and later a student at Göttingen, had been on the staff of the Army of the Cumberland in the Civil

FROM MAUMEE TO THAMES AND TIBER

War.[3] Colonel Prentice always furnished wine at our Greek symposia, and his fine residence also housed the excellent classical library of his deceased father-in-law, Mr. Robert Kelly. That library was ideally fitted for the meetings and readings of the Club. Dr. Sachs, a devoted lover of Greek Literature, was also a member. Later on, the orientalist Isaac Hall joined the Club. Some twenty-eight years after my entry, in 1907, when the Club had become a memory, I wrote[4] as follows:

"Those indeed were *Noctes Atticae* more genuine than those of Aulus Gellius, gatherer of antiquarian and grammatical herbaria, botanist of the flowers of the Classic Past.

"Most of those scholars to whose weekly meetings the present writer was invited twenty-eight years ago, have passed into the Silent Land, but four stand out above the others: Henry Drisler, Greek lexicographer, placid and imperturbable, successor to, and eminent pupil of, Charles Anthon, curiously non-perceptive of the aesthetical and historical side of classic letters, exponent of the Second Aorist; Howard Crosby, charmer of souls, vivacious and earnest, free-lance of all debates, versatile and incalculable in his sallies, quaint and obstinate defender of faulty and impossible readings; Isaac Hall, Oriental and Greek scholar, endowed with the genuine scholar's swift and keen perception of the crucial point or of the sore spot in any critical controversy, pugnacious and defiant of mere authority; and Charlton T. Lewis, whose scholarly ideals and earlier training were gotten from Theodore Woolsey and James Hadley of Yale, of the much cited class of 1853[5]—Lewis, I say, whose forms of relaxation included

---

[3] He soon invited me to give lessons in Latin writing and speaking to his older son Robert K., who was to go to Princeton in 1880.
[4] In the *New York Evening Post*, September 7th, 1907, *American Classicism II: The Higher Ranges.*
[5] Of which were Chauncey Depew and Andrew D. White.

Sanscrit and papers in the highest mathematics, Latin lexicographer, translator, essayist, organizer of reforms in public correction and reformatory institutions, activities in all of which he excelled without apparent effort. Lewis was the best reader in the Club, advancing without a trace of hesitation or stumbling, ignoring no difficulty nor airily vaulting it, covering more ground than any reader in that company.

"The Club read and reread many of the Greek classics, most of those called *classic* by Hadrian's renaissance, Pindar no less than Xenophon. It was not desultory in choice and procedure, but generally pursued each author to the end. Of post-classic authors we took up Polybius, Josephus, Plutarch, Lucian, and a few others. It is a curious and significant fact that one of the later members, an eminent authority and well known to his generation as a publicist and economic writer, Horace White, brought out an altogether admirable version of Appian. The Greek Club then and its life and work were, and deserve to be, recorded in this year (1907) of a half century's retrospect as the finest vindication, right in this traders' Babylon, of the nurturing strength and the mysterious charm of classic reading: a veritable graduate school antedating any one formally begun in America, and, in its constituency and incentives—*sit venia verbo superbo*—perhaps superior to them all, for all were masters and all were learners as masters ever are."

The ethics, academic and social, of the Club are a sweet memory. To question or to doubt was a privilege freely accorded the oldest or youngest member—of course whoever interrupted the reader was expected to make good his point. It was bad form to appear sensitive or to display the slightest degree of displeasure. Elementary matters of course were taboo. When my turn came to entertain, I paid the expenses of the table in some member's house, until, a few years later, I could welcome the Club in my own modest domicile. My first reading at the Club came at Professor Drisler's, on December 19, 1879: Demosthenes *In Midiam*, 1-42.

On New Year's, 1880, there were still the New Year's calls of that era, now a mere memory. It was then still *de rigueur* for the lady of the house to receive the callers, while table and sideboards were groaning under the load of viands, ices, and wines. But many of the visitors could not maintain wise moderation, and this old social custom, too, soon after passed into innocuous desuetude.

On the evening of December 16, 1879, by invitation of the treasurer of the Philological Society of New York, I delivered a lecture in the chapel of the University on Washington Square before some fifty hearers, on "Plato's Use of Myths." In the audience were General Loring and Colonel Long, the latter recently of Egyptian service and originally a reporter on the *Tribune*.

I was beginning to put much of my time and knowledge, without money and without price, at the service of Professor Drisler, chief editor then of Harper's Classical Series, and also American collaborator of Liddell and Scott. Thus he requested me to make an English version of the commentaries of Classen and Böhme on Thucydides VI and VII, for the use, I believe, of an American editor-to-be of these books of the great historian. Furthermore Dr. Drisler asked me to read Thucydides through with special attention to the fine lexical points. Liddell and Scott were at my elbow; the idea being to make some additions or improvements to go into the next edition of the lexicon. The Columbia professor asked me to keep an account of my time and labor. The Commentaries named were done by March 27, 1880, on 240 pages of MS., in about one hundred forty hours of work; the lexical revision of Thucydides consumed some eighty to ninety hours of hard work, from November 18, 1879, to April 15, 1880. I also made an abstract of Holm's work on Sicily. My reward was not in money, but in the scholarly trust and good-will of the Jay Professor of Greek at Columbia. I also became very friendly with Seth Low of Brooklyn, once a favorite pupil of Professor Drisler's at Columbia. Several times I took his turn in reading in the Club when his counting room on the East River made greater demands on his time.

Of course my wistful eyes kept looking abroad—with vain yearning. On June 16, 1880, my Diary records that Lanman goes from Baltimore to Harvard, C. H. Toy to Harvard, Frederick D. Allen from Yale to Harvard, Tracy Peck from Cornell to Yale.

For the American Philological Association, in July, at Philadelphia, I had prepared a paper on "Vergil and Plato," discussing the feature of pre-incarnation of future Roman worthies in *Aeneid* VI with pertinent material from Homer's *Odyssey* XI, and from Plato's *Gorgias*, *Republic*, *Phaedrus*, also from modern authors like Sellar, Conington, and Nettleship. The paper was well received, and was published in the *Transactions*. Among those in attendance were Crosby, Whitney, Humphreys, March, and Cattell of Lafayette.

The greater part of the summer I spent at Wurtsboro, Sullivan County, New York, in the Shawangunk mountains, as tutor to a son of Judge McAdam of the Marine Court, recovering there my normal physical vigor.

After a brief visit to my parents and my native city on the Maumee, I began my second year of "Prep" teaching in New York on September 13, 1880. In that second year came a curious *parergon*. During certain noon hours I gave historical lectures at a distinguished private school for girls at 63 Fifth Avenue, a welcome addition to my slender honorarium. A new door was opening. Almost all

FROM MAUMEE TO THAMES AND TIBER

my evenings were devoted to my forthcoming edition of Plato's *Protagoras* in Harper's Classical Series. Often I read proof at the famous publishing house in Pearl Street. I worked very hard, and I soberly doubt whether I could have done much better at fifty or seventy than I did then at twenty-eight. The volume, destined for Juniors in good colleges, was ready in the autumn of 1881. One irksome blunder of my own escaped even the trained eye of the chief editor. The book eventually was reissued in 1892. Since then Greek studies in America have entered the consumptive stage. I quite justly, though vainly, hoped that this work would open for me the door of some reputable college.

I was married about this time, on September 5, 1881. It was a sad time in our land, when the tragedy of President Garfield's long suffering was drawing to a close by the ocean breezes at Elberon. Two eminent scholars graced our nuptials in Harlem. One was Dr. Gustavus Seyffarth, the noted Egyptologist, formerly of the University of Leipzig, who gave the bride a valuable ring of rubies, an heirloom of his own mother. Professor Drisler brought a set of Shakespeare in a box, twelve small volumes. When the matrimonial coach left the bride's home, Dr. Drisler threw an old shoe, but broke the glass in the gas lamp before the house. I shall always rate him a true friend of my early manhood, although I may honestly say that I *earned* his friendship.

We two, after our return from our wedding tour to Ellenville, New York, were not long in our modest apartment in East 120th Street when a thief entered during my wife's absence and stole her watch. Fortunately he did not see the *honorarium* of $150 for my *Protagoras* which reposed quite near the timepiece.

Greek then was still in honor in the colleges in America, and my *Protagoras* was well received by many of our best scholars. May I be permitted to transcribe here a letter then received from the author of *Greek Moods and Tenses*?

Cambridge, Nov. 10, 1881.

Dear Dr. Sihler:

I thank you very much for the copy of your new edition of the *Protagoras* which you have been kind enough to send me. I hope it will prove the first fruits of a long and plentiful harvest on your part.[6] I wish we had had this a little sooner, as we should have recommended it to one of our classes which is reading the *Protagoras* now. It will be a comfort hereafter to know that we have a good American edition to use when we want it.

Yours very truly,
W. W. Goodwin.

But to return to my work for my daily bread and my young wife. Her domestic virtues made a home for me to which I returned every evening with deep satisfaction. My daily tasks of five and a half hours, now at 38 West 59th Street, were of course performed with increasing smoothness and efficiency. At the same time, the ever widening sphere of private tuition grew so much that on Saturdays I left my Harlem home after breakfast and saw it no more till nightfall. My income from that source in that year (1881–82) was equal to two-thirds of my regular salary.

The summer of 1882 we two spent in Vermont near Jericho, east of Burlington. It was a dairy-farm where no summer boarders had ever been before; and we lived, literally, on the cream of the land. The landscape was charming: toward the west the noble chain of the Adirondacks, towards the east Mt. Mansfield dominated the panorama, and Camel's Hump greeted us on the southern horizon. I spent all the forenoon hours on Plato, having the ambition, entirely on my own volition, to leave a second and more perfect copy of my doctoral thesis in the archives of the Greek department at Johns Hopkins University.

[6] How cheering were those words then!

FROM MAUMEE TO THAMES AND TIBER

In those earlier eighties, there began a movement in New York City to do something for the higher education of women. Miss Bessie Minturn, of that noted New York family (Fifth Avenue near 12th Street), was particularly active in this agitation. In her company was an academic Englishwoman from Girton or Newnham. My services as classical tutor were brought into play in a quasi-official way. Among my most enthusiastic pupils was Mrs. John Curtis of East 34th Street. Dr. Curtis was a professor in the College of Physicians and Surgeons of Columbia, and a half-brother of George William Curtis. The lady was a sister of the "Fighting McCooks" of Ohio, of the Civil War. Whether these sporadic beginnings of offering Greek to New York women proved the original germs of the later Barnard College, I am unable to say.

Returning now to the main interest of my life, classical scholarship, I come to the birth of the *American Journal of Philology*, virtually promised by Dr. Gildersleeve in his Presidential address, July, 1878, at Saratoga. It began to appear in January, 1880. I find an entry in my account book, for March 15, 1880: "*American Journal of Philology*, Vol. I. $3.00." Of course the editor had to secure, *ab limine*, contributors of acknowledged eminence as far as possible, those on whom fitted the Pindaric[7] $τηλαυγὲς$ $πρόσωπον$. He *did* gain contributions from distinguished British scholars like Robinson Ellis, Nettleship, Lewis Campbell, Rendel Harris, and others. Of course the reports on foreign journals and the reviews of books called for many diligent helpers, for at first the *American Journal* was really as comprehensive as the term *philology* can well be. I mention among those earliest helpers: C. D. Morris, Humphreys, Allinson, Bloomfield, Garnett, Savage, Thomas Davidson, Merriam of Columbia, James D.

---

[7] "Countenance beaming from afar." Gildersleeve used that expression in a letter to me, of those years. Cf. Pindar *Olympian Odes*, 6, 5.

HOPES DEFERRED

Bright, A. M. Elliott, Toy, Lanman, Minton Warren, Martin L. D'Ooge of Ann Arbor. The *Hermes* of Berlin for many years was entrusted to E. G. Sihler. Now a good review or report has a certain chastening or refining influence on the reporter or reviewer. Why? It must not be done hurriedly, perfunctorily, superficially, but carefully, patiently, *honestly;* it postulates protracted and genuine toil and a kind of self-denial on the part of the reviewer, who must be something more than a mere condenser or abstractor. I will now dare to say something—utter an experience not rarely experienced: some of the supra-clever and condescending papers by Wilamowitz in *Hermes* proved a trial: I mean the characteristic manner, from a higher level and *ex cathedra:* thus I noted of Aristarchus, "dagegen helfen Aristarch's schaale Exegetenkünste nichts."[8] I recall that Gildersleeve once, in referring to this trait in the noted Hellenist, quoted the familiar Horatian line: "omnes eodem cogimur," etc. The heavier articles, the original papers in that initial year, were contributed, as far as America was concerned, by men like Franklin Carter, Lewis Packard, and Gildersleeve himself. Charles Short wrote heavy reports on the New Revision of the King James Version of the New Testament.

In the earlier volumes of Gildersleeve's *Journal*, as I suggested before, in addition to the Greek and Latin Classics, Semitic, Romance, Comparative, and Germanistic work was well represented. In the very first year, the *Journal* had subscribers in thirty states of the Union. A survey of "Periodicals received" is significant. I find: from Greece, 2; from Germany, 37; from England, 11; from Italy, 4; from France, 6; *from America*, 1; from Holland, 1; from Russia, 3 (published in French).

There is certainly in the life of scholars and scholarship the fundamental human principle of "passing on the

[8] *American Journal of Philology*, vol. I, page 265.

torch." *It is men who stir men:* if American Classicism owes more to Gildersleeve than to any other American, it seems fit that we should note to whom Gildersleeve ascribed most of his incentive. It was to *Ritschl*. Now, even at Saratoga in 1878, Gildersleeve had referred to Ritschl with deep feeling. Later the two heavy volumes of Ribleck's biography of Ritschl (1879, 1881) drew from Gildersleeve's pen one of the most elaborate papers that he ever wrote for the *Journal*. I venture to assume that I may serve the readers of this volume by transcribing a few passages from that deeply felt and nobly expressed farewell: "No man could go out of his school without a thorough conviction of the necessity of exhaustive study ... But what seems to me even now, at the distance of more than thirty years, the best thing about Ritschl, was not his accuracy, not his method, but the personal spirit which breathed out of his lectures. Böckh was a great man, doubtless, but he read his yellow lectures with a serene sublimity and uttered his classic sentences with a quiet self-satisfaction that awed, but did not inspire." Especially would I beg to stress the following monition by Ritschl, true as ever, though repeated by Gildersleeve some fifty years ago: "Philology is a science and must be studied as a science, even by those who are only going to do elementary work as teachers. The good teacher must ever, as a teacher, hear more and know more than he needs to impart, both in quality and quantity; and the *quantum* that is chosen and weighed out for immediate information, for a practical purpose, must be brought out of abundance, out of depth." Here are stated axioms and ideals, which, from my Berlin days onward, I pursued with ever deepening purpose and consistency.

The birth of my first son, Henry, February 4, 1883, I cannot entirely pass over. It was an anxious and distressful time, followed by a half-year of anxiety, when the souls

HOPES DEFERRED

of the parents were ever distracted between hope and fear, and when the material calls on my slender professional income more than ever drove me to private lessons after school hours.

In 1884, I took an intense interest in the nomination and election of Grover Cleveland; and, in my last visit to my father in July of that year, I delivered an impassioned plea for that candidate, a real political speech of one and a half hours, in the largest hall of the courthouse of my native city. There was a band, and the mayor introduced me. My good father cordially approved. The Greek Club was much divided that autumn, but of course maintained its sound tradition of good-will and peace. We had now received a new member, a distinguished Southern scholar, Thomas R. Price, called from the University of Virginia to Columbia, he having succeeded Gildersleeve at Charlottesville in 1876. There was one feature of our club to which I must turn for a moment. Even more than in the readings was the innermost *ego* of the members unfolded at the symposia which followed. We had no Macaulay to monopolize the conversations, although Dr. Crosby with his wonderful humor and his incalculable sallies, blending mirth with serious thoughts, naturally commanded our willing attention beyond all others.

The year 1885 ushered in a series of summers when real vacation and the rest-period of our profession, for me, came to an end. In the first two summers I fairly filled the weekdays tutoring in the summer houses of the patrons of our Collegiate Institute along the lower Hudson and on Staten Island. In the long vacations of 1887, 1888, and 1889, I took upper class pupils to Vermont to Massachusetts, and to a pleasant place in the foothills of the Adirondacks, near Crown Point, New York. The forenoons were devoted to vigorous work in the classics, the afternoons to games like tennis or baseball in which I regularly joined. Then there were excursions into the charming landscapes all around us. Thus most of my summer pupils entered college a year earlier. Of course, as I realized later on, the whole summer-plan reacted unfavorably on the professional interests of the principal and proprietor at home, which ultimately brought on the most important crisis in my life and career. It was in fact a cleavage of interests. In the autumn of 1890, having put in a laborious summer of tutoring at Long Branch, I found myself at the beginning of the school year in that autumn utterly spent, weary in body and soul, a state of exhaustion hitherto entirely unknown to me. Since 1885, I began to see, I had given myself no genuine rest, no real vacation, due at the bottom to the *res angusta domi.* So then, on December 17, 1890, I told my employer that this must be my last year.

In the summer of 1890 there had been born to me a second son, to whom I gave the name of Howard Crosby, my paternal friend and benefactor. The child's mother had undergone extraordinary suffering and trials, which continued for a long time after Howard had come to us. My outside tutoring had been called upon for income as never before. As to the minor incidents which led up to the final cleavage with the Collegiate Institute on Central Park, I shall not dignify them with any recital, important as they were in the epic of my life. It is a common saying that we must all be prepared to eat a peck of dust or dirt in the course of our lives; but *my* allotment, to speak with great moderation, had been long exceeded.

But I must now return from the teacher's desk to the work of the scholar's pen. In the summer of 1885, Dr. Drisler summoned me to his study where he sat, as usual, before a mass of texts, deeply engaged in his lexicographical labors, a spot where I had often enjoyed his kindly conversation when my *Protagoras* was going through the press. This was his news: "I desire to have an edition of Caesar's

HOPES DEFERRED

Gallic Wars for the Harpers." But I shrank from the prospect of adding a school edition to the endless series of editions already performed and perpetrated in our own and in other lands. He admitted this, but added: "What we really need, is a real *Lexicon* to Caesar; the current editions end with vocabularies hurriedly put together, without any philological value." So I began my *Caesar-lexicon*, i.e., a real concordance. This task occupied much of my leisure time, from summer, 1885, to December, 1888, some thousand hours of intense labor. It proved the severest trial of endurance of all my laborious life. There were some 45,000 references. The precise discrimination of usage, the range of meanings, the syntactical work on conjunctions like *cum* (the ancient *quom*), demanded the most scrupulous care. Still there was a great benefit to me personally: I gained far more in finer Latin scholarship than if I had excerpted twenty of the best Latin grammars in existence. Something almost tragic (for me) occurred soon after my completing this long task. The Harpers declined to publish, disavowing therein their own chief editor, Professor Drisler. Perhaps they were then approaching insolvency. Dr. Drisler even offered to reimburse me out of his own pocket, which of course I declined. I shared the cost of the publication with a noted publishing firm, dedicating the concordance to my old teachers, Hübner of Berlin and Gildersleeve of Baltimore. Other severe and untoward experiences crowded into my life about this time which I will pass over here. They left some scars.

Let me return to the autumn of 1885, a year in which I began that laborious task, apparently so thankless, but only apparently. A telegram called me to my native city to which I promptly hastened, in order to share in the funeral honors of my father, whose counsel and conduct had been to my soul like a second conscience from early childhood onward. He entered into rest on October 27, 1885. On the morning after my last arrival in St. Paul's parsonage, I entered into his study and, with deep emotion, scanned those noble and revered features now so calm and chiseled in the marble of the final repose; somehow certain lines of St. Paul flashed before my spiritual eyes, in my reminiscent survey of this particular life: "and that He died for all, that they which live *should not henceforth live unto themselves, but unto Him which died for them and rose again.*"[9] The material fortune which the Reverend Dr. Sihler left consisted of some three hundred dollars and a theological library; but, besides this, a bequest imponderable and imperishable, a noble life for memory and example. The funeral cortège was over a mile long.

In 1885, the annual meeting of the American Philological Association was held at Yale. My monograph on the orator Deinarchos was published in the *Transactions.* Professor Goodwin thought that I was then connected with New York University. From 1885 onward, Caesar naturally began to assume a larger place in my studies. In 1887, at Burlington, Vermont, I presented my first fruits: *The Tradition of Caesar's Gallic Wars from Cicero to Orosius,* and still later my *Studies in Caesar* appeared in the *Classical Review* of England. I became convinced that something more than stubbles could be gathered in that ancient field.

At one time I planned to spend a year of rest and recreation in Baltimore, and Dr. Gildersleeve actually suggested some service like that of a *Privatdozent* for me, with Polybius as my theme; but in May, 1891, I received a call to Concordia College, a Lutheran gymnasium at Milwaukee. I had indeed, in my physical condition, approached somewhat closely to the danger line of what is called "nervous prostration"; but at Cleveland in the home of my brother Christian, a physician too, of wise counsel, I recuperated completely.

[9] II *Corinthians,* 5, 15.

HOPES DEFERRED

Addendum. In one of my last years of service in the Collegiate Institute in New York, I prepared for my advanced pupils a *Vocabulary and Syntax of Xenophon's Hellenica IV, 1–5, on which are based the Exercises in writing Greek for Entrance at Harvard* 1890–91, *arranged and analysed by E. G. Sihler, Ph.D. Johns Hopkins, 1878, Classical Master at Dr. J. Sachs's Collegiate Institute, New York*, virtually a Greek grammar *en miniature*, the entire vocabulary properly set down and grouped according to inflection, with many etymological clues; the particles, case-syntax, the prepositions. I find also that, in the syntax of Conditions, I used the Gildersleevian terminology: Logical, Unreal, Anticipatory, Ideal. Greek indeed was still in honor in our land at that time.

Further, in the last February of my New York secondary work, the following craves record. On February 27, 1891, the last birthday in the life of Howard Crosby, an important meeting was held at the house of Mrs. Stuart on upper Fifth Avenue. It was called by the Reverend Dr. John Hall, pastor of the Fifth Avenue Presbyterian Church, then still Chancellor of the University of the City of New York. The "uptown movement" for this institution, urged particularly by the Vice-Chancellor Henry M. MacCracken, was there and then discussed and determined upon. And as regards the Latin Chair there, Dr. Crosby, as far back as the silver anniversary of the Greek Club, December 30, 1882, had spontaneously intimated to me: "You will be called!"—a prospect which, treasured in silence though it was, had now sustained me through many years.

Not long after the meeting just referred to, on March 29, 1891, Dr. Crosby passed away from pneumonia. He was only sixty-five. As my wife and I passed by the casket in his church, the Fourth Avenue Presbyterian, I felt that I had lost a powerful and consistent friend, almost the

FROM MAUMEE TO THAMES AND TIBER

only friend I still had in the wide world. Dr. Drisler was in Europe. My last months in New York, from April 1st to June 20th were a period of deep gloom, my family being sent west two months before I became free. My incessant labor with voice and pen in the twelve years then consummated often seemed utterly vain and fruitless; even the vigorous optimism of many years seemed shrivelled and dead.

X

A PRELUDE IN WISCONSIN

THE Concordia College on the west side of Milwaukee on the Milwaukee river, ten years old in 1891, had been organized precisely like the mother institution in Fort Wayne, from Sexta to Prima with heavy accent on the classics. The immediate environment was Lutheran; Milwaukee then, in proportion to the population, was (and is) perhaps the most Lutheran city in America, unless we include Fort Wayne. By far the greater number of students expected to study Divinity at St. Louis after graduating from Prima. The sound tradition of thoroughness in the classics was all to the good; but I was surprised at one feature: bilingual though many things were in the most German city of the Union, I found that even the Prima students had great trouble in making English versions of Horace's Odes, instead of German. My compensation indeed was modest, but it included a whole house some three-quarters of a mile cityward from Concordia. I strove to console the dear partner of my life for this western exile, as she insisted on calling it, by refurnishing our new domicile with generous effort. It was all in vain. She would say: "If only we had remained in New York, I would have been content if you had peddled books there! O why did you come out here?" Many chafing shackles indeed, for me, were gone. I felt it with daily joy and manifold satisfaction. The greatest of all names could be freely brought in whenever historical or cultural or spiritual associations called for it. But the allotment of work was peculiar. The faculty sitting in conference, voted the courses. Every one knew that Greek was my specialty, both by academic training and by my production, such as my edition of Plato's *Protagoras;* still the elementary work in Greek was assigned to me. It was an odd welcome. I was grieved. Coming home from the first faculty conference, I asked my good wife whether the many small boxes in which I had brought my library from New York were still in the attic? They were. "Well then," I said, "do not use them up for kindling. I may use them again; perhaps sooner than we now can tell." However, for the sake of peace and the wider good which Concordia served, I taught the Greek elements as I would have taught Plato. I bore that and many other things as cheerfully as possible. As for domestic things, I soon realized that the kitchen larder now could be replenished much better and more economically than in New York. My account-book tells me that at Thanksgiving, 1891, the turkey cost about $1.08, and many other commodities were equally reasonable; a domestic servant could be had for $10.00 a month! It seems incredible to-day. The gas bills were 90 cents or $1.00. Electric light had not yet come.

I return to my classes. I had Horace with Prima, but also *mensa* with Sexta. I sometimes felt like a novice in a monastery to whom the menial duties are assigned by the *fratres conventuales.* I had a course in Modern History with Secunda and Tertia which I enjoyed very much, giving in English the free narrative of a fully digested lecture. This seemed something novel to my new western students, and I know that they were gratified. We could weigh in the scales of moral and political valuation the great movements like the Reformation or the French Revolution and its chief product, the pestiferous career of the Corsican. All this seemed to my students stirring and thought-moving to a degree. They became conscious of powers dormant and undeveloped, powers now called into joyous and deliberate action. There are few studies as

A PRELUDE IN WISCONSIN

pregnant with positive educational good as history; and the analysis of decisive personalities has a charm exceeding all novel-reading.

But I must now turn to a larger and more widely important theme. A law, called the *Bennett Law*, had, in Illinois and Wisconsin, laid a heavy hand on Christian day-schools. The political result had been that the ruling party in those two states had been beaten and that the law had been cancelled by the legislatures of these States. It seemed to be a palingenesis or a recrudescence of the Know-Nothing Movement cut short by the Civil War, thirty years before. Wisconsin, whose farmers in great measure were German immigrants or sons of such, in the critical four years of 1861–1865 supported the Union with consummate loyalty. Their patriotism had been tried and tested. Carl Schurz had begun his public career at Watertown, Wisconsin. Here, then, there seemed to be at stake the principle of religious freedom guaranteed by the Constitution of our nation. For this very cause, many Lutherans of Saxony and Pomerania had emigrated, viz., to maintain and enjoy their religious freedom and to escape from the secular control of religion. One could very fairly quote the parallel of the Pilgrim Fathers and Plymouth Rock in 1620. Now Governor Hoard, the famous dairyman of Wisconsin, had perhaps by the Bennett Law intended to quicken the process of assimilation. But the Christian day-schools were not intended at all as means to maintain any living bond with the Fatherland. Their instruction in the essentials of citizenship was efficient. They justly resented intrusion and secular control. Then too, apart from religious freedom, there was another basic thing in that controversy. We may call it that of ancestral self-respect. Only a fraction of the primeval settlers in the Middle West hailed from Scotland and England.[1] Had the Ger-

[1] In the South, of course, it is very different. Still the Huguenots of South Carolina and the Creoles of Louisiana also have their own memories.

mans of Wisconsin been as clannish as the Scandinavians of Minnesota and the Dakotas or the Hibernians of New York and Massachusetts, they could easily have maintained political control of Wisconsin. But, while they were content to preserve some of their ancestral habits or traditions, they saw their sons and grandsons losing German speech. Still they insisted, in this controversy, on cultural and religious self-determination. So the Democrats in Wisconsin—ordinarily in the minority—elected Peck Governor and sent Mitchell to Washington as Senator.

When I came to Milwaukee in the fall of 1891, the coals were still glowing under the ashes. In that contention, even the parallel of Sparta was brought in by the nativists—with the thesis that children belonged not to the parents but to the state, an unhistorical absurdity. There cannot be any—even the slightest—similarity between Lycurgus and Thomas Jefferson. I gave a lecture that winter (1891–92) on the absolute state socialism of Sparta, and demonstrated the absurdity of such parallels. I am indeed a Jeffersonian of deep conviction, believing that to be the best government which most keeps its hands off from the personal self-determination of the citizens.

Near Milwaukee, I believe at Wauwatosa, there was (and is?) a National Soldiers' Home, splendidly and generously equipped. My visit there was twenty-six years after Appomattox. The Superintendent very courteously permitted me to delve into the bulky ledgers of the Home. These ledgers registered names, regiments, and the original residence of the veterans there cared for. With the exception of a few from the New England States, I found that the majority of the veterans at Wauwatosa were of German and Irish descent. As a newcomer, I abstained from utilizing these observations in the controversy of that time.

I now return to my study and to my classes. No one, I

A PRELUDE IN WISCONSIN

dare say, will ever guess or reason out to which branch of the classics, in that western winter, I chiefly devoted myself—private tutoring there being none whatever. It was Aristotle's *Politics* which wholly absorbed me then. What is more, this study also had a practical side. Even before leaving New York I had begun making a written abstract —in English—of Bekker's text[2] of the great Stagirite. And now I gave my survey of Aristotle's *Politics* to Prima as a course in history. One is likely to forget that the very terminology of Political Science is largely derived from Aristotle: Aristocracy, Democracy, Oligarchy, Monarchy and Monarch, Polity, Demagogue,[3] with the fundamental thesis that "Man is a political creature," (p. 3. line 16) and the wealth of statements which mankind has come to accept as fundamental: e.g., that coinage is a sovereign function of the State; that primitive society is one of the hunters; that the nomadic and cattle-raising stage is higher, and that the agricultural is the highest; then slavery, trade, money, the genuine production of wealth being quite different from banking and exchange. Of course I limited myself to being the interpreter of the great Analyst, whose range of illustration reaches from Persia to Carthage. I dictated summaries and then discoursed freely and joyously on the modern application and the enduring truth of his theses. It is worth while to be a pupil of an Aristotle. In passing, we may remark that Aristotle was no admirer of "democracy," the Greek type, where the *demos* often oppressed the "Best" (as in the French Revolution, or more ruthlessly in Russia, in recent times). Even in Athens, the *demos* displayed few traits that he admired. Self-sufficiency[4] ($α\dot{υ}τάρκεια$) he designates as the most desirable quality for a strong state. The sense of all right and

---

[2] Purchased in Leipzig, April 29, 1874.
[3] The Demagogue is a flatterer of the *demos*. VI, 4.
[4] Which to-day probably could be predicted most truly of our own land, far less so of England, Japan, Italy.

wrong, he urges, is the property of man alone, above the lower creatures; but, when man abandons moral principle, he is the *worst* of all living beings. There is no atavism of goodness. Aristotle's rejection of Communism is absolute and keen; to the peculiar communism of Plato's ideal state he is unfriendly. On the other hand, he holds that money-making ($\chi\rho\eta\mu\alpha\tau\iota\sigma\tau\iota\kappa\acute{\eta}$) as the chief occupation of a given state is "contrary" to Nature. As for coinage, the state merely guarantees the metallic content, no more; it does not create values. Thus teacher and students were continually stirred and stimulated to deal with fundamentals.

Another result of this course for myself was this: I discovered that Aristotle (very differently from his teacher Plato) viewed the political system of Sparta quite critically, nay, unfavorably. I determined to examine this point with care. But books and monographs? Here I record my gratitude to the Public Library of Milwaukee. For me—I may say for me alone—they ordered many treatises, mainly from England, dealing with the Aristotelian problems, promptly, without regard to expense. My working-desk in my home on State Street was loaded with valuable works drawn from the Library. Twice a week I found myself in the office of the chief Librarian, and never failed of her aid.

This matter of books brings me quite aptly to the final stage of my brief sojourn in Milwaukee. There was then an established custom in the Concordia College which I disliked and disapproved. The students whose ages ran from fourteen to twenty or twenty-one, had what was called a "students'" or "pupils' library" (Schülerbibliothek), juveniles, biographies, German and English classics, etc.; but the students were rigorously excluded from the books of *learning;* these were reserved for the faculty. I insisted, in faculty meetings, that we should gladly welcome our students to the latter class of books. Ultimately

A PRELUDE IN WISCONSIN

I made a little endowment myself, one-fifth of my little fortune of $5000, the savings of many years. Why did I do this? Let me explain. This was one of the many occasions when good comes out of evil.

Late in January, 1892, I received a letter from Chancellor MacCracken in New York, a letter which my dear wife hurriedly brought out to the College to me—a letter intimating, a bit cautiously as yet, that there was a probability that I would be called to the University of the City of New York.[5] Early in March, 1892, came a letter from the Secretary of the Council informing me that I had been chosen "Acting Professor" of the Latin Language and Literature, provisionally for two years, with a stipend of $2000. Rarely did I see my dear wife so supremely happy; she fairly snatched the important epistle from the letter-carrier's hands. This letter proved the most important event in my professional life—*vita nova!* I mean the life I had yearned for during the last thirteen years. I was now thirty-nine years old. Up to this time, Mrs. Sihler had barely endured Milwaukee; but now the sun of her life was once more beaming above her, and her soul looked eastward once more. She departed from her social seclusion and gave a coffee-party to all the ladies of the Concordia circle, surpassing her own culinary efforts. In due time, of course, my coming departure from the Milwaukee Concordia was duly announced in the church papers; and around me, expressions of regret were mingled with felicitations. But one semi-official letter came from a clerical officer of the Synod—he died in 1907—which seems to have been filled with great bitterness. My good wife, after opening and reading it, actually burned it. I readily forgave her, when I learned the point and purpose of that maledicent missive. The writer called me *inter alia*, a "hireling." It was the first time in my life that any one

[5] The name was officially changed to the present form in 1896.

had applied that terrible term to me. All of my life—so I felt deep within my bosom—had been one of industry and devotion, where *lucrum et damnum* had not figured at all. There were foolish whisperings near me that my New York salary was to be not less than $4000! I was too proud to say anything about it to the members of the Faculty. What I now at last looked forward to was this: a full and free employment of all my powers, powers incessantly trained for some twenty years, ever since Theodor Mommsen had matriculated me at Berlin. The prospect now opening before me made me very happy. A "hireling"? I really forgave my good spouse. It was her affection which made her destroy the maledicent letter, but I could not sleep the next night. I found a solution. I went out to the College and summoned my colleagues—it was a Saturday—and told them this: I would return the $1000 of my salary as a little capital for permanent investment, one-fifth of my little fortune, to be called the "Dr. William Sihler Fund," the income to be used for the purchase of works of standard worth, while at the same time honoring the memory of my dear father.[6]

After my departure for the East was settled, the slightest suggestion or wish on my part was promptly heeded and carried out. So, too, a large flagpole was erected on the campus, with a fine national banner waving from it, and was dedicated on Decoration Day, May 30, 1892, with appropriate exercises, under the management of Prima. I delivered the main address, dealing with the preservation of the Union—a discourse published in one of the evening papers of Milwaukee. For me it was a welcome opportunity to attest the loyalty of Wisconsin Lutherans to the laws and welfare of our common land. And with this event we will take leave of Wisconsin.

[6] Thirty-three years later I revisited the Milwaukee Concordia, and was delighted with the excellence and the lasting value of the books gathered by the Dr. William Sihler fund.

XI
VITA NOVA. WASHINGTON SQUARE AND UNIVERSITY HEIGHTS (1892–1923)

IT fell to my lot to teach two years at Washington Square (1892–1894), the last two years of the old University building facing the northeast corner of the Square. The environment was a curious one. The Square in olden times had been a parade-ground; still earlier, according to local antiquarians, a potters' field. Our American academic annals are indeed shorter and newer than the European; but their movement, through cultural stages, has been much faster. The outward appearance, the Oxford type of the building, was indeed correct and impressive. But there were many drawbacks. The ground floor was not used for instruction. Central heating was unknown. In my classroom, to which I alone (and the janitor) had a key, there was an old-fashioned iron stove in the corner. I found curious odds and ends in the drawer of the professorial desk, such as cancelled mortgages belonging to my predecessor. In his earlier years, Ebenezer Alfred Johnson had been a tutor at Yale, associated then with Alphonso Taft, father of President Taft. After the crisis of 1837–38, he was called from Yale in 1838, at twenty-five, and held the chair of Latin to 1891, for fifty-three years, when, in the summer of that year, he died suddenly while visiting his garden in Yonkers. Professor Johnson's classical library came to us soon after my accession. It contained many works of value, even of German erudition. These were bound through the help of William Allen Butler, class of 1843, the eminent jurist and an author also: his "Nothing to Wear" (*Harper's Weekly*, 1857) became an American classic. Thus I followed a Latinist whose tenure of his chair has but rarely been equalled in our land. But to return to the limitations of those primitive classrooms. I now cite from the memories of the Reverend Dr. Zabriskie, '50, where he referred to the classroom of the Grecian, Tayler Lewis. "His was the favorite room for incense offerings of asafoetida, red pepper, and tobacco." In my two years at the Square this particular form of student intermezzo and juvenile prank did not occur. There was, however, a different form of juvenility. Firecrackers were sometimes tossed in over the door through the transom which had to be open for the sake of ventilation. Youth will adopt such practices if possible and make its record. All this silliness passed away with our migration to University Heights in the autumn of 1894. As for my own students, my ambition was to gain and hold their devotion to the work in hand to such a degree that occasions for discipline simply should not arise. I may as well set it down in this place, that in all my thirty-one years of service, I did not once make a disciplinary report to Chancellor, Dean, or Faculty. My Grecian colleague, Dr. Henry Martyn Baird, upon my entry at the Square, gave me a piece of wise counsel on this point.

I may as well pass in review some of my colleagues—now gone—as they appeared to me in that autumnal beginning of my long service, in September, 1892. Dr. Baird was Dean of the College of Arts, a Greek scholar of intimate familiarity with that language and that literature, from Homer to Pausanias. In his early manhood, he had been a traveller and investigator on the soil of classic Greece. (His *Modern Greece, a Narrative of a Residence and Travels in that Country* by Henry M. Baird, M. A., illustrated by almost sixty engravings, New York, Harper Brothers, 1856, was published when the gifted author was about twenty-four years old.) He had traversed the soil

VITA NOVA: NEW YORK UNIVERSITY

of Hellas from Athens, in more than one excursion. He had not only sketched the ruins of the Acropolis, such as the Erechtheum and the Parthenon, but he had done much more. He did not hesitate to call the transfer of the Elgin marbles to the British Museum "British Vandalism." The city and university of Athens under Bavarian Otho were set down with charming clearness. This work of direct investigation and the volume recording it long antedated the American School at Athens. But this was not his most important achievement. He was, in the autumn of 1892, not very far from the completion of his real life-work, the six volumes dealing with the Huguenots of France from Francis I and from Catherine de' Medici onward to Louis XIV and the Revocation of the Edict of Nantes, the standard work to-day, I dare say. I was privileged, during my first Christmas vacation (1892–1893), to spend a day as his guest in his study at Yonkers. Sometimes, as he then told me, he had to wait ten years before securing some rare quarto or folio written by contemporary authors in France or Switzerland. His personal manner was scrupulously courteous and dignified, especially when presiding at faculty meetings.

Of the other members of the faculty of September, 1892, I may speak more briefly. John J. Stevenson, in many ways an exponent of the *ingenium Scoticum*, was an alumnus of the class of 1863—the Gettysburg year. He owed, I believe, most of his academic training or incentive to John W. Draper,[1] in whose private laboratory he had gained his Ph.D. In the multitude of his didactic fields he had, officially, been "Professor of Chemistry, Geology, and Physiology." Personally he nursed a deep aversion for the classics. His father, a Presbyterian clergyman, had *compelled* him, at an immature age, to begin Latin and Greek (nay Hebrew too, if my memory serves me) in his own study.

[1] He died in 1881. Dr. Stevenson died August 10, 1924.

149

But, when I came from Milwaukee, his Chemistry and Physics had already been segregated. Biology was detached in 1894, so that Geology alone remained for Dr. Stevenson, which really was his forte: he had done much in West Virginia in determining the site of coal-measures.

Chemistry was now, in 1892, in the hands of *two* professors. Morris Loeb, Harvard 1883, later a Ph.D. from the laboratory of the eminent Berlin chemist Hofmann, was now "acting Professor" of Chemistry in general, while Robert W. Hall, A.B. Princeton, and later of the Columbia School of Mines 1876, was Professor of Analytical Chemistry. Still the laboratory facilities were, at the Square, of necessity of a very slender kind. But in this as in other inherited deficiencies, we looked patiently and hopefully to the "Uptown Movement" which we all knew must come soon.

So, too, in English: Francis Hovey Stoddard (Amherst, 1869), who had specialized in Anglo-Saxon and related studies at Oxford, and later taught at Berkeley, California, had been called to Washington Square from the Pacific in 1888. He later on had very large classes in the Graduate School, and retired in 1914.

There were three names in the faculty of 1892 pleasantly associated with my academic past. One was Daniel W. Hering, C.E., one of the original Twenty Fellows of Johns Hopkins. Dr. MacCracken had brought him, in 1885, from the Western University of Pennsylvania, as professor of Physics. His equipment at the Square was scanty; but like the rest of us he drew most of his inspiration from his outlook on the future. In Mathematics there was a Canadian, Daniel A. Murray, M.A. Dalhousie College, Halifax, N. S., who had studied higher mathematics at Baltimore under Thomas Craig, and was completing his Ph.D. thesis while teaching at Washington Square. He had a room for his bachelor's quarters in the tower of the

VITA NOVA: NEW YORK UNIVERSITY

southwestern corner of the University building. I never had a friend who blushed so easily. He was often a welcome guest at Mrs. Sihler's table in Harlem on Sundays. Her culinary skill was appreciated by all her guests, most of all of course by myself; her allowance always was modest. The youngest of us four Hopkins men was John Dyneley Prince, pupil of Gottheil of Columbia, of Sachau and Dillmann at Berlin, and of Paul Haupt at Baltimore, where he gained his Ph.D. in 1892; he had also taken part in Hilprecht's expedition to Assyria, and in New York University was professor of Semitics and Comparative Philology. He was (and is) one of the most gifted men that I have ever met or known. To call him a *polyglot* genius would be moderate praise; one could fairly call him *pantoglot;* for him the acquisition of a new language was child's play. I called him the modern *Mezzofanti*. He belonged to that rare or small class of academic persons who are born into comfort or what most professors would call *wealth*. To the University on the threshold of better things he did a great service. With the aid of his father-in-law, the noted physician Alfred L. Loomis, he secured one of the most notable libraries in the Semitic and related fields. It was the library of Paul de Lagarde, one of the brightest stars in the academic firmament of Göttingen, a collection which remains one of the most precious possessions of our University. When it arrived and was temporarily ranged at the Square, I was requested to make an investigation of its classic side, and soon realized[2] that our slender resources in my own field had been fairly doubled.

I must here say something of the newly established School of *Pedagogy*—now of Education—begun with a notable gift by Charles Butler, which really moved into

---

[2] I could not then foresee that the Lagarde Collection would one day prove a treasure-house when I was engaged on the last of my greater works, *From Augustus to Augustine* (1916–1922), published by the Cambridge University Press, 1923.

life in March 1890. Jerome Allen was the first dean. This school was not to duplicate the existing normal schools. It was to afford actual teachers incentive and guidance towards advancement in their own profession; to give to teachers, in a word, more professional substance and dignity: the entire course ended in a degree of "Doctor of Pedagogy" (Pd.D.). There was no Teachers College at that time.

May I be permitted here, as a veteran teacher, both of boys and of men, to insert a *commentariolus* of my own? A teacher should be equipped to follow the history of Education, from the life-story of great educators, from Socrates to Quintilian, to Comenius and beyond. This by itself is a great task. Paul Monroe's Encyclopaedia had not yet been written. It is undeniable that the enormous expansion of "subjects" in our land is bewildering. In pondering on the one great aim, the training and development of the essential and normal powers, we are bound to arrive at certain definite and irrefragable conclusions. Studies that mean merely a temporary introduction to a body of facts, briefly and imperfectly held for a threatening examination, are vain and deceptive. May I not here turn to the original and primary word coined by the Romans, which they endowed with a much stronger meaning than our "study"? "*Studeo alicui rei*," with the Tiber folk meant this: "I devote myself to an object—any object—with the application of all my faculties both of thought and will." To-day, with the "credit" system everywhere prevailing, when "hard" courses (with small classes) and "easy" courses—"snap" courses—are ranked as equal, I say to-day we have actually allowed our educational system to drift into a Serbonian bog and are often pursuing an *ignis fatuus*. We have "lunch-counter" education, as Dean West of Princeton has felicitously called it.

Let us turn back two decades. On November 29, 1907,

VITA NOVA: NEW YORK UNIVERSITY

was begun at the College of the City of New York the "Twenty-first Annual Convention of the Association of Colleges and Preparatory Schools of the Middle States and Maryland," presided over by Woodrow Wilson, President of Princeton. I then held and still hold that we continually indulge in educational experiments, ever trying out some new or novel mechanism, withal a scattering process, instead of concentrating on a limited number of *great* subjects. With all our continental self-sufficiency we are really *insular*. May I cite a passage from my address at that convention: "The Canadians in the Rhodes Scholars' Competition, as well as the Australians, have made us blush by the shallowness and the poor classical knowledge of the young men we have picked out and sent to Oxford. And then we were told to console ourselves: that our young gentlemen could jump high with their legs, that they could run very fast within the ten seconds and do other things as relevant as these." Another passage: "We must bring our high schools down to a smaller number of great subjects. Of course the idea of bringing the university and the college into high school—the policy strikes me as a paradox of crudity, as absurd, deleterious, and pernicious." Further I said: "You cannot know, you cannot divine at what moment the scintilla of concern and profound interest may be evoked from your class . . . that is the moment to forge, that is the moment to build. It is your duty to kindle the spark, to bring interest to that moment of life and growth. If you have *wide* knowledge at your service, that will produce the glorious genetic rebound in the intellectual life of the class . . . but if you are merely a machine that presses certain buttons, that has pressed them often, then . . ." Woodrow Wilson[3] in his address in the evening—I had gone home—said: "I sympathized so deeply with Dr. Sihler this morning when he said we shall be obliged to re-

[3] Who introduced the preceptorial system at Princeton.

duce our education for each person—not for all, but for each person—to a small body of great subjects, and until we have done that, we will not have returned to the true process of education." So much for the meeting of 1907. May I add one more point: the true teacher—not least the college professor—is *in loco parentis*.[4] At the bottom the teacher's work and aim must be spiritual, without regard to his own gain or fame.

Among the members of the Council of 1892 we should here once more name Charles Butler[5] a younger brother of Benjamin F. Butler, Attorney General under Jackson and Van Buren, founder of the University Law School. The latter's son, William Allen Butler, I have already introduced to my readers. Then there was William Loring Andrews, whose father made the first gift of considerable amount for endowment in honor of his mother Sarah Andrews. The gray stone mansion at University Heights, now Graduate Hall, was, I believe, originally built by the elder Andrews as his own country home. Another member of the Council in 1892 was the Reverend Charles Deems. He organized the "Church of the Strangers" whose worship was long held in the chapel of the University. Further it is a great pleasure to name the Reverend John Hall of the Fifth Avenue Presbyterian Church, Chancellor from 1881 to 1891, who did so much for the institution in saving it from closing in the crisis of 1881. Then there were David Banks, law publisher, soon to be a generous patron of gymnasium and athletics at the Heights, and William F. Havemeyer, who gave the Chemical Laboratory at the new site. Two survivors only to-day recall the Council of 1892, the Reverend Dr. George Alexander, long pastor of the University Place Presbyterian Church, and the jurist, Mr. Joseph Auerbach.

[4] Quintilian II, 24: "Sumat igitur ante omnia *parentis* ergo discipulos suos *animum*, ac succedere se in eorum locum, a quibus sibi tradantur, existimet."
[5] Who served from Chancellor Matthews to Chancellor MacCracken.

VITA NOVA: NEW YORK UNIVERSITY

When one looks for the homes whence came the undergraduates of my initial year, one realizes at once that the college at the Square was still a merely *local* college, was in fact, as every one admitted, a *day-school*. There was no athletic field, of course, no gymnasium, no opportunity for athletic training. Were there any games? Professor William K. Gillett, the athlete in our faculty, told me of lacrosse matches, when the team first had to journey to Staten Island; he personally was a fine hand at tennis and baseball. Nor were there any dormitories. The students who were candidates for A.B. came, as noted before, from a very narrow periphery: Manhattan, Brooklyn, Jersey City, Newark, Elizabeth, or Yonkers; one each from Pennsylvania, Michigan, Illinois, Delaware. Now the classroom *alone* does not and never did knit together as with bands of steel, in friendships often enduring for life, enduring loyalties, often strengthening, or giving new life to Alma Mater. I have been told by alumni of the latter and last years of Washington Square, that they were much pleased when they were taken for Rutgers men.

One of the gravest mistakes of the past had been this: Dr. Crosby, at the beginning of his administration (1870), had put through a statute from which he expected much, *Free Tuition*. The effects of this policy were the opposite of those hoped for. More than ever the great colleges of New England and the College of New Jersey (Princeton) drew on New York City and Brooklyn. Dr. MacCracken, until he brought about the migration to University Heights and the rebirth of New York University, was esteemed by many men in the academic world of America as one condemned to make bricks without straw, or as a brave soldier who had assumed a forlorn post. As a matter of fact, free tuition proved a grave injury to the college not merely by the loss of income but also by the social effect—a "charity-school" some called it. At this point it may be proper to save from oblivion an incident of Dr. MacCracken's first or second year, after he came from Pittsburgh in the autumn of 1884 as successor to Professor Benjamin Martin. He told me this in 1912–13, after his retirement from the chancellorship. It was in the lower corridor at Washington Square, which was very dark. There were two members of the Council discussing the status of the much tried college. He, unseen by them, unwittingly caught mention of his own name: "If this man from Pittsburgh cannot get the college going better, we will have to close it anyhow."

I now come to an innovation realized through Dr. MacCracken, then Vice-Chancellor, in 1886: courses for graduate students, "the Graduate Division." He himself, devoted as he was to philosophy, offered courses in the comprehensive field, as e.g., on the philosophy of theism, meeting his students in the evenings in his own residence in Irving Place. Moreover all A.B. men, students of divinity in or near New York, had free tuition in any graduate courses. I need not say that I consider the Greek courses offered by Dr. Baird among the most valuable. The University also had received an endowment for Comparative Religion, the Lectureship being then held by Dr. Ellinwood, a course especially valuable for future missionaries. Needless to say, I did not assume the courses in Latin Literature scheduled in the catalogue by my predecessor. Rather I now prepared to choose my own work, work for which I had trained my best powers and ideals for twenty eager years. At last! it was the pealing of a silver bell opening the gates of his best life for E. G. Sihler. It is true: voices reached me from the older, stronger, and richer sister in the academic field, questioning our right to offer these higher courses. Particularly do I recall such an intimation from my paternal friend, the Jay Professor of Greek at Columbia, in a remark he made to me on my return from Wisconsin, in October, 1892. I shall deal quite

VITA NOVA: NEW YORK UNIVERSITY

fully with this important matter in my next chapter. As for myself, I was deeply resolved to put all my ambition and the fullest measure of unrelenting industry into this very field, unwilling, as far as I was concerned, to have the junior institution rated a mere Cinderella. The drawback which I felt most painfully in those initial years, was in the lack of *books;* and I was ever devising new channels for irrigating this particular arid field.

Another feature of these two last years at the Square was this: there were not two semesters but *three terms:* it was almost impossible to do justice to any important subject. When things began to move right and the class had been brought to consistent work and interest, the curtain came down for term examinations. It was all a hurried and feverish procedure. Here too I was happy in looking forward to better things in the autumn of 1894. For those initial two years I had also assumed the work in history, work in itself congenial to me and carried forward with enthusiasm. The students had to learn to take well-connected notes, which had to be recast and polished at home, while I examined the "books" from time to time. Of course some indolent "men" were caught in copying notebooks or even in passing off the books of others as their own. I also introduced the use of historical geography, being a pupil of Kiepert.

The Baccalaureate sermon of June, 1893, was delivered at the University Place Church, to a small and quiet company. At the Commencement proper, too, there was but a slender attendance, and afterwards some refreshments at the Chancellor's residence in Irving Place. When one, in the present time, tries to measure the more than 20,000 guests at the Commencements on the slope above the Harlem, that day of little things appears as a legend of long ago.

I had to begin the work of teaching at the Square very

gently, cautiously, and tentatively. Still even then I laid down the law to which I firmly adhered for the thirty-one years of my service: every student in Latin had to hand in Latin prose weekly. I marked the books in my study, book for book. These weekly tests revealed or exhibited individual scholarship incomparably better than the translation of the authors. I succeeded in making the use of translations[6] very unprofitable, very discreditable. At University Heights, of course, these things became familiar laws. My mode was simple but efficient: with texts closed at the beginning of the hour, I would select the rarest and the hardest words in the text and present them to those men whom my preceptorial tact suggested for this preliminary test. "Standardization," the much-vaunted principle of these later days, has its limits. I found that classes and years bore some positive resemblance to crops. The husbandman the same, but the soil *not* the same; although the farmer must do much with seed-grain, with plough and harrow, the results will differ. I need not carry the parallel any farther. A further point: in dealing with freshmen I sought particularly to cheer and help those who were weaker or had poorer preparation. The mere moral or spiritual reaction and rebound on the part of the grateful student often achieved wonderful and deeply gratifying results, not to speak of the soul-joy of the student when he became conscious of powers hitherto dormant, and felt that his own wings in time would carry him high and far. Many important points must be reserved for the next chapter.

Among my students in history at the Square were also the "scientific" men who had no classical preparation. In one of my very last courses at the Square, I noticed some peculiar spellings in the final examination: *othodox* for orthodox, *Ganzery* for Genserich, *Goeths* for Goths, *Capi-*

[6] Working in the "Bohnyard."

VITA NOVA: NEW YORK UNIVERSITY

tal for Capitol. I was not ill-pleased in May, 1894, to bid a final farewell to these "scientific" men.

The year 1894 proved an incisive one not only for my domestic *Lares et Penates*, but also for the institution itself, with which my academic life, both of voice and pen was to be connected to the day when I retired from seminar-room and lecture-desk forever.[7]

But to return to that historical spring of 1894: For March 4th, I find an entry in my account book: "birds warbling in Park, mellow sunshine." But on the very next day there came a bolt from the blue. An official letter came from the Secretary of the Council, the Reverend Dr. John Reid, informing me that from September 1, 1894, the salary of the chair of Latin was to be reduced from $2000 to $1500. Only gradually we learned that the Corporation had assumed a very large mortgage both on the property at the Square and on that of our future home at the Heights. The mere annual interest charge, I believe, was more than the (reduced) salaries of the College Faculty. I, for my part, was in a state of consternation and economic helplessness. My mathematical colleague, Dr. Murray, was so discouraged that he sought and found a modest provision at Cornell. It is fit and proper that at this point of my life-story I should record the bravery and the domestic virtues of my dear wife,[8] and how she distinguished herself in that bitter and unforeseen emergency. She did not tell me on that occasion what she would or could do. I learned it only after many years. Being an expert needlewoman, she crotcheted fine bridal handkerchiefs which she sold at Ladies' Bazaars and with the proceeds bought her own clothes for years. As she is gone, I may well give her the proper setting in my life-story.

April 18, 1894, was Founder's Day. The entire college,

[7] September 1, 1923.
[8] Who has entered into rest some time ago.

teachers, students, made a joyous excursion to the "new Site," to bid good morning to the Future. The Seniors, among whom was the oldest son of the Chancellor, came up in tallyhoes and also brought up some gargoyles from the old building in the Square. Mrs. MacCracken set a luncheon in what soon was to be called Butler Hall, the mansion of the Mali estate. At the east end of that country place there still was a porter's lodge surrounded with larches. Featherbed Lane nearby skirted the Croton Aqueduct. It was indeed a rustic neighborhood. I will here insert a poem written not long before by a student, published originally in the *Violet*, lines that fairly throb with the spirit of the migration:

> Whe'fo' hang yo' harps on willows? Sing de song of Jubilee!
> Massa Cracken he hab promise fo to set his people free.
> Mine eyes is old and feeble, but dey tells me what is true,
> A vision strange and mighty, ob de joy of N.Y.U.
> De changes and contrivins, which de wise men all hab plan,
> Fo we's gwine across de ribber to possess de promis lan.
> We's gwine to march in orders, each one prouder dan de res,
> All the fessers will be handy, eb'ry one rigged up his bes.
> Massa Pardee wid de medics and de bearers ob de saw,
> Massa Russell all a smilin wid de ladies ob de law
> An dey'll wear their robes of purple, wid de hoods of violet hue,
> An de city's population will be takin in de view.
> So we'll sing and blow de trumpets as we march along Broadway,
> Shoutin' loud de praise an glory ob de beauteous breakin' day.
> Den when we's above de Harlem, oh de fun dats sure to be,
> Wid de campus broad and spacious and de frolics wild and free;
> When de boys get out de baseball or de football for to play—
> Jes' de idee sets me itchin fo' de coming ob dat day.

The academic year closed before the end of May. The venerable pile at the Square saw the last meeting of the Alumni in the Chapel. I recall an utterance of John E. Parsons: "We older men have done our share in the past: things are changing mightily, but we will entrust the future to the younger men." It is not my task here to go over the

VITA NOVA: NEW YORK UNIVERSITY

annals in detail of the new life at the Heights, some 165 feet above the Harlem and Hudson. For me too it was a new and most wholesome life. Every morning I went north on Amsterdam Avenue, and walked across Washington Bridge and then a good mile farther north on a country road skirting the Harlem—healthy exercise at all seasons. The recitations in that October, 1894, were at first held in the first gymnasium the college ever had, constructed in part from the two barns or stables on the Mali estate. There were many small rooms in the gymnasium surrounding the central space where new gymnastic apparatus was set up. Several times my Latin room was very cold; did I dismiss my students? No, I told them to do what I did, to keep on their hats and overcoats. In January, 1895, with a satisfaction rarely exceeded in all my didactic life, I moved into the new and admirable Hall of Languages on the western side of the new campus, where, in the northeast room on the third floor, I taught my undergraduate students in Latin up to September 1, 1923, nearly twenty-nine years. Now the Hall of Languages had one important feature which at once reminded me of Johns Hopkins. Each professor had a study or "office" fairly commodious, contiguous to his lecture-room. Here he could easily be found by his colleagues or his students. The latter saw me there often, but almost exclusively on matters pertaining to their studies or their standing, very rarely indeed on disciplinary matters—which virtually never happened. May I add at once what I had quite correctly foreseen? The joyous freer life, the splendid opportunity for physical training, the gymnasium, Ohio Field, the rustic outlook, especially northward—never in my life did I recall a contrast so sharp as that between Washington Square, so near to Broadway, and this noble campus. Here we really felt as if the mercantile metropolis with its roar and rattle, its cramped life of trade, were a hundred miles away. The

Palisades beyond the Hudson closed the western horizon; and from my own study, in clear weather, one could see the blue hills of Long Island. Later, at Christmas, 1906, the generous bounty of Mrs. Russell Sage added to our campus the Schwab estate on the south. Then indeed the outlook on all the four points of the compass became our own, the Heights dominating everything.

In the autumn of 1895, I transferred my entire private library from Harlem to my study at the Heights, where it remained to August, 1923, twenty-eight years. A single room with many stacks held the general library up to September, 1900, somewhat enriched by the Italian library of Professor Vincenzo Botta, a collection especially rich in Dante. I was commissioned to sift it with care—a somewhat dusty task. The new Library, a noble gift of Miss Helen Gould, designed by a famous architect, was announced in the spring of 1895. Ground was broken by the Chancellor in October, 1895, a notable academic occasion. Seth Low, then President of Columbia, was among the guests. In the classic perfection of its general lines and with its superb rotunda of green marble columns, surrounded by the seminar-rooms with pertinent collections, it seems indeed to be "a possession for all time,"[9] not a competitive production for the moment. But, like Rome itself, this noble edifice was not built in a day. Even more familiar to the wider world than the Library itself is the Colonnade that forms the western fringe, the Hall of Fame for Great Americans. It was early in the autumn of 1900 that I, with very great satisfaction, could now move to the Latin Seminar-room on the gallery of the Library. Meanwhile, on Thanksgiving, 1896, had occurred the housewarming of the beautiful new dormitory on the eastern side of the campus, Gould Hall, with its music-room in the basement, where the glee club could practice, en-

[9] Thucydides, I, 22.

VITA NOVA: NEW YORK UNIVERSITY

riched with a Steinway grand through the munificence of the donor.

In the summer of 1899, through my initiative, the American Philological Association held its annual meeting at University Heights, under the presidency of Clement Smith of Harvard. The attending members, among whom was Francis A. March of Lafayette, were mainly lodged in Gould Hall.

Of course to the majority of the undergraduates, campus, gymnasium, and fraternity houses and the social opportunities ever there engendered, were more impressive than books and study. Scholarship does not convey fame among the undergraduates. I have not changed that conviction. "Debates," it is true, seem to convey some distinction on the campus. The main thing there—as intrinsically obvious in physical spectacular competition—is display and a little transitory distinction or notoriety. The banjo, the mandolin, the glee club, tennis, basket-ball, intercollegiate gymnastics, track-meets, excellence with clubs, weights, parallel bars, and, above all others, in baseball and football, sports whose coach outranks all the faculty, daily notices in the Press, all these are the main interests and ideals of the young men in our colleges, whereas studies and scholarship, the imperceptible training of soul and mind, are not adequately or even *fairly* rated and esteemed. No "quick reputation" is here attainable. *Stover at Yale* is full of typical truth; and the doings of the football and baseball teams, to the undergraduate mind, dwarf into insignificance all the scholars, authors, and scientific men embraced within the faculty. I shrink from any comparison with Oxford and Cambridge, where physical training is by no means neglected, but where the scholarly forms of distinction duly predominate. I think for the moment of Gladstone; with one or two exceptions, every prime minister of England laid his foundations on intellectual and academic training in *"dulci iuventa."* One observation I must not leave unwritten. I noticed that the young men at the Heights who excelled in gymnastics gained a supple and gracefully symmetrical body fairly comparable to the bodies of Greek athletes preserved for modern eyes by the sculptural art of Praxiteles, Lysippus, and others.

In May, 1901, the first twenty-nine tablets commemorating Great Americans were unveiled amid a degree of wide and deep national attention such as New York University had not experienced in all her seventy years' history. Chancellor MacCracken had prepared an "Official Book" (Putnams) and for this volume had commissioned me to contribute brief biographies and also to gather estimates by competent and eminent critics dealing with their characters and lives, especially non-American critics. Some of these were men like Guizot, Chateaubriand, Byron, Mignet, Mirabeau, Hallam, Carlyle, Goldwin Smith, Mohl, Mittermaier, Colonel Chesney, Gladstone, Humboldt, Hermann Grimm, and many others. About this time also appeared the first *History of New York University* (Herndon, Boston), largely done by me.

Soon after, we acquired and, in the winter of 1902–3, installed a classical library of the first order, the Hübner collection of Berlin, offered us through the mediation of Hübner's friend Gildersleeve. There was nothing in all my service, for which I had striven so persistently and so earnestly, in season and out of season, as for this particular kind of equipment. My compensation had been moderately rehabilitated; but the Hübner collection, now ranged in the Latin and Greek seminar-rooms, made me feel rich. It meant almost everything for my academic and literary life, the detail of which, however, is to be told in future chapters.

In the autumn of 1909, the bountiful legacy of John S.

VITA NOVA: NEW YORK UNIVERSITY

Kennedy, utterly unforeseen and unexpected, made it possible to cancel the mortgage which, for some fifteen years, had so heavily lain upon the University. Who will fathom the deep joy of the Chancellor and all the friends of New York University, at this unloading of that burden? Dr. MacCracken resigned at the Commencement of 1910, and soon with Mrs. MacCracken started westward on a tour around the world. In his absence, but on his seventieth birthday, September 28th, we gathered near the northern end of the Hall of Fame and solemnly witnessed an act of cremation: it was the burning of that academic burden, the mortgage.[10] I will limit myself in this place to a few words from the chapter which I contributed to the volume *In Memoriam* published in his honor in 1923, where I endeavored to sum it all up in these words: "It is something to assist at the birth of a child and to foster its growing and adolescent years with loving care; but men are widely agreed that it is a far greater task and a more felicitous achievement to save an adult abandoned by his very kindred and given over by those of his own household, and not merely to save his life, but to place him and it in an environment where new friends, new strength, new hope come to him and where he not only can with grateful eyes look back upon so much desolation actually traversed and concluded, but can look forward with a quickening trust to an ever brighter future."

Of my domestic history I will add but one item. In May, 1910, we moved at last into a quasi-rustic home of our own, in Mt. Vernon, New York, where all the four seasons passed by us with pleasing change; it was the last moving of fifteen in all in the annals of our household.

After an *interregnum* of one year (1910–11) under the efficient management of John Henry MacCracken, there

---

[10] Dr. MacCracken lived eight years longer, passing away at Christmas-time, 1918, in Florida.

FROM MAUMEE TO THAMES AND TIBER

followed in November, 1911, the notable inauguration of the Seventh Chancellor, Elmer Ellsworth Brown, Ph.D. Halle-Wittenberg, 1890, who had been United States Commissioner of Education 1906–1911. I will not say more of my twelve years' service under him than this: my own work and the consistent pursuit of my own ideals went on and on to the end of my service, September 1, 1923, with his cordial approval and support.

XII
UNDERGRADUATE TEACHING AND GRADUATE LECTURES

In setting down these memories, I must not be tempted to excerpt the printed catalogues of those happy years, nor, as a rule, will I be tempted to compare classes with classes. Of course I was bound to stimulate the gifted and ambitious men; but not less, as I have intimated before, was I eager to help and encourage the weaker or less well-prepared students found in every class. My great aim was this: to proceed slowly and lay my foundations soundly. Every freshman class is sure to be a Joseph's coat of many colors; but it was my aim that in time it should be a garment of even texture. It was my fixed policy to change the initial unevenness by steady and consistent procedure. Here the weekly Prose figured large. Prose was never optional in my thirty-one years of service. I did not indulge in giving points and warnings in advance; no, here, if anywhere, each student had to learn the great lesson—the lesson not of the classroom merely, but of life itself—that he must stand on his own feet and that he must gain strength by his own efforts; we must recall the old adage: *"Non scholae sed vitae discimus."* The *way* the student learns is often more important than the *subject* itself, as that great teacher Quintilian has so aptly said.

For several years I had to begin rather humbly in prose, with detached sentences of an elementary British book. American textbooks for prose I used but rarely. Why? I learned with great surprise that some publishers furnished *Keys;* I asked for whom? Of course not for the students. Still the acquisition by some student of such a *pons asinorum* might simply ruin everything; it would be like swimming with a bladder under each shoulder. Hence those keys could only be meant for the professor or some junior assistant. I considered the whole thing an insult to my profession, from Bowdoin to the Golden Gate. I finally chose a British book of more advanced character, where in the rear were found connected pieces such as are set at the "Moderations" at Oxford or Cambridge; and this application of transatlantic standards proved a most excellent thing. This work, or this grade of work, was maintained for each and every student from the first week of freshman to the end of senior year. Thus the students had to learn to *make* Latin and incidentally acquire mastery of Latin syntax: a power which immeasurably outranks the ability to analyse a complicated period of any given prose author. My students readily learned that poets are often driven by metrical necessity to resort to irregularities or immunities[1] impossible to a Cicero, Livy, Tacitus, or Pliny.

With Latin optional after the first year, those who continued were of course always a chosen band. I often resorted to Latin themes for free composition—the real ideal of the whole matter—when individual ambition and genuine scholarship shone forth even more, because here the student really gave utterance to his own thought in classic garb. Sometimes I also resorted to Bacon's *Essays*. A fine of twenty-five cents was established for remissness in handing in: the fund so accumulated and paid to the librarian being applied to the purchase of classical books by the General Library. For especially strong upper classes I sometimes did the following: I selected a *vita* from Plutarch, of some Roman worthy—as of Cato the younger or of Caesar: this biography I presented *viva voce*

---

[1] The so-called *Licentia Poetica*.

UNIVERSITY TEACHING

in Latin; of course more slowly at first, with repetitions and explanation, but rigorously avoiding the use of English.

From 1896 to 1900 a friend of mine gave $50 annually for a Latin Prize. This prize I bestowed for excellence in written tests, in which the competitors were limited to expressing themselves, in their own way, in Latin. Why have we not in America competitive honor examinations in which the colleges of a given state could unite? What is the inherent obstacle or objection? Would not that be a sounder test than the competitions of spectacular athletics? I appeal to the presidents of our institutions of learning.

I come to the texts. When I looked at some catalogues[2] printed in our broad land and saw, e.g., Tacitus' *Agricola* assigned to freshmen, or Juvenal to sophomores, I paused. My reflections were full of doubt and questioning, the more so, as I more and more realized that the training in writing and speaking Latin, if ever it flourished elsewhere or anywhere, was rapidly disappearing or had never been attempted.

As for the real father of Roman prose literature, Cicero, I proceeded with great circumspection; the anatomical exercise of parsing the Catilinarian speeches of the brilliant Arpinate I well knew had furnished the chief pabulum of almost all the freshmen before they came to me. Cicero as well as Caesar had functioned chiefly as a Latin speller, especially Caesar, than whom no great politician and strategist ever wrote more exclusively for men, particularly for the keen politicians of his day. I sometimes saw letters of Cicero offered to freshmen. It is true that not many of my colleagues did give Tacitus to freshmen, driving them to the Bohnyard; but, at the same time, they thought too much of any syntactical "ease" or "difficulty," ignoring the *matter* in the texts. Now the letters of the

[2] Paper is patient.

Arpinate to his bosom friend Atticus have a unique value as source-matter revealing the long drawn-out agony of the Roman Republic, incomparable as constituting the very pulse-beat of those sad times; but the continual allusions and citations in *Greek* found there, would make one hesitate to offer these documents to freshmen in Latin, with Greek the Cinderella everywhere.

Cicero's *De Officiis*, his Stoic essay on right living, I sometimes used with freshmen. But I realized that the full powers of the great orator—great orator *pace* Theodor Mommsen—were perhaps nowhere revealed in so manifold a manner as in that fiery invective against Mark Antony known as the *Second Philippic*,[3] of which I said in one of my later and greater works: "If within the compass of all moods and strains of man's soul or emotion there is one not found there, then I am greatly mistaken. There are passages of pathos, of lofty sentiments, not surpassed by pure tragedy; there is low and lowest comedy, mimicry of tenderness, scenes of low life, buffoonery, and farce. There is jest, humor, mirth, but also flaying ferocity. In time this discourse became one of the great classics in the rhetorical schools of Rome and the Roman world."[4]

I found in coming closer to my freshmen that they had never been trained to read a Latin text aloud with any real expression or correct intonation, emphasis or point—in short not trained to read aloud at all, let alone with any sense or sympathy. Of their scanning of Vergil I will say nothing. There is a certain charity in silence.

I come to Livy. When reading of *Cannae* (216 B. C.) and the genius of that incomparable strategist, Hannibal son of Hamilcar, the victor on that field, there indeed I was not at all content with my own text, the historian Titus Livius Patavinus. I presented, with diagrams on the

[3] Which later I published in the Gildersleeve-Lodge series.
[4] *Cicero of Arpinum*, p. 430, Yale University Press.

black-board, the narrative and in it the strategic lucidity of a much greater historian than Livy, Polybius, who equals Thucydides in the higher postulates of historiography but greatly surpasses him in political experience and in the width of his philosophical vision. Generally also I used the last twenty minutes of the recitation to read forward myself, whereby an incomparable opportunity is given of teaching and guiding one's students as when a painter in his studio operates on his own canvas in sight of his pupils.

As to Horace, I generally put his lyrics (*carmina*) in the second semester of the freshman year.[5] Here I took occasion to emphasize the dependency of Roman *belles-lettres* on their Greek models and predecessors; and I often scanned Alcaeus and Sappho for them.[6] The mere labeling of the prosody I considered inadequate. The term "dead languages" I did not endure. Often I trained my classes to scan Horace's Odes in chorus; and I know from one of my most distinguished veterans, that they greatly enjoyed this metrical exercise. Whenever I could, I enlisted candidates to enter the Greek field with its great language and sovereign literature. I showed my young friends how Greek names, places, poets, history, myths, were in the warp and woof of these odes—Leuconoë, Clio, Pallas, Pindus, the Atrides, Lydia, Salamis, Castor and Pollux, abounded in these imitations of Greek models; how the master of the *Sabinum* actually designated his butler as "Thaliarchus" (master of the feast). I showed my students with what consummate skill Horace knew how to reward his patrons and liberal benefactors, Augustus and Maecenas, and further how his *Weltanschauung* or philosophy was again and again revealed in his lyrics; but of course that was not the place to present the other famous

[5] His *Saturae* (miscellanies) reveal the personality of Horace much more than the Odes, but contain, also, elements of grosser paganism.
[6] From Bergk's noted collection.

FROM MAUMEE TO THAMES AND TIBER

Roman follower of the Garden, Lucretius, who belongs to graduate work alone, few ancient authors more so. His *de Rerum Natura* is perhaps the greatest didactic poem of antiquity; but any serious study must turn to Democritus, Epicurus, and Diogenes Laertius X.

The sophomore year of my work at University Heights remains in my memories the golden year, the annually recurring period of deepest satisfaction. The men entering my classroom in the last September days were students whom I had trained and had tested in many ways. They knew *me*; I knew *them*: we were friends. I knew with moral certainty that no disciplinary matter would ever arise to disturb the harmonious affection of our lives in teaching and learning. While writing and speaking Latin advanced with steady pace, I gradually came to settle down on two writers by preference: Pliny's *Letters* and Terence. In the case of the former, the Rome of Domitian, of Nerva and Trajan, seemed to lie before us once more; the pleader in Roman courts, the pupil of Quintilian, the member of the Senate, the patron, in generous endowments, of his native city of Comum on that beautiful lake, the bosom friend of Tacitus, the high-minded gentleman who abominated the memory of the tyrant Domitian, the admirer of Greek culture, the proprietor of the seaside villa, the nephew and heir of his uncle the admiral whose death in the catastrophe of Stabiae he alone has related to us, and above all the Proconsul of Bithynia who dealt most harshly with the primitive Christians.[7] In concluding the course, I generally called for essays on Pliny, when the students could dwell upon some of the chief topics readily suggested by that life and that character.

The case of Terentius Afer is radically different. So closely did that gifted freedman reproduce in Latin the society of Athens dramatized by the genius of Menander,

---

[7] The editions by a distinguished American scholar, Elmer T. Merrill, need no attestation from me.

UNIVERSITY TEACHING

that even those of my students who were innocent of Greek, could fairly move about in that city at the time when its political and moral decadence had set in. We studied the art of Menander together, with consummate enjoyment. My sophomores readily appreciated the art of character-drawing and particularly the irony of fate and change that so often overtakes the cocksure leading persons, humiliated in the end. And real romance even occurs, as in the *Andria*. Often I instituted dramatic readings after a play was concluded, each student having some one definite character assigned to him, in the original text; and the amount of real preparation was readily discernible in the elocution and the spirit with which the different rôles were read. Further there was another form of ending the semester: each member of the class had to prepare and read an essay on one of the plays previously read by the class—a test vastly more of a test than the final examinations themselves.

The upperclass work varied much. Of course the numbers were small, and the work of the teacher often assumed the form of a lecture. Juvenal, Tacitus, and Seneca were often chosen; and my habit of reviewing the matter in hand through the medium of Latin questions and Latin answers proved very fruitful. The ear and voice were brought into play; and also a much greater degree of intimacy with the person of the writer was attained. The greatest reward, after all, in this mode of teaching is this: that a sense of power is engendered in the student and the human element echoes in his own soul. Seneca in a way is a curious encyclopaedia of what men call Greco-Roman civilization and a mirror of that civilization from Homer to Nero. Simple and epigrammatic in statement, he still postulates—especially in his *Epistulae Morales*—a positive familiarity with that culture, particularly in letters and philosophy.

FROM MAUMEE TO THAMES AND TIBER

One of my last ventures was also one of the most profitable: the history of Octavian-Augustus delivered in Latin with Latin notes and summaries by my class, which I need not say was the élite of the undergraduate body. The Ogden Butler Classical Fellowship always was a real distinction even though the stipend was modest.

I now come to that part of my didactic service which meant most for me—I mean my graduate lectures. In these, apart from my authorship bound up with them, the greatest happiness of my academic career was sought and found.

My very first course dealt with the source-writers giving the history of the Emperor Tiberius, my first two students being one an A.B. of Columbia and one, of New York University. Very often, of course, the substance of my lectures suggested the theme for a dissertation for the doctorate. Very many of the Latin teachers — women teachers—of the Normal College of New York, now Hunter College, availed themselves of my courses. One of these teachers followed my courses for eight years, and finally wrote a thesis of sound learning dealing with the didactic metaphors in Quintilian.

I will now recall one of the earlier years of my service in the winter of 1894–95, when the new structure at Washington Square was in progress of erection. Amid the steel beams around us, temporary rooms with partitions of pine boards had been contrived for the teaching needs of that winter. My work was on Lucretius, whose interpretation, of course, implied continual excursions into Greek philosophy. I had in that winter one solitary disciple, but a student of uncommon maturity, a clergyman whose charge was in Morristown, New Jersey. Still, with all the drawbacks of that winter, and just because there was but one student, a student of ideal devotion, I now deem that course, in the retrospect of thirty-four years, one of the

UNIVERSITY TEACHING

most successful in all my career. Ultimately Dr. George P. Eckman[8] published his thesis, *The Controversial Elements in Lucretius*, in 1899, at a time when publication was not as yet an official desideratum. Of course the available source-matter of Epicurean philosophy figured very largely both in my course and also in Dr. Eckman's monograph of one hundred and twenty pages. I need not say that, in all my service in the thirty-one years, I urged the essential and fundamental importance of Greek, whenever and wherever I had the opportunity. The majority of my women students were content with gaining the A.M. degree. Of the thirty-one Ph.D. theses that I suggested, guided, and approved, only four were by women.

In my own practice, I carefully maintained a certain point of what I may call academic ethics. There were always certain aspirants for the highest of academic honors who, I knew, lacked capacity or perseverance. These I privately warned to abstain. On the other hand, I was happy in guiding through private conferences those capable and willing to follow me, both as to the process of research and the necessary limitations. My aim and ideal was that when the candidate was finally summoned to the critical examinations, the first-hand knowledge spread in his thesis and his familiarity with the related fields should be obvious and demonstrable.

It was in March, 1900, when I was returning from a brief vacation from over-work, and from renewed personal contact with Dr. Gildersleeve in Baltimore, that I formulated a principle that I successfully urged on my colleagues in the next session of the Graduate Faculty. It was this: "Unless our American colleagues in university work see the dissertations of our Ph.D. aspirants *in print*, our work will not — cannot — have that standing and acceptance which it must have. Other scholars must have the oppor-

[8] He died in 1920.

tunity of sitting in judgment on our work—a judgment which we must not only not shun but must welcome and invite." I must not here enumerate theses and candidates; but, apart from Dr. Eckman, I beg to speak a little more in detail of two of my Ph.D's of whom our University may well be proud. Both closed their eyes in the epidemics that came closely upon the heels of the Great War. Both were husbands and fathers; neither of them was a native American. Edoardo San Giovanni had received his earlier training at the *Liceo* of Corregio near Parma, in upper Italy. Coming to New York in the last years of the nineteenth century, he found at first a modest post as truant officer; but his uncommon Latin scholarship soon found better employment at the College of the City of New York and later on in one of the Brooklyn high schools. He wrote and spoke Latin with great purity and elegance. His thesis, in Latin, and published, dealt with the difference between the hexameter of Statius and that of Vergil. Also he was one of the few masters of writing Latin verse in these latter times. After the Peace of Portsmouth, 1905, he published a little volume of his own Latin verse, using especially Horatian measures and also the elegiac distich, and choosing for his themes poems of American, English, German, French, and Italian origin, such as Whittier's *Maud Muller* and *Snow Bound*, Longfellow's *Excelsior* (which in his version became "Excelsius," a grammatical necessity), in Asclepiads; also many of the briefer lyrics of Heine; then *Woodman spare that Tree* (in Sapphics) by G. P. Morris. For my personal taste, I rank very highly his exquisite version of Christina G. Rossetti's *When I am dead, my dearest*. I shall honor the memory of San Giovanni and please some of my readers by transcribing both the exquisite lyric of the English-Italian poetess and the Latin version of the Italian-American scholar.

UNIVERSITY TEACHING

> When I am dead, my dearest,
> Sing no sad songs for me;
> Plant thou no roses at my head,
> Nor shady cypress tree;
> Be the green grass above me
> With showers and dew drops wet:
> And if thou wilt, remember,
> And if thou wilt, forget.
> I shall not see the shadows,
> I shall not feel the rain;
> I shall not hear the nightingale
> Sing on as if in pain;
> And dreaming through the twilight
> That does not rise nor set,
> Haply I may remember,
> And haply may forget.

Now follows the version by San Giovanni:

> Ne forte maerens carmina concinas,
> Fatum rapit si delicias tibi,
> Ne forte dent umbram sepulcro
> Ulla meo rosa vel cupressus.
> Tantum sed illic roris et imbrium
> Gramen sit udum munere. Flebilis
> Licet memor vivas amicae,
> Immemor et licet, ut feret mens.
> Par hoc erit tunc. Nam tenebrae tegent
> Sensu carentem, scilicet imbrium
> Ignoram et in silvis querentis
> Carminibus philomelae acerbis.
> Premar supernis dummodo somniis
> Caliginosum muta per aera
> Oblivio mergat iacentem
> Ambiguum an meminisse det fors.

The rare little volume was inscribed to me, and in transmitting it he did so with a brief Latin letter, such as the Italians of the Renaissance were wont to indite. This too I would here like to save from oblivion:

> Ern. G. Sihlerio, Ph.D.
> Athenaei Neo-Eboracensis Professori

FROM MAUMEE TO THAMES AND TIBER

E. San Giovanni S. D.
Qui modo spe vacuus gaudebam nobilis oti
Haut bene vitandum me tenet officium,
Sihleri, et ingenuus vetat una munere fungi
Ornas quo iuvenes. Tu, bone, parce, Vale.

The poem at the head of this little volume is entitled: "Ode to the President." It is a fit tribute to Roosevelt for his mediation in bringing about the peace-treaty between Russia and Japan at Portsmouth, New Hampshire, in 1905. These noble lines are no version, but all San Giovanni's own. I transcribe the first two stanzas:

> Hoc tibi Pax tribuit: nomen, Roosvelte, perenne,
> Dixit enim properans
> Caesariem foliis redimita virentis olivae
> Aethera per liquidum:
> Surgite vos, nuptae! Matres, en surgite, castae,
> Quas viduavit atrox
> Mars. Lacrimis tandem vultus tergete madentes.
> Pax ego nata Deo
> Adsum.

The other one of this distinguished pair of graduate students was Louis Delamarre (d. 1919), a native of France, who had studied at Paris under eminent Latinists like Havet and ultimately became professor in the College of the City of New York. His thesis became a veritable volume of two hundred fourteen pages: *Tacite et la Literature Française*, Paris, 1907, a work combining sound scholarship with much grace and skill of presentation, which that grateful soul dedicated to me, April 15, 1905.

One more non-American Ph.D. I would beg to mention in this connection: Eric Boström who came to us from the Baltic University of Dorpat and published (in Latin) his thesis dealing with the Greek words found in Plautus, 1902. It was for me a felicitous rounding out of my work in this field, that my last three Ph.D's entered classic teaching in the very University I had served so long.

UNIVERSITY TEACHING

A curious but notable extension of my work was this: Through the invitation of Austin Abbott, Dean of the Law School (d. 1896), I gave, from 1895 to 1902, a weekly lecture of two hours, in the Law School at the Square, on the Roman Civil Law. I based my work on the texts of Gaius of Berytus and of the Institutes of Justinian's Commission combined in Gneist's *Syntagma*. Nowhere, I dare say, is the *ingenium Romanum* more clearly revealed than in those terse definitions revolving around Persons, Property, and Contracts. Sometimes I laid more stress on the historical and antiquarian side, sometimes more on the logical and ethical.

As intimated repeatedly before, I urged, whenever I could, the precious value and the intrinsic preëminence of Greek. May I not give more body to this chapter by transcribing from an appeal of my own: *The Rehabilitation of Greek in the Colleges of the United States*[9]:

Pia Desideria

The best College teacher of Latin—and I am speaking as one of the veteran classicists of America—is he who is the best Greek scholar among any given number of aspirants for a chair devoted to the language and literature of Rome. From the Greek freedman Livius Andronicus of Tarentum onward, Roman letters (*satura* apart) were patterned after the Greek; and I defy any one to do justice to Horace, e.g., without close knowledge of the Stoic and Epicurean systems of Greek thought, without knowing all now knowable of Greek lyrics, of Greek mythology, or the moral lessons of the Homeric Epics. You cannot follow Cicero's life and the very phrasing and sentiment in many of his letters, unless you have a solid grasp on what was the solidest of all his possessions, viz., his Greek culture, in which his soul sought ever such spiritual rest as was available from it or in it. This matter could be pursued from Plautus and Ennius down to Augustine whose struggle with Neoplatonism never seems to have had a clear-cut issue.

Must Greek die in our colleges? Nothing particularly glorious or auspicious in such a bereavement. Greek often seems moribund and there are those who recognize the Hippocratic face. Or do we naïvely believe

[9] *Johns Hopkins Alumni Magazine*, June, 1919.

that these things may really be conserved by second-hand scholarship with manuals and translations? There is precious little difference between second-hand "scholarship" and second-rate scholarship. One of the gravest defects of our actual classicism in the colleges frequently is premature specialization by the teacher, often accompanied by lifelong limitation. The interests and cultural sympathies of such men must needs remain narrow. Their powers and influences are bound to be so. But, on the other hand, to gain an ever wider and truer vision of classical antiquity—there seems to be no other way than to *hold the contents of the texts familiar*—is indeed a very full and liberal task for a lifetime of unremitting and devoted labor. The man who sets out to gain this direct and true vision and—may I say—*personal* relation to the ancient world, will, I am sure, never become indolent or inefficient, will never stagnate —his instruction as well as his academic personality will always have the grace and power of a certain perennial vigor and freshness so desirable for *all teaching* but indispensable for the energy and enthusiasm with which classical teaching must be carried on.

The main thesis for this insistent appeal—the historical sovereignty of Greek in the development of Roman culture—can best be illustrated by a close study of Quintilian, on whom I gave a graduate course in my latter years, faithfully tracing incidentally the dependency of this eminent teacher of the Flavian era from his Greek predecessors, his marvellous familiarity with the currents of Greek rhetoric, grammar, letters, and philosophy, from Gorgias of Leontini, and from Plato's *Cratylus*, and from Aristotle, down to his own time, when the professional preëminence of the Greek professors in the metropolis of the Mediterranean World was a condition accepted by all, however unwillingly endured by the *rhetors* who came to the Tiber from the western provinces.

One more point before closing this very professional chapter: I had long realized that in graduate schools, Caesar, Cicero, and Vergil had small place. I am speaking about conditions as they were about 1900. If distant nations turned to parse English by making a *corpus vile* of Burke, Milton, Tennyson, what then? The temptation to conceive those Roman writers and personalities in a distinctly elementary way, was of course very great. They were generally rated as "high school" authors. The response on the part of high-school teachers of Latin to my graduate courses on these three Latin writers was encouraging. As some of my most important works grew out of such courses, I must ask my indulgent readers to inspect chapter fifteen.

May I not fortify my contention by enumerating some of the points bound up with "graduate" study of Vergil, even at the risk of giving this very professional chapter a kind of technical conclusion? The *vita* by Suetonius (Donatus); Servius of Rome the conserver of precious exegesis; the *Bucolica* and their model, Theocritus; the patrons of the youthful Mantuan, Varus, Octavianus Caesar, Pollio, Cornelius Gallus; the *Georgica*, the most finished of Vergil's works; the incentive of Hesiod; why the fourth book was recast; the *Aeneis* which became the national schoolbook of the Roman world; Homer's *Odyssey* the main model for the first half, while the last six books in a manner reproduce the *Iliad*; the adroit introduction of Actium; Turnus and Pallas corresponding to Hector and Patroclus, while Aeneas is endowed with the main attributes of Achilles. I suggested as themes for doctoral theses: traces of non-revision in *Aeneid* VII–XII; the element of Pathos ($\pi\acute{a}\theta o\varsigma$) especially in IV, the Dido book; the similes of Vergil compared with those of Homer; the Vergilian exegesis in Macrobius. Although Heyne, Conington, Nettleship were open on my seminar-table, still the very great care with which I sifted and put in order all the material preserved in Servius, endowed my own work with a certain calm self-determination and —*sit venia verbo*— comparative independence. Whenever my students urged me to write a volume on Vergil, I declined, and contented myself with pointing to Sellar of Edinburgh.

XIII

MY FIRST VISIT TO ITALY AND FARTHER

I HAD to wait until 1897, when I had turned forty-four. It was not my fault that I had to wait so long. I had long felt that my professional training was laboring under a grievous deficiency. My resolution was fixed and determined the day after the Silver Party, led by William J. Bryan, had been defeated in November, 1896, and the Gold Standard reaffirmed. I was now sure of the purchasing power of my slender resources. At once I plunged into Italian, not so much to read Dante in the original as to be able to converse with real ease with the natives of the classic peninsula, whether professor or peasant. I wrote exercises continually; I read Italian New York journals; I conversed with Italians whenever opportunity offered. I find at the end of December, 1896, the following entry in my account book: *"Il conto di questo anno e chiuso e fermato, si non sara aperto di nuovo."* The Greek Club was still alive; but, after Dr. Crosby's death, March 29, 1891, it had changed its meetings from weekly to fortnightly. I entertained the Club at my Harlem home on April 23rd, but I could not then know that the end would come late in that same year.

I sailed for Naples on May 18, 1897, by special permission of the Chancellor. It was a slow ship, the *Sarnia*, of the Princess Line, owned in England; the fare was only some $56.00, the time of passage some twenty-one days. The officers and crew were Italians, all but the Captain and the Chief Engineer, who were British. Of course the conversation at table was exclusively Italian, which was entirely agreeable to my general plans. The ship's physician was an M.D. of the University of Pisa; we exchanged some friendly lessons in English and Italian. He struggled desperately—and vainly—to pronounce any English word beginning with an H. *House, hand, heart* became *ouse, and, eart*. But he was a cultured gentleman and could quote Dante by the dozen lines on any occasion. I realized as never before what a national poet and educator the great Florentine really is, comparable to Homer in the Greek world. Of course we had Italian wines at lunch and dinner, and I readily accustomed myself to dishes prepared with olive oil.

The Azores were a dream of rare beauty. The fishermen's huts, snow-white with the deep green background, the churches and hamlets standing out so strikingly in landscapes where winter is unknown, reminded me of pearls reposing on green velvet. The little island of Flores was the last of that exquisite archipelago, as we now were heading for the Spanish main. One morning the ever courteous Captain invited me to come up to him on the bridge, and, giving me his telescope, asked me to scan the eastern horizon. "Why, I see nothing but clouds," I said; but what I did see were the distant mountain-ranges of the southwest province of Portugal, Algarve; and in due time we passed Cape St. Vincent. High up on that famous promontory nestles the monastery of that saint. I thought of Columbus and also of Lord Nelson in 1805, for we were sailing through Trafalgar Bay. Tangiers with its mosques and minarets was the first greeting of the Old World; the Crescent, once ruling from Delhi to Granada and Seville, suggested a flood of historical reflection. Of course the Pillars of Hercules were greeted with deep satisfaction. Dr. Gildersleeve once told us that our national dóllar-sign ($) was devised from the Spanish "pillar dollar," a serpent winding around the pillars of Hercules. I at once sketched the African side; and from then onward to Sep-

MY FIRST VISIT TO ITALY AND FARTHER

tember, to the mouth of the Clyde and Lough Foyle, my pencil was never idle. The sketch of the African Pillar of Hercules, made thirty-one years ago, bears this inscription: "Bullones Mts., height 2800 feet, E. G. Sihler, from S. S. *Sarnia*, African side of Straits, June 4th, 1897." Everywhere the golden gleam of ripening wheatfields greeted us from Africa: in early September I observed them near Edinburgh. The noble range of the Sierra Nevada[1] of Spain on the northern skyline also offered many fine views, with the blue Mediterranean in the foreground. The Romans were wont to call it *mare nostrum*, which indeed, once upon a time, they ruled from the Tiber, until Goths, Franks, and Vandals ended the *Imperium Romanum*. The aftermath of the Great War (of 1914–1918) was then, in 1897, still in the womb of Time.

The south coast of Sardinia we skirted with fairly close vistas, cutting straight across the gulf of Cagliari: in Caesar's time it was called *Caralis*. Soon after, one morning, passing by Capri and Ischia, we approached Naples on that gulf of paradise. The golden gleam of the morning sun illumined that panorama, of which the exquisite heights of Posilipo form the most striking feature. On the very first forenoon, I visited the University, not yet housed in its present modern edifice. There I had long conversations with Enrico Cocchia, with Fadda, professor of Roman Law, and especially with the Rector, Commendatore Miraglia, who then lectured on the Philosophy of Law. The vigorous gesticulation of the Italian hands I observed then and ever afterwards. Some students in the rear of his lecture-room were smoking cigarettes, a form of academic freedom which I had never witnessed before. In a visit which I paid to Professor Miraglia in his official abode or office, he expressed to me his wonderment at one

---

[1] *Sierra* is derived from the Latin *serra*, a saw: the series of mountains, to the eye, reminds one of a saw.

particular feature of things academic in America: he marvelled that Harvard, Yale, and other universities were *private* foundations, and quite free from state support and state control.

Horse-cars took me out and up to the Posilipo whence there is the famous entrancing prospect towards Misenum, Ischia, Capri, Vesuvius, and Sorrento, a view unparalleled, or as the Italians put it, *"senza paragone."* On the Toledo —the name a reminder of Spanish rule—I found an excellent *ristorante* where I enjoyed an excellent *pranzo* with choice of red or white wine (*bianco o nero*) for the Italian equivalent of thirty-five cents! That was in the happier days of European peace.

I must not dwell on the archaeological treasures of the Museo Nazionale.[2] There I was particularly interested in the carbonized parchments, curious relics of the catastrophe of August 24, 79 A.D., which destroyed Herculaneum, Pompeii, and Stabiae. Mau (whose bust now adorns the entrance to Pompeii by the Porta Marina), the German archaeologist, has devoted his life to the work of repristination and reconstruction; our own Kelsey of Ann Arbor has often been called the American Mau. At the Museum of Naples, I secured a *permesso* for Pompeii, giving me the privilege without fee or guides to move about freely in that cemetery of a deceased civilization, visits which will stir reflection and fix our vision of that pre-Christian civilization as nothing else can. I must not here dwell on any detail, particularly on certain features in which the paganism of the Mediterranean world fairly cries out aloud to us—amid all the curious detail of baths, theaters, *triclinia* (dining-rooms), basilicas, markets still preserving the funnels that carried off the blood of poultry, or the honors shown to municipal benefactors, temples and evi-

---

[2] I also purchased from a copyist, for a song, an excellent figure out of the *"Bevitori"* by Velasquez.

dence of emperor-worship, shop-fronts with the measures for oil and wine, but, above all, the corpses preserved in plaster in the very attitudes in which they were smothered in that catastrophe, also the domestic safe, the *arca*, stoutly built and still defying Time.

On one of the two days I then spent there (lodging in the excellent Pension Suisse, just outside the Porta Marina), I was sitting on the remnant of the old city wall, a wall recalling Sulla, Cicero, Seneca, and Nero, and also one greater than these, Paul of Tarsus. It was not long before sunset; a gentle breeze from the Mediterranean fanned my brow; stillness was everywhere, the silence of the grave—everything dead, dead, dead; no life but this: the gentle wind moved the chalices of numberless poppies; and lizards darted amid the flowers. Greek travelling artists furnished the frescoes in the *triclinia* of the well-to-do who restored so much between the earthquake of 63 A.D. and the catastrophe of August 24, 79 A.D. After all, I pondered, *slaves, women, emperor-worship, gladiators:* who would wish to bring back all these and so many other things like these? Before leaving Pompeii, I made a very careful drawing of the Apennine range as viewed from the station there.

On the third day, I engaged a one-horse carriage to carry me over the heights between Casellamare and Sorrento, by way of Vico Equense, down from Punta di Meta to the Cocumella, a tour bewitching in its vistas of the sapphire sea far below on the right and of the stern contours of the Sorrentine Apennine on the left. My end and aim was the famous hostelry called "Cocumella" from the little dome of the church connected with the pension—all of it once upon a time a Jesuit sanitarium, with the park-like garden full of lemons and oranges, on its own plateau some one hundred and fifty feet above the Mediterranean. On the first morning after my arrival, when I peeped through

FROM MAUMEE TO THAMES AND TIBER

the Venetian blinds of my chamber, I marvelled: for on the trees near my window there seemed to be almost as many lemons as leaves, nor did I fail to hear the gentle cooing of the turtledoves. It was here that Goethe's famous lines would again and again echo in my happy soul (the version here given is that of the noted scholar and poet, Dr. Carol Wight of Johns Hopkins):

> Know'st thou the land where lemon blossom blows,
> Where 'mid dark leaves the golden orange glows?
> Soft sighs the wind from out the azure sky,
> Nor myrtles move, nor waves the laurel high:
>   Know'st thou it well?
>   For there, for there
> I would with thee, O my beloved, fare.

I swam in the sea at the foot of those almost perpendicular cliffs; on this gulf, too, my pencil was active to enrich my sketchbook, a patient and painstaking labor, which rewards the traveller who can do it much more than the kodak.

On my way Romeward, I spent another day in the ruins of Pompeii; and then from Torre Annunziata, without stopping at Naples, I went on to Rome. On that tour, the railway following largely the Via Latina of ancient times, I passed by town after town, of ancient site and ancient name, slightly changed if at all from Hannibalian or Ciceronian times: Capua, Teano, Cassino, near which was Varro's villa—while above is the famous mother-convent of the Benedictine order—Ferentino, Frosinone, Anagni. A glorious landscape presented itself as we stopped not far from Monte Cairo. Around that summit of the Apennines dark storm-clouds had gathered, while in the sunny foreground women with sickles were harvesting the wheat. I observed also—remembering Horace—that, in many a grain-field, elms planted in definite system of the "quincunx" like the five spots on dice were carrying the grape-

MY FIRST VISIT TO ITALY AND FARTHER

vines—grapes, amid the wheat—wine and bread being thus gained in the same field. Every town had its arable area for agriculture, while the towns themselves had their sites on dominant elevations, so that the workers daily had to descend in the morning, and ascend in the evening, a severe addition to the daily task of their lives. The women of Valmontone were just doing their washing in a large basin, a picturesque form of community labor.

Soon we passed into the wider plains of the Roman Campagna. I remembered then that Roma was really the last foundation among the Latin communities, and that the choice of site immediately on the Tiber was really a challenge to the Etruscans. A restaurant "For Hunters" was the last thing that I noticed before running into the main station of the "Eternal City" and finding excellent lodging in the heart of Rome not far from the Quirinal. In and about Rome, ancient, mediaeval, and modern history claims the attention of the student in a degree unparalleled elsewhere in the world. I called at the German Archaeological Institute in the Palazzo Caffarelli above the Forum. There I gained many valuable suggestions from Professors Petersen and Hülsen, especially the latter, whose charts of Ancient Rome are so indispensable to all students. I also noticed the busts of Bunsen, Niebuhr, and Henzen, to which I was sure that Mommsen's would soon be added. Many inscriptions that I saw were conserved by being immured, mostly funeral inscriptions found when the German government built the edifice housing all this rare material; also there was a library of supreme excellence. Scholarship is something almost spiritual: it is most enriched when giving most. I have no space here for the wealth of matter conserved in my diary of that summer, and so must limit myself to a few of the most striking matters. One was this: the Roman municipal government had (and probably still has) the habit of identifying itself with the grandeur of the Past in this way: the official notices of the Mayor (Sindaco) were headed by classic letters, S.P.Q.R., "Senatus Populusque Romanus." Almost daily, going down from my pension on the Quirinal, I passed the remnants of the temple of Mars Ultor (Mars the Avenger) erected by Augustus Caesar in honor of his adoptive father Julius Caesar,[3] really in commemoration of the Ides of March, 44 B. C. Those ponderous columns are now fenced in like a tomb, around which there flows and seethes the daily life of a modern city.

I pass on to the glories of the Renaissance: Michelangelo's *Last Judgment* in the Sistine Chapel in the Vatican: the Saviour in the upper centre, conceived by the great Florentine sculptor-painter like a Greek Hercules or youthful Jove about to hurl a thunderbolt; angels below with mighty trumpet-sounds; far above, two groups of angels bearing upward the implements of our Lord's suffering and crucifixion, a whirlwind of glorious triumph in that part of the vast composition.

Another bright memory: "San Paolo fuori le mura" (St. Paul outside the walls of Aurelian). When I had satisfied myself with the majesty of the colonnades in the basilica commemorating the greatest of the Apostles, I wandered about the contiguous Benedictine Cloisters completed in 1241, the Latin inscription in mosaic fixing that date. My own footfall was the only sound now, save for innumerable swallows twittering in the azure of that June evening. But my attention was drawn to the center of the quadrangle: a great bed of roses there, their last faint fragrance perfuming the air. I thought of Tom Moore and the last rose of summer; also of Horace (Carmina I. 38, 3):

> Mitte sectari, rosa quo locorum
> Sera moretur.

[3] With the financial aid of my Latin classes, I purchased at Rome a choice collection of photographs, mostly of busts of Roman historical persons, which on my return

MY FIRST VISIT TO ITALY AND FARTHER

On the evening of that June day, I gained my first direct association with Oxford. Professor Minton Warren (who had gone to Harvard from Baltimore) was just closing his year as Director of the American Academy at Rome. He urged me very earnestly to call on the noted Latinist Robinson Ellis, Corpus Professor at Oxford, who had just been examining certain MSS. in the Vatican Library before the summer closing, and was staying at the Hotel Molaro. After a few hours of delightful and strictly classical conversation, Dr. Ellis invited me to visit him at Trinity College, Oxford, in early September, on my homeward journey.

I pass on to the Villa Borghese, to reach which I first traversed many a dusty fathom in a parching afternoon of the summer solstice, June 21st, being weary from the daily contemplation of the fragments or monuments of the mighty past. From coffers of the popes through many ages flowed to their kin the gold which all Christian Europe, for so many centuries[4] before the Reformation, kept sending to Rome. Thus, then, especially in the Renaissance, Roman noblemen in their palaces in the city and in their villas in the country surrounded themselves, by preference, with the art of classic, often distinctly pagan type, also of neopagan brush or chisel. In a room of the Borghese there is a cycle of five splendid pictures from the *Aeneid*, with Dido's tragic death as the entire piece. Then Titian's Sacred and Profane Love, or Napoleon's sister Pauline Borghese done in marble by Canova. Vanitas Vanitatum! She died of cancer of the stomach, as did her brother. The distinctly Christian subjects are few and far between, swamped by the Olympian world.

In the Flavian Amphitheatre, the so-called Coliseum, I

---

were framed and hung in my classroom at University Heights, adding much to the directness of my work during the next twenty-six years.

[4] Philip le Bel, in his struggle with Boniface VIII, forbade the exportation of gold from France.

admired the architectural craft that could calculate and execute such ponderous proportions, the mathematical computation and the practical engineering involved in actual construction. If the Coliseum had not so long been used as a quarry or a brickyard, it would be as well preserved to-day as Agrippa's Pantheon, preserved as "Santa Maria Rotonda." I found the view from the upper lobbies towards the Alban mountains and the Sabine Apennine and the Etruscan Sea striking and fine. One's head swims—and still it is only when one patiently examines a few architectural details, that the solidity and unity of the stupendous total dawns upon the visitor.

On June 29th, St. Peter and Paul's day, I visited the stupendous basilica of St. Peter's where High Mass was celebrated by Cardinal Rampolla in person. It was all a gorgeous spectacle. The singing of the eunuchs in the Sistine choir impressed me unpleasantly. The garbing of the hierarchy from Cardinals down to the Seminarists of many nationalities—from generals to privates—is very instructive, highest to the lowest being gathered into a single scene. Wooden bars separated the general public, the clergy proper constituting the congregation.

Naturally nothing arrested my attention so much as inscriptions—the surviving utterance of the past. Most of them of course are in Mommsen's great *Corpus*. Still I seemed to touch ancient history as though I were a contemporary, when copying them myself. Here I saw that Greek freedmen and freedwomen kept their original name but appended it to their Roman name, the *libertus* thus permanently preserving both the memory of his former servitude and his obligation to his *patronus*, even when the latter had ceased to be the *dominus*. I made particular note of a bust of Cicero, one of the time when he was about forty-eight, say in 58 B.C. His countenance reveals a soul highly mobile, quick, intuitive, the mouth lacking

MY FIRST VISIT TO ITALY AND FARTHER

the characteristic Roman firmness and decision; the features are not set; humor and the power of quick repartee seem to lurk in the eyes and in the lines of the forehead. Caesar's features—he aged very fast—were in striking contrast. The temple of the Vestals, even though preserved only in the foundations, suggested to me the interweaving of this particular worship with *all* of the Roman institutions, nay with the very perpetuity of the Commonwealth, all conceived as bound up with the common *hearth*. The bakers who supplied these foremost ladies became wealthy, as certain inscriptions still suggest. The fearful penalties visited on a lapse of virtue on the part of a Vestal Virgin are familiar to students of Roman antiquity. The Forum comprehends vast expanses of time: from the temple of Castor down to the column of the Byzantine Phokas, more than a thousand years of European history seem to be marshalled before our eyes.

On the afternoon of July first, I went out northward to the Pons Mulvius (Ponte Molle) where I discovered a "stabilimento di Bagno" under one of the arches of that famous bridge, famous through the Catilinarian Conspiracy, where in 63 B.C. the incriminating proof was secured by Cicero's agents. Here then I swam across the Tiber, a classic spot forsooth. I fancied also, at the time, that this little feat was a bit classical too. I found the current very swift and powerful, and was a bit tired when I rested on the Etruscan bank. I learned also why Horace calls it *flavus* Tiberis. The swimming back *seemed* to be three times as long and quite exhausting. The Pons Mulvius is preserved in my sketchbook. The view eastward towards the Sabine Apennine was fine, though the mountains did not appear with that sharp distinctness which I had observed of the Campanian Apennine. On that blazing July afternoon, the Sabine range seemed to be very far away —silvery gray, a few white clouds resting on the summits.

FROM MAUMEE TO THAMES AND TIBER

On July second, before five, I arose and walked by the Banca d'Italia, down through some narrow lanes out into the open by the Coliseum with its yellow-reddish tints, which the Travertine stone seems to assume with age, by the *Meta sudans* and the arches of Constantine, and then through an avenue of locusts which fringe the via San Gregorio. This runs north and south, and skirts the Palatine on one side. How much like a fortress indeed is the very site of the original Roma Quadrata! Further south I approached the site of the old Porta Capena (leading towards Capua) in the old Servian Wall, the road opening into a region which is all within the Aurelian Wall, but now (1897) covered with fields and vineyards largely hidden from view by the jealous high garden walls of Italy. To my right, the giant remnants of the Baths of Caracalla rose into the blue morning sky, vast and massive. The sun had not yet begun to send down its burning rays. The *pauper colonus* even here and now was in evidence. Some poor people were moving, a woman carrying on her head a table and over her left arm two huge flasks. Mules rushed by, drawing toward the city two-wheeled carts loaded with country produce. Behind the driver, astride on the bags, sat an official of the *dazio* (consumers' tax). At last the southern end of the Aurelian Wall was reached, the greater half of my excursion having been through what we should call "country." Then came the arch misnamed "of Drusus" (brother of Tiberius), the stones in the arch being fitted together without mortar. Next came the gate of San Sebastian, capped with a bulwark of the Middle Ages, witnesses of the passing of the Pagan world, witnesses also of the rise and fall of feudal and hierarchical times. Here I saw the frescoed wall of an ancient *Columbarium* (receptacle for funeral urns) under the shelter of protecting eaves: "Ne tangito, o mortalis, reverere Manes Deos!" ("You must not touch, O mortal: hold in awe the gods of the

Dead!") Presently I came to the little church commemorating the Neronian persecution and St. Peter fleeing from it, the legend commemorated by the Inscription: D.O.M. [Deo optimo maximo] Haeic [hic, here] Petrus [a] Xsto petiit: "Domine, quo vadis?" A fountain nearby slaked my thirst: it was 6.40 A.M.; but even then the sun began to shed burning rays. Soon, on the left, came the ponderous monument of Caecilia Metella—the inscription calls her "Crassi," i.e., widow of the nobler Crassus son of the Triumvir Crassus who perished in his Parthian campaign beyond the Euphrates, 53 B.C. Near by is the long oval of the race-course of Maxentius who perished at the Mulvian Bridge in 312 A.D., defeated by Constantine. Far away in the East are the broken arches of the Aqua Claudia and the Aqua Marcia. I thought also of Paul and his faithful secretary Luke of Antioch who approached Rome by this road, the via Appia, as they came up from Tres Tabernae in March, 61 A.D. (Acts 28, 15).

A few days later, in the museum built among the huge arches of the Baths of Diocletian, I marvelled much—as I still marvel—at the curious symbolism on many sarcophagi: why are garlands of fruit and flowers, and why Bacchic scenes on these receptacles of the dead? On July 5th in my excursion to Tibur (Tivoli), I observed in the Campagna that sometimes the *pauper colonus* actually lived in caves or burrowed (in tufa?) like a rabbit.

Of my journey to Florence I have no space to tell. Florence lies in a bowl, and it was now fearfully hot on the Arno. That famous city of Dante impressed me as being much more mediaeval than Rome, e.g. in its City Hall, while, again, the Renaissance is also more obtrusive—the name of *Medici* carries within itself entire generations of that era. Further, the Tuscan Capital certainly is much more a monument of her own sons, her own wonderfully gifted sons, than is the Rome of the Renaissance which summoned the painters and the sculptors from a distance. I spent much time and study in the Etruscan Museum with its vases, arms, fibulae, *safety pins,* and tombs, and that last item is really all that remains of human pride and human ambition. One need not be a Carthusian, to have *Memento Mori* often, nay daily, reverberate in one's soul. The older history of Italy came before me, when the Etruscan League still was a power; and the antiquities at Florence called to mind the names of the member-cities: Populonia, Volsinii, Volaterrae, Arretium, Clusium (Lars Porsena), Luna, Tarquinii, Telamon, Volci.

But the intolerable and enervating heat drove me to hasten northward, and, after a brief stay at Milan and a refreshing swim in the city-baths, I crossed into Switzerland by way of the St. Gotthard. What a relief to come down on the northern side of the Alps to Lucerne, to pine trees and cow-bells and cooler skies! I transcribe from my diary: "As I write this, the rain is slowly pattering down on the avenue of chestnuts that fringe the beautiful Lake of Lucerne; my lungs inhale the cool fresh air of the morning with grateful delight: the garb of nature everywhere is copious, luxuriant, full of life, sap, and growth." I had fairly overdone it in Italy. My constant observing, study, inspecting, and reflecting in the ever more exhausting temperature of those southern climes, incessantly registering observations in the morning and doing much sketching on the spot, ever striving to fix and hold fast *multum in parvo:* it had indeed been the most laborious summer of my life.

I now mused much on those simple herdsmen and peasants of the fourteenth and fifteenth centuries who had beaten down the chivalry of Austria and the golden pride of Burgundy on many a glorious field, and had gained their independence themselves, alone, as at Morgarten 1315, Sempach 1386, Morat 1476. There is no greater achievement of man than the creation of a well-knit common-

MY FIRST VISIT TO ITALY AND FARTHER

wealth; in the end it is the hard fibre and the power to endure, that counts in the building of a small republic. As to Thorwaldsen's Lion of Lucerne, the inscription on that noble monument is almost of equal beauty and dignity with the sculptured symbol itself: *"Helvetiorum Fidei ac Virtuti."*

In turning over a volume of the *Fliegende Blätter* of Munich (1893), I came upon a lyric of rare beauty and universal human import—astonished as one would be at finding some noble lines of Tennyson's buried in a volume of *Punch*. I will not risk a translation:

> Im Lenzgrün, als die Vöglein sangen,
> Sind wir zu zweit durchs Thal gegangen,
> Du lehntest dich so warm on mich:
> Mein theurer Freund, wie lieb ich dich'.
> Im Lenzgrün, als die Vöglein sangen.
>
> Und als der Herbst begann zu prangen,
> Sind wir zu dritt durchs Thal gegangen,
> Du trugst mild lächelnd unser Kind:
> Ob andre auch so glücklich sind?
> Als goldner Herbst begann zu prangen.
>
> Und jüngst, als ferne Glocken klangen,
> Bin ich allein durch's Thal gegangen—
> Es stob der schnee und pfiff der Wind—
> Ob andre auch so elend sind?
> Und ferne Trauerglocken klangen.

An exquisite elegy. I abstain from exegesis.

Of course my sketchbook grew apace, especially after I crossed the Brünig Pass to Interlaken, where the Berner Oberland, from generation to generation, reveals its majesty to the traveller, the white robes of the Jungfrau overtopping all that wonderful chain. Some of my reflections were like this: "How many millions of tons of granite or limestone or gneiss (or whatever it may be) are here upreared into the colder sky, so that the sun cannot melt the icy shrouds of those famous peaks." But after a little reflection I returned to an important truth, viz. this: *relatively* those spires of rock rising above the rind and crust of our planet are great; but *absolutely*, there is no *life* there: a worm, a crab, a butterfly will show much greater marvels under the microscope of the biologist. The ever-proceeding palingenesis of living or "organic" nature, seems to me an unspeakably greater revelation of the Divine Power and Purpose[5] than those upheavals in the rind of our earth.

Why the absolutely level promenade at Interlaken with its walnut-trees should be called "Höhenweg," I never could understand. The company strolling there is gathered from all parts of the world. Still it is a fine place to observe the giants beyond. In the evening, when already the lower world of valleys, foothills, lakes, river, and plain was sinking into dusk, the spotless Jungfrau in blazing whiteness alone reposed in the light of the setting sun; presently in golden tints of majesty she was robed; imperceptibly she assumed hues of pink, then violet—a sight so vast and beautiful, that every restful heart was fairly hushed in contemplation, as though gazing up at the very footstool of the eternal majesty of God. A rapture far too great for feeble words enthralled my soul in silent love and awe.

After stopping at a place in the Black Forest—Badenweiler, with hot springs known even to the Romans—and at the University of Freiburg, I made some stay at Heidelberg, visiting the famous University and adding the castle (destroyed by the French in 1689) to my sketches as well as the exquisite panorama above and beyond. Let us recall Melac, who, acting under the orders of Louis XIV, created the most picturesque ruin in Europe, one of the enduring monuments of Louis le Grand. At Mayence I examined

---

[5] The present writer, with Aristotle, is a teleologist.

MY FIRST VISIT TO ITALY AND FARTHER

Roman *pila* (javelins) and even dental implements of Roman times found in the bed of the Rhine. "Kastel" across the river recalls the Roman bridgehead or *castellum*. From Mayence, of course, I sailed down the Rhine by Bingen, Bonn, and Loreley—what an enduring power in a brief poem! It is the beaten path of Europe.

From Cologne I took a fast train to Berlin, my first visit to Berlin since March, 1875. The semester had just closed. Of course my first visit was to the University, the cradle of all my academic life-purposes. Dr. Hübner had gone to a watering-place on the Baltic; the great Hellenist, Adolph Kirchhoff, now seventy years of age, was taking his vacation in the Harz Mountains. So I could not thank them personally any more. As best I could, I once more sought the places and associations that I had so warmly treasured for a quarter-century. As most of the persons were gone, I had to content myself with the places. Many things were changed or changing, but the historical monuments of Prussia and Germany were still there. Gazing once more on the *Schwarze Brett* in the dear old vestibule of the University, I was amazed at one notice: a course for Greek beginners! Most unwillingly though it was, I had to realize that even here Mercury was gaining on Minerva—even here where Böckh, Bekker, and Kirchhoff had presented Greek letters. Still I felt a dominating impulse: my visit to Italy had brought closer to me the importance of archaeology, and my pencil found occupation in a new sketchbook. Especially did I resort to the Museum, Old and New. I made not merely "sketches," but very careful drawings, which some of my friends have called etchings, which now lie before me as I am writing. Euterpe with all her flutes, the temple of Apollo at Phigaleia in Arcadia, Preller's fresco, which so often had entranced me during those vernal semesters (1872–74), Agrippina, the wife of Germanicus, the Boy with the Goose, the Giant-figures of the Zeus-altar of Pergamon, and an outside view of the New Museum itself, taken from the Kupfergraben, August 25, 1897; Wolf's mounted warrior spearing the lion, on the front of the Museum. I also drew the "historical corner-window" of William I, where, during my student days, I had so often seen the old gentleman greeting the colors.

From Hamburg I sailed to London on a small steamer, *Uranus*, Captain Schade. Even on the North Sea, I succeeded in getting a few marines for my sketchbook. Arriving in London, I soon found acceptable quarters near the British Museum. Of course, I once more visited the notabilia: Westminster, St. Paul's, the National Gallery at Trafalgar Square; but most of my time was devoted to the British Museum. I gained for my sketchbook the two most perfectly preserved figures—apart from heads and arms—of the Elgin Marbles, the work or design of the great Pheidias himself. I then and there gained a direct vision of the great sculpture of the Parthenon, a much more satisfactory conception than through books, even those of Pausanias, the classic Baedeker.

By far the most important incident of this belated tour was my visit to Oxford early in September, 1897. I promptly called on Dr. Robinson Ellis, who had invited me at Rome. That eminent scholar bade me cordially welcome and spent several hours of the forenoon in acting the *cicerone* for me on the banks of the Isis, taking me from college to college. I paused especially before New College, its walls grimy with the centuries. A good part of the afternoon, I wandered about alone. There had been a cattle-market that day, and the farmers in their smockfrocks, before returning home, were curiously entertained by a kind of jugglers new to me. These artists, moving about on very high stilts, and wearing peaked felt hats, exhibited an agility that I never had witnessed before. They caught the copper coins tossed to them by the farmers, high or low,

MY FIRST VISIT TO ITALY AND FARTHER

right or left, far above their heads or very low between their legs, using their felt hats as receivers. They never fell from their stilts nor did they miss a single coin. It looked like fun, but was a very hard living after all. There are many other clownish forms of existence, even in periodical literature, such as *Punch:* men prefer to smile or laugh, rather than to shed tears over King Lear or his youngest daughter Cordelia. Now this outdoor show of these stilted artists was performed—where? Of all places in the world, near the *Martyrs' Monument*, erected in memory of Cranmer, Latimer, and Ridley, who perished at the stake, at Oxford, victims of Bloody Mary, on March 21, 1556. This juxtaposition of the Reformation with the humdrum working day of the moment was curious and impressive.

In the evening of the same day, Dr. Ellis, Corpus Professor of Latin in the University, gave me a dinner at Trinity College, both viands and wines being of the choicest. It was not in term time. Several scholars, one of them of international eminence, had been invited to meet me. Of course, the conversation was more significant than dishes and decanters. The eminent guest, whom even now—he is gone—I shall not name, was then perhaps the greatest master of English philology, unless we except Sweet. He even knew the etymology of *Mugwump* and *bulldoze*. A curious incident may here be recorded. After our cigars, when the symposium was drawing to its end, I begged for the autographs of this choice company, to be a keepsake for the future. Then the eminent scholar, himself a guest, ventured this curious remark: "I suppose you Americans sell such autographs when you come home." Zeus *Xenios* mercifully guarded my tongue and I remained silent. Simonides the wise Greek poet called silence "a distinction of danger void."

Of Edinburgh and Glasgow there is nothing here to record but this: before our steamer of the Anchor Line passed away from Greenock on the Firth of Clyde, I secured a landscape of the northern bank of the Clyde with hills and spires of Scottish churches and heather, which remains one of the best leaves in my collection; another I made when we lay in Lough Foyle on the Ulster coast of Ireland.

In due time the *Furnessia* steamed up the Hudson; and I found every one in my little domicile in Harlem sound and well, especially her who ever was the crown and pillar of my household.

XIV

THE HAPPINESS OF MY SEMINAR-ROOM

(1900–1923)

CONFERENCES in that room were rare. It is true that I sometimes conversed with lame ducks and showed them that they had the power to swim and to swim alone. *Solitude* is by no means the same as loneliness. But still it is a serious state of being, and the *sine qua non* of real study and deeper thought. The best of my life, when taken as that of a scholar and author, was bound up with that pentagon fireproof room, glass and steel being the chief material of its structure and equipment, while two spacious tables, joined by their longer sides, allowed a goodly array of volumes to be set up before my note-book. We often use the term "ideal spot," but the seminar-room, with the Hübner collection largely in it and the Greek Seminar close by, was for me, for twenty-three years, really the ideal spot of my life: no hindrance there, no interruption to the application of my best powers: material of all degrees of authority and authorship all around me; the deepest wishes of my life here actually attained—what more could I wish for, nay dream for?

The Gould Memorial Library, as intimated before, like Rome itself, was not built in a day, or year; almost half a decade was consumed, from autumn 1895 to summer 1900. It was designed by one of the foremost architects of America. Now even architecture has often followed a *mode:* the very terms of *baroque* and *rococo* connote modes of the past. Who will compare Louis XIV with his high heels and wig of state with the Apollo Belvedere? I must not quote the too familiar line: "A thing of beauty is a joy forever." Much more to the point are certain German verses written by the eminent scholar Philipp Wackernagel:[1]

> Das Schöne kommt her vom schonen, es ist zart,
> Und will behandelt sein wie Blumen edler Art,
> Wie Blumen vor dem Frost und rauher Stürme Drohen,
> Will es geschonet sein, verschont von allem Rohen.

No vulgar or vile thing was to enter the edifice. Chancellor MacCracken chose a noble passage of Milton's for the inscription in mosaic which runs around the rotunda; and as you descend to the auditorium below, you see in six languages the words: "The Fear of God Is The Beginning Of Wisdom." Behind the stage of the auditorium, the organ for which I was commissioned to select, there is a superb window by Tiffany, a triptych, where female figures of spiritual beauty personify the virtues of Justice, of Fortitude, of Charity. The symbolism of the last-named is brought out by the artist with exquisite felicity: behind that noble and gentle head there are showers and a rainbow: "for he maketh his sun to rise on the evil and on the good, and sendeth rain on the just and on the unjust."

One of Dr. MacCracken's best devices was this: the names of the greater authors and leaders were placed close to or near the seminar-rooms housing the books or departments to which the names are pertinent. For Latin, I was given the selection and I chose: Cicero, Lucretius, Vergil, Horace, Tacitus, Jerome. Some of my readers may question the propriety of the last-named being thus honored. But I chose him with deliberate design, for Jerome, in a way quite of his own, represents the transition from the Ancient World to the Middle Ages, and the very grammar of his writings betokens that transition. The Chancellor

[1] Whose best works may be consulted in the Ottendorfer Germanistic Collection in the Seminar near by, devoted to it.

THE HAPPINESS OF MY SEMINAR-ROOM

also asked me to find a motto for the loan-desk in the rotunda. I chose, from Seneca: *"Satius est se tradere paucis auctoribus quam errare per multos"* (It is better to devote yourself to a few writers, than to stray aimlessly through many). Immediately below the noble dome of the rotunda with its rosetted squares are placed four figures of the Muses, of the highest Greek art. Kleio remains the tutelary spirit of the present writer.

The view from my seminar-windows toward the setting sun and the "grim, gray Palisades"[2] was always a wholesome interval or interlude of restful reflection when I was a bit weary from hard reading or excerpting. The sky above the Palisades generally was an unfailing index of weather probabilities. When the Palisades seemed hazy in the morning, it was almost certain that showers would come before nightfall. But when each rib of those mighty basaltic cliffs stood out sharply chiselled in the morning sun, fine weather was a certainty.

But to come closer to the main theme of this chapter: the deeper cause and substance of my happiness was quite independent of the weather and in fact of physical things in general, independent also of the current futilities of our political contentions and controversies between the "Ins" and the "Outs." Then again the noise and roar of Broadway and Wall Street were really far away from the peace and calm that were around me. A scholar's work really could not be carried on better anywhere in the East of our broad land. As for Morningside, the northward expansion of our American Babylon had quite deprived that part of New York of its quondam rustic surroundings.

Dearest indeed to me was my cabinet, not so much in the Indian Summer time when the foliage of that northern prospect was red, golden, and bronzed, nor in the spring

---

[2] See the noted college-poem by one of the most loyal sons of N. Y. U., the Reverend Dr. Duncan McPherson Genns, of the class of '99.

when the lilacs began to embroider the walks on the campus, but rather in December and January when the ice-floes were floating on Hudson and Harlem, and Nature was buried in hibernation. Then the seminar was at its best; then the spirits of the mighty Dead assembled on the shelves around me and near me seemed to whisper to my eager ears of their struggles and problems. It was then that my soul was entranced by the famous lines of Robert Southey:

> My days among the dead are passed;
> Around me I behold,
> Wherever these casual eyes are cast,
> The mighty minds of old:
> My never failing friends are they,
> With whom I converse day by day.[3]

And they will go on speaking when this pen is laid by forever.

My didactic hours or lectures were merely a pleasant diversion from book and pen. I certainly did not eat or sleep in that pentagonal room where I was surrounded by the men of old; but otherwise, until the shades of evening drove me home, *there* was my real abode and environment of existence. There indeed I felt and I was—rich. Why? Because there I could delve and follow up any problem arising; there I could place one text after another on the scales of analysis, comparison, and reflection; there I could assign them rank and precedence, and generally, in the end, they would tell me what I wanted to know. Sometimes too their silence was significant. Their testimony might appeal to my sense of the beautiful or of the ugly, or to higher perceptions—to my sense of political or moral truth. So too there came about in me a gradual emancipation from great names, hallowed though they might seem to be by academic tradition or cultural standards—*auctoritas* that

[3] *The Scholar.*

THE HAPPINESS OF MY SEMINAR-ROOM

often seemed to be guaranteed by manuals or cyclopaedias, the voice often of compilers who chiefly glean after the sickles of the great reapers like Mommsen or Bentley.

At the risk of writing a technical paragraph, I will stop for a moment with Horatius Flaccus, and show by a concrete example how the resources of my seminar-room enriched—or *could* enrich—my undergraduate or my advanced work: how the tragic death of Antony and Cleopatra is reflected in an Ode (1, 28), which to-day is the earliest extant document of that crisis which introduced the Augustan age; or how he warns Pollio to abstain from writing a history of the Civil Wars of the recent past, reminds him that he is treading on living coals hidden under treacherous ashes (II, 1); how keenly he ever feels his inferiority to his unattainable Greek models Alkaios and Sappho, whom I sometimes scanned to my freshmen; or to the incessant betrayal of the anxieties of the valetudinarian poet, or the efforts of Augustus to add Arabia Felix to the Empire (I, 29), or to the Epicurean disdain for erudition (I, 28). On the whole, the echo of those famous poems is sad, extremely sad:

> sed omnes una manet nox
> et calcanda semel via leti . . .

For readers who do not read Latin I may refer to the version made by my friend the late Professor C. E. Bennett of Cornell[4] and recall at the same time the name of one of our most distinguished Latinists: "But a common night awaiteth every man, and Death's path must be trodden once for all. Some, the Furies offer as a sight for cruel Mars; the hungry sea is the sailor's ruin. Without distinction the deaths of the old and young follow close on each other's heels; cruel Proserpina spares no head." How many of my readers know that in Roman schools the poets were often, literally,

---

[4] In the Loeb collection which he sent me in June, 1914. He died at Cornell, April, 1921.

FROM MAUMEE TO THAMES AND TIBER

reread by the pupils in the sequences or order (*ordo*) of prose?

But to return to my seminar-room: I shall have more to say in my next chapter which I am fain to believe and hope will prove the most important in the story of my life. Beyond all, like the vaulted sky above our world, was this conception which lifelong contemplation and study from every angle deepened into a firm conviction: the civilization which is our own, whether pre-Christian or Christian, came to us from the Mediterranean, from the blind minstrel of Chios to Augustine of North Africa. Now the following reflection often engaged my mind in my seminar-room: A mighty array around me—a thousand years and more of production in prose and verse, of very uneven worth —though much of it quasi-hallowed by the adjective 'classical.' What *shall* I do? What *can* I do? How shall I form my judgments, my valuations? Shall I merely take over and assume the *ipse dixit* of the greater men in our scholars' profession? The mere multitude of greater names from Plato and Aristotle[5] down to Scaliger, Casaubon, Mommsen and Kirchhoff, may well appal a young scholar, or an older one for that matter. The great texts often are buried under a crushing mass of erudition, like veins of gold under strata of non-auriferous rock. I looked upon the exegetes of many generations with a certain feeling of sadness. I knew distinctly—in those musings—that Homer would live, that so would Sophocles and Euripides, and even Aristophanes, the serio-comic critic of his own day. But what has become of Aristarchus, of Krates of Mallos, of Didymus of the brazen bowels, of Eratosthenes, of hundreds of names preserved in Suidas, or of the exegetes of the National Epic of the Roman world, Vergil? What we have in the Scholia or in Servius are mere rem-

---

[5] As recorded by Sir John E. Sandys in the three volumes of his *History of Classical Scholarship*.

THE HAPPINESS OF MY SEMINAR-ROOM

nants. But their modern successors have heaped up veritable mountains of commentaries and monographs. After the Hübner collection came to us in the winter of 1902-3, the great quarterly journals were ranged on the shelves in the Gallery near the Greek and Latin Seminar-rooms: *Hermes*, *Rheinisches Museum*, *Philologus*, *Bursian*, etc., etc. Of course I welcomed them, but the contents were by no means of equal value. When one examines Bursian's *Jahresbericht* (which never covers the whole field for the year), one may well be discouraged in contemplating the mighty streams of German learning, to which English and French must be added, not to speak of the *Mnemosyne* of Holland. One might feel that, on our side of the Atlantic, we were condemned to be excerptors, excluded from the service of original contributions and forever reduced to the status of European pupilage. Still I did not despair: I found that, by patient and untrammeled study of the texts, an objective and sometimes noteworthy attainment of sound—i.e., first-hand—learning was still possible, not less on the Harlem and the Hudson than on the Spree or at Oxford, Cambridge, Göttingen, or Paris.

Now there *are* indeed editions that may seem to take the wind out of our American sails: we have had as yet no Madvig, Haupt, Kirchhoff, Wilamovitz, Munro, Lachmann, Bentley, Porson, or Tyrrell in his monumental edition of Cicero's correspondence; nor have we had any one who would dream of vying with Mommsen or Grote. To pause for a moment with the great Berlin historian: One of my most careful monographs dealt with *Augustus Princeps*, published in 1902 in the volume of contributions dedicated to B. L. Gildersleeve on the completion of his seventieth year, (Baltimore, 517 pp.), monographs written by forty-three of his former pupils both of Charlottesville and of Baltimore. Sixteen were in the Greek field, sixteen in the Latin; the rest dealt with Sanscrit and Comparative Philology and with English and Germanic themes. This massive volume probably is to-day a landmark in the history of American scholarship. I had been led to reëxamine this subject (Augustus Princeps) from the sources, because I was struck by the fact that Mommsen differs not only from the almost unanimous opinion of students such as Hoeck, Madvig, Peter, Merivale, and Ranke, but also from Cassius Dio whom he criticizes severely. None of the historians named determined me in advance to reach the following conclusion: that Augustus assumed the political headship, with that deliberate adroitness which marks all his domestic management, by simply taking the first place in the Senate—simply continuing, apparently, the practice of the Censors in the Republican era, when they made up the quinquennial list. I found my material in Cicero, Livy, Dio, the *Monumentum Ancyranum*, etc. In my conclusion, I had on my side not only Madvig and Ranke, but virtually all the texts of antiquity and some great inscriptions.

Often too I compared Mommsen and Madvig in their delineations of the constitutional history of Rome. I found that Mommsen often formulates paragraphs of almost mathematical precision, when the available tradition of antiquity is but fragmentary and inadequate. In the sober pondering of my seminar-room, I was sometimes reminded of a famous French zoölogist—was it Buffon or Cuvier? —who, when given a few bones, could reconstruct the entire skeleton of the animal in question. Now then, in this and similar work amid modern authorities and ancient texts, I came to these conclusions: that, apart from Quintilian's *ars nesciendi*, sober and patient examination of the ancient material could be undertaken on our side of the Atlantic as well as on the other; and also that often a merely negative conclusion was the only one attainable. A chiaroscuro is very often the only vision possible.

THE HAPPINESS OF MY SEMINAR-ROOM

Looking away from the texts, there were of course many other tools and aids in or near my seminar-room, the very names of which now in my sunset years stir up sweet memories. The Byzantine Greeks produced little, but they conserved much: think of Photius. Or what do we not owe to Suidas—in lexical matters, in history, geography, grammar, biology, mythology? Then there were Liddell and Scott, Passow, Georges, Lewis and Short, and the *Stephanus* of the Dindorfs and Hase: how often I lugged the formidable folios—printed on vellum—out of the Greek seminar-room into my own! My "never-failing friends" were they: how often did they clear up obscurities and doubts, and point to a better exegesis! Of course, I was never so conceited as to believe that I could dispense with lexicon and concordance. I sometimes bestowed a full fortnight on a single word or phrase. Speaking of lexicons, I discovered that Liddell and Scott relied on the last *Stephanus*, and once or twice I actually discovered an omission or mistake in that treasure-house—always proving the dependency of the British lexicographers. Then my Latin *Forcellini!* I cannot say how much I owe to that Italian work, even though it has been antiquated by that gigantic venture, the *Thesaurus Linguae Latinae*, begun in 1900 and launched under the auspices of the Universities of Berlin, Göttingen, Leipzig, Munich, and Vienna, where the history of every word appears, from the Scipio Inscriptions to the beginning of the Middle Ages, published by B. G. Teubner, the foremost academic publisher of modern times. The vast enterprise almost foundered in the aftermath of the tragedy and desolation produced by the World War. My study of the Roman Civil Law, mentioned before, a study sustaining my lectures at Washington Square from 1895 to 1902, made me fairly conversant with the *Corpus Juris* and with Gaius of Berytus. The wealth of history sleeping in the Imperial "Constitutions" from Hadrian to Justinian opened my eyes to treasures rarely touched in America. As for Cicero, I had from the beginning of my service in 1892 determined to surround myself with an apparatus of the greatest comprehension; and I believe that I fairly succeeded. But vastly more helpful than the many editions and the countless monographs was the work of Merguet of Königsberg, his two concordances: four heavy quarto volumes dealing with the Orations and three dealing with the philosophical writings of the Arpinate, with the most liberal and exhaustive presentation—seven precious volumes purchased from the "James Loeb Fund." The *Lexicon Plautinum* by Gonzales Lodge (B. G. Teubner), which has been in production for more than a quarter of a century, is a monument entirely *sui generis*, and it is a monument to American scholarship. Here I have great pleasure in adding the admirable concordance to Horace done by an American scholar, Lane Cooper of Cornell, published by the Carnegie Foundation, Washington, D. C., 1916. As my work—never determined by the narrow exegesis of the class-room—extended, I began to gain a real grasp on the entire field from Romulus to Alaric, the decadence and collapse of the Roman Empire, and so took up certain authors which are in themselves unfitted for the lecture-room. Such a one is Ammianus Marcellinus of Antioch, an officer under Julian, whose Latinity is the oddest thing in all Roman literature: of him we have an excellent recent edition by Charles Upson Clark, Yale '97. Another one of these later and last "Classics" is Ausonius of Burdigala (Bordeaux). From him we may learn how Latin *and Greek* teaching, with municipal salaries, had extended to the Bay of Biscay. Also he exemplifies how actual paganism then was often blended with official or outward conformity with the Christian creed.

At this point, I may as well insert some more American data of importance. Elmer Truesdell Merrill, long at the

THE HAPPINESS OF MY SEMINAR-ROOM

University of Chicago, is distinguished as a critical editor of Pliny's Letters (Teubner, 1922), whereas the other Merrill, William A., has edited the didactic poem of Lucretius (University of California Press, 1917) which William Ellery Leonard of the University of Wisconsin has done in an English version in blank verse (1916). One is tempted to make a slight change in Bishop Berkeley's famous line—thus:

> Westward the course of Learning takes its way.

At this point I must make an annotation: the Regents at certain of our state universities in the Middle West practice a bountiful support of American scholarship: they publish (*ex munere publico*) the learned work of their professors, such as that of Oldfather on Seneca's tragedies and of Pease on *Cicero de Divinatione*. Homer has had eminent students in the Western World such as Thomas D. Seymour (d. 1907), John A. Scott of Northwestern University, S. E. Bassett of Vermont; and on Plutarch, my late friend Bernadotte Perrin of Yale (d. 1920); G. L. Hendrickson of Yale is a master of the Roman satura. As for the American collaboration in the Loeb Series, we note that here, under the direction of Capps of Princeton, American scholars are coördinated with British classicists. Our American Academy at Rome and our American School at Athens are strongly established, and for them Greek and Latin are no "dead languages." It is difficult to enumerate even all the editions of Egyptian Greek Papyri—where that of Henry A. Sanders of Ann Arbor holds high rank. I have been tempted to rename that university *Papyropolis*. Nearer to me are Westermann and Kraemer in this field, while our archaeologists have done great work, such as Theodore Leslie Shear whom I am proud to call an old pupil, and David M. Robinson of Baltimore. The successor to my own chair, Dr. R. V. D. Magoffin, is President of the

FROM MAUMEE TO THAMES AND TIBER

Archaeological Institute of America. American funds and scholarship carried forward the great work of Sir William Ramsay in Asia Minor; and William K. Prentice of Princeton (Ph.D., Halle, 1900) studied on the spot Greek and Latin inscriptions in Syria. But I must not, though an old man, be tempted to become a mere *nomenclator Philologorum Americanorum.* I am only *one* among them. The field is too large.

May I then from this wider sweep return to my personal life and work in my seminar-room at University Heights, immediately above the American Hall of Fame, where, I repeat, the happiest, i.e., the most deeply satisfying, years of all my life were spent: *"ohne Hast, ohne Rast."* I should like to set down a few pertinent matters before I close this chapter. It was a life of solitude, yes; but the gnawing sense of loneliness, let alone of aimlessness, was ever far from me; that gloomy spirit never darkened the door of that pentagonal room. It would be questionable taste to enumerate the titles of all the monographs elaborated in that room—after 1900. There is a temptation for an old scholar to count the sheaves in the stubbly field of life and labor now almost traversed. I shall not yield to that temptation. For German readers and fellow-classicists, I published in 1902, in the *Neue Jahrbücher* of Leipzig, a survey of American Classicism, its teaching and learning too, as well as the greater figures in our annals then recordable.[6] Perhaps I may be permitted to name my *Collegium Poetarum at Rome* (1905), in which I believe that I succeeded in throwing some new light on the brief life-story of Terence. The odd term thetikoteron[7] ($\theta \varepsilon \tau \iota \kappa \acute{\omega} \tau \varepsilon \rho o \nu$) had long puzzled Ciceronians from Aldus Manutius (Venice, 1554) on to the most eminent one of our own time, Robert

---

[6] Used by Sir John E. Sandys in his American Chapter, in vol. 3 of his *History of Classical Scholarship.*
[7] In Cicero, *Ad Quintum Fratrem,* III, 3, 4.

THE HAPPINESS OF MY SEMINAR-ROOM

Yelverton Tyrrell (d. September, 1914). But to conclude this hurried survey and also this chapter: There is a famous French canvas, "the Gleaners"—peasant women bending down to their humble work in the stubbly field. What, after all, are we, the classicists of these later times, but *gleaners?*

XV

FROM HOMER TO AUGUSTINE: THE CHIEF THEMES OF MY PEN

I NOW turn away from monographs and from the often laborious tasks of threshing a little grain from husks often threshed out before, not to speak of the fruitless controversies often assuming a personal tinge so common to our profession,[1]—controversies and feuds for which I entertained an ever-rising aversion—sometimes pin-pricks and endless forms of belittling some rival. There are here and there threshers on our barn floor who use flails, but often they are beating the empty air.

I had not long been installed in my seminar-room in the Memorial Library in the autumn of 1900, when a large and ever-expanding theme began to take possession of my soul. It was indeed a great theme: Classical Civilization as a whole; what, if any, are its spiritual elements? My inner prompting was not derived from theological writers like Tholuck, like Uhlhorn, like Dean Milman, or Lightfoot and Westcott, nor from the earlier Christian Apologists like Justin Martyr or his successors. I had spent a goodly part of my life from nineteen to forty-eight on the letters, philosophy, and political history of Greece. One must not forget, however, that only a limited part of the Hellenic race, largely that which is contained within the Ionic-Attic branch, has any genuine cultural significance. As for Sparta, Elis, Aetolia, Corinth, the Locrians, Thessaly, Messenia, Arcadia—what have they bequeathed to us? As for Rome, she was largely the mediator or trans-

---

[1] As when Mahaffy charged Jebb with cribbing from Blass.

mitter of Greek culture, the superiority of which the Romans willingly conceded,[2] while glorying in their universal empire. As I approached or was crossing the meridian of life, I frequently fell into deep revery and questioning of myself. I often sought clearness and some solid ground in that elastic and indefinite domain which academic language calls "Philosophy of History." I also sought a satisfying definition of "history." I sought a true scale for the weighing of *spiritual values*. I found myself unable to adopt Herbert Spencer, or Herder, or Goethe, or Lessing, or Comte the Positivist, or Buckle, least of all Hegel, while I found much in Lotze to attract me. I positively refused to see any manifestation of the Hegelian "Weltgeist" in Alexander or Caesar or in the pestiferous Corsican Napoleon. I refused to believe with Lessing that, given time, mankind will somehow evolve, out of itself, a rationalistic millenium. Taking the moment when I am now writing, the general drift of human history from 1789 to 1919 must incline any sober thinker to question Lessing's automatic evolution to ideal perfection. I also found that the line between Pantheism and Deism was a very slender one, not much more than a spider's web. Further, I sought to reduce to its true limits the cult of the Beautiful. I found that the overwhelming majority of mankind was excluded from that cult, that the daily toil in shops or fields kept them from reading the classics, or from visiting the galleries of Florence or Rome, or from contemplating with Winkelmann and his disciples the perfect and ideal lines of Greek sculpture. Superior to all this must be the spiritual verities gathered fairly within the limits of the first Christian century in the canonic books of Christian faith, the New Testament. Its modest garb of style[3] and its post-classic Greek did not disturb my own valuation of it as the great self-

---

[2] Vergil, *Aen.*, VI, 847 *et seq.*
[3] In which respect the Epistle to the Hebrews, I believe, outranks them all.

attesting body of spiritual verities and values. I could not fail to see that *all* souls are meant for spiritual objects, and could therein find surpassing felicity, whereas aestheticism and its cult must ever be limited to a narrow group, an élite favored by fortune or study or artistic endowment.

To return for a moment: in this determination of enduring values, in this seeking for some Archimedian point of a positive foundation, I gained an ever-deepening conviction that it was indeed impossible, in spite of Pheidias, of Rafael and Michelangelo, to find a compromise between the spiritual and the aesthetical values. In this long pursuit, I had come across a work that much impressed me. This was the monumental volume of Ignaz Döllinger: *Heidenthum und Judenthum, eine Vorhalle zur Geschichte des Christenthums*, Regensburg, 1857. Friends of mine like the late Reverend Dr. Talbot W. Chambers had told me in the old Greek Club days that the British version was long out of print. I seriously planned making a new version of my own. I nursed this idea for several years. Early in July, 1901, visiting Harvard to attend the meeting of the American Philological Association, I called on my old colleague of the Baltimore days, Josiah Royce, and told him of my project. "I would write my own work, Sihler," was the gist of his advice, which, I need not say, chimed with my deeper inclination. So I put my hand to the plough, not knowing at the outset how deep and how long the furrows would prove to be, and that full seven years would be spent on this first one of my greater and strictly personal works. The clarity and the objective precision of the great Munich scholar Dr. Döllinger were indeed models: no vague or sweeping generalizations, but every judgment fortified from the best sources. The essential features of Greek religion—or better, religions—the mysteries, forms of cult, images, the epics and heroic legends; the philosophical schools, the essential traits of the religion of the Romans, the impressive absence of myths and legends; the curious blending of gross superstition with rigid state control and official determination of rites and ceremonial; then Stoics like Seneca, the Emperor-cult, and the official apotheosis of Hadrian's Ganymede, Antinous; decadence and decay, slaves, women, the intrinsic desolation of all true humanity: such were some of my themes in this long task. I might indeed have been dismayed by the encyclopaedic and searching work of Döllinger with its bristling detail.

Still, adhering faithfully to ancient material and classic texts, I worked out a series of chapters from Homer and Hesiod to Neronian Rome as mirrored by Seneca's caustic pen and ending with the deathbed of Hadrian. My second chapter, introductory like the first, dealt with Humanism and the Humanists. On this theme, I spent nearly two years, greatly aided by the resources of Columbia University. I really immersed myself in the Renaissance. Unwilling merely to compile Voigt, Symonds, and Burkhardt, I excerpted the leaders of this much extolled and much misunderstood culture-movement from their own writings whether Latin or Italian, from Dante guided by Vergil, to Petrarch, to the unspeakable Boccaccio, to the still more unspeakable Poggio and Beccadelli, Bruni, Pius II, and particularly Filelfo. The neopaganism—admitted by Symonds—destroyed for me the idealization of a fancied Golden Age which still widely prevails. Then came Homer and Hesiod and the efforts of the later Greeks to endow their Olympus with some remnant of moral dignity—all this I traced with great care and with an open mind. As to many of the Greek lyrical poets, Seneca aptly summed up their moral character in this terse judgment: "illi ex professo lasciviunt"[4] (wantonness is their deliberate theme). One chapter was devoted to Aeschylus and Herodotus, who

[4] *Epistulae Morales*, 49, 5.

FROM HOMER TO AUGUSTINE

almost equally exhibit their belief in the anger and envy of the gods; another to Sophocles; another to the Sophists and the new learning and its mouthpiece, Euripides; then came the Triad of Greek Thinkers, a severe chapter. The funeral inscriptions gave much in the domain of religion, as did the oracles and the mysteries, Eleusinian and other. The whole of this, by far the greater part of my volume, the Greek part, I concluded with a few lines of my own, in which, I dare say, much of the hopelessness of it all is condensed:

> A god to whom I cannot pray,
> Pray, what is he to me?
> Montblanc is he, or star afar,
> Pentelic marble, Tigris clay,
> Or isle in southern sea.

The Roman part was, of course, much shorter: I drew clear lines, I believe, of the Roman spirit and Roman character. The very nomenclature of the Latin folk betokens the hard and sober, the utilitarian trend of the Romans in striking contrast with the idealizing type of Greek names. The Roman virtues were largely economic, and their institutions, e.g., when dealing with slaves or revolting provinces, were cruel and harsh to a degree. In Rome there never was any real democracy: the battles of Rome were won, her administration determined, her children begotten, and her blood shed, for the interests of a small number of great families. I then presented four portraits: Cicero, Cato of Utica, Lucretius, and Horace. The entire volume closed with a chapter on "L. Annaeus Seneca, the Versatile."

My original quest was to determine and know the *spiritual elements* in classic civilization before Jesus Christ. It was not my fault that my results largely bore a negative character. The title *Testimonium Animae*, I need not say, I borrowed from Tertullian. For many classicists, I well know, it is almost a professional article of faith to idealize everything pertaining to Greece and Rome. A distinguished Berlin scholar in a review became abusive instead of being merely condescending. He is no longer living. Here too, as often later on, I gained a valuable experience, namely this: judgments and estimates of a serious book vary almost as much as the personalities and idiosyncrasies of the various critics. I learned as an author, not to be too greatly elated or too greatly depressed. The *Testimonium Animae* was and is largely meant for theological readers in our own land whose hold on Greek has become somewhat frail or rare. A close vision of the civilization of the Mediterranean world must always show that the Christian religion was not, and could not be, evolved from that civilization, and that, with much of it, no compromise was possible. But, to conclude this survey: Is it not better to content ourselves with a sober, an objective survey of that civilization, and leave mandatory ecstasy to the aesthetical enthusiasts and popular declaimers, whom, like the poor, we shall have always with us? I will merely name the *Gesta Christi* of Loring Brace, and pass on after transcribing a passage from my epilogue: "I would not bring back classic paganism, if every idol described in Pausanias could be recovered in flawless perfection, if every Corinthian bronze once decorating the villas of Roman senators could be set up again, if every scroll cited by the Elder Pliny, by Athenaeus, Diogenes Laertius, by Gellius or Macrobius, could be placed in the British Museum." As for the critics, old or young, I would beg to invite them to examine my source-material with a fair degree of care. "Contempt solves no problem." I too was young once, and, as an old man, am fond of recalling an utterance in Macrobius: "tum cum admirabamur, nondum iudicabamus" (then when we were wont to admire but not yet to exercise judgment). I may, in taking leave of my favorite child, append the condensed estimate of the most eminent reader of this volume, Dr. Gildersleeve:[5] "The book is, as I expected it to be, a true expression of yourself with your tireless industry, your astounding reach of reading, your honest purpose to get at the fountainhead of knowledge, at the head of things, your perfect openness, your forceful and imaged utterance."

Not long after the conclusion of this work which absorbed all my powers for seven years, I began my Caesar-biography. The great historical subject (and problem) of Gaius Julius Caesar had occupied me off and on since 1885, when, by the invitation of Henry Drisler, I had begun to work on my Concordance: I went forward steadily to gain something far more necessary than intimate familiarity with those conquests. I was determined to leave no stone unturned, and in the entire process of investigation to maintain the mean between critical aloofness and making a hero out of this uncommonly gifted and unscrupulous politician. I also well knew that in our national practice Caesar had been a Latin speller and parsing book, and that, in consequence, he had little or no place in the graduate work of our land—Caesar, one of the most controversial figures in universal history and historiography. Cicero's place, academically speaking, in America, had not been very different. The life and work of the latter, covering every aspect of those times, the long-drawn-out agony of the Roman Republic, with us had likewise been held and treated in a most elementary way.

There was a further consideration in my own reflection: the Königsberg historian, Drumann, with the astounding detail of his investigation, with his personal design of extolling Monarchy as the ideal and finality of all political forms, had striven for something additional. He had been a special pleader for two ends, to elevate Caesar and to debase and degrade Cicero. Mommsen, whose prestige and authority were world-wide, had gone even farther in this

[5] Dr. Gildersleeve died at Baltimore, January 9, 1924.

policy of apotheosis of the one, and of depreciation and belittling of the other. Although the bulk of my students, before whom this volume was originally delivered as a series of lectures, were high-school teachers of the metropolitan district, I set for myself the severest standards of *critical* historiography, and told the story *sine ira et studio* (to use the famous phrase of Tacitus) from Caesar's birth and schooling to the Ides of March, 44 B. C., without the bitter partisanship of an adversary or the zeal of an uncritical admirer. Of course in the relation of the Celtic campaigns of the great Captain and the endless problems of verifying battlefields and towns on the soil of modern France and England, or Belgium, I maintained modest silence, while appreciating the work of L. Rice Holmes and French antiquarians. The treasures of the Museum of St. Denis near Paris I was never permitted to inspect, nor to gaze upon the giant statue of the national hero Vercingetorix near Alesia.

I showed that, in a long series of incidents in Caesar's life, the ancient sources are by no means harmonious, e.g., in the matter of the pardon granted to young Caesar by Sulla. Such points I discussed in many an excursus in small print. Of Cassius Dio I said: "Here then we come upon the imperial historian Dio and henceforth are dealing with a pen and purpose more personally acute than the transcriptions of Appian or the psychological and moralizing electivism of Plutarch."[6] The bulk of Greek source-matter in the tradition of Caesar's life probably outweighs the Latin. Of course Caesar himself could not be impartial: he dared not say anything of the millions of Gallic gold which he captured, and in which certainly he himself grossly transgressed his own Lex Julia Repetundarum,[7] on which undoubtedly he would have been indicted and found

[6] *Op. cit.*, p. 59.
[7] *Ibid.*, p. 86.

guilty at Rome, had he not begun a civil war against Pompey and the aristocracy.

In my American edition of January, 1911, I added something substantial as I then thought and still think: an appendix dealing with Mommsen and Froude. Of course I must even now at this late day apologize for coupling these historians at all. Both were born in 1817; both, in their earlier manhood, were decidedly non-conservative in their outlook. The sympathies and antipathies of Mommsen as well as his belief in the Hegelian "Weltgeist" crop out everywhere in his famous and justly famous *History of Rome*, cut short at the battle of Thapsus 46 B. C. As for Froude—largely an excerptor of Mommsen—the case was different. A man who could glorify the British Bluebeard, Henry VIII, could make or support any thesis whatever. Many of his parallels are absurd, as, e.g., when he compares Sulla[8] with Graham of Claverhouse. Furthermore I pointed out a long list of blunders in Froude's "Sketch," with specific exactness, to which here I must now return. I concluded this review of Froude's hasty performance with the words, "But to go on to the end would be like counting the pustules on a small-pox patient"[9]—which brought upon my head a bitter assault by a British reviewer, whose admiration of Froude's style was great, but whose knowledge of the subject in hand was small. As I intimated before, my authorship—with reviews running the gamut of praise or blame for the same work—in the end endowed my soul-life with a high degree of equanimity; for, no matter what the general merits of a book may be, a single sentence may utterly upset the complacency of the reviewer, who sometimes devotes a few hours to a book which has cost the author many years of earnest toil.

At the conclusion of my Preface, I wrote in my seminar-

---

[8] Not "Sylla": that is the spelling of Greek historians, like Plutarch.
[9] *Op. cit.*, p. 319.

room, October 28, 1910, a passage that *might*, but should not, be understood as a challenge: "In conclusion may I not express a hope—not oversanguine it is true—that our British and Continental fellow-classicists may begin at least to realize that first-hand classical study on this side of the Atlantic has reached a point of earnestness, a stage of exact and sustained effort, which may deserve some attention from them too, and some return for the European pupilage, which among us is rapidly coming to an end." I was in my fifty-eighth year when I wrote those words. The London *Athenaeum* was particularly generous in its review and was not offended by that paragraph.

One day in April, 1911, as I was standing in my little study or "office" in Language Hall and casting a loving glance at my youngest literary child lying on my writing-table there, the thought then and there flashed through my brain: "Why not send a copy to B. G. Teubner in Leipzig?" I did. But nothing seemed to come of it. Still, "habent sua fata libelli." One day in September, 1911—Chancellor Brown had but recently assumed office—I received a letter from the great publisher offering me a contract for a German version of the *Annals of Caesar*. I will make no bones about it: I was proud and happy. It was left to me whether to have the version made by another or to make my own. Of course, I determined to do it myself. A hard drive it was, and an English-German lexicon was not rarely consulted: the German idiom had gently and imperceptibly been drifting away from me during the decades since 1875.

When, early in 1912, I sailed for Naples with my good wife, the last proof had not been read. The mail at Naples was in disorder. So I warned B. G. Teubner to send everything to Lucerne, this being the nearest point to Leipzig that I reached on that tour. I read the entire last proof of the book in a few weeks at the Villa Maria, not far from the borders of that lovely lake, and also made the index in

FROM HOMER TO AUGUSTINE

Switzerland, the country of my ancestors. Work in vacation time! Later on, leaving Geneva, I made a tour of Provence, the Gallia Narbonensis of the Roman Empire, and there added many new vistas of history and landscape to a new collection of my drawings begun with the castle of Chillon at Montreux. Caesar began his Gallic Wars at or from Geneva. From that historic town I went to Lyons. Going thither I observed that the train reached a point where the Jura-range is sharply stopped by the Rhone (Rhodanus). At this very point I could personally and directly ponder on Caesar's strategy in dealing with the emigrating Helvetians. He says (I, 6) : "There were altogether two routes, one through the country of the Sequani, *narrow and difficult* between the Jura-range and the Rhone river, where hardly one cart at a time could pass; moreover a very high mountain rose hard by, so that a handful of men could check" (any marching column). The railway now, in 1912, was passing the precise point: I seemed for the moment to be living in 58 B. C. And again at Lyons, when I was standing by the confluence of the mighty Rhone and the sluggish Saone (Saconna or Arar), the very words of Caesar rose to my mind: "There is a river, the Arar, which flows through the country of the Aedui and the Sequani into the Rhone with an incredible slowness, so that by mere eyesight one cannot make out in which direction it flows" (I. 13). It was literally true: the waters of the Saone were really as sluggish as the great captain wrote: I threw a piece of wood into the affluent of the Rhone, and lo and behold! it seemed not to move at all. Again I seemed to stand by the side of the extraordinary man who later on did cross the Rhine, the British Channel, and the Thames itself, and established his diadem in Thessaly, on the Nile, in Africa, in Spain. But to return to my own work—in two tongues—*Caesar*. The attestations of European scholars, especially in England, could not but be highly pleasing to the western author—scholars such as the late Professor Haverfield of Oxford and the Senior Classical Tutor at Merton College there. To these were added voices of critical scholars from Germany, Holland, Sweden, France, Austria, Italy. The American Edition, *per se*, I speedily inferred, would have been ignored, if the Teubner imprint had not been superadded. Both editions were inscribed to my dear friend Bernadotte Perrin of Yale (d. 1920).

As for my expectation that American high-school teachers, or those who train them, would eagerly procure and study this volume, I was deceived. The truth seems to be that most of the teachers in our secondary schools are burdened with all kinds of bookkeeping and related forms of routine duties, which consume time and inhibit real scholarship; and their contributions to American scholarship in consequence are slight or negligible. Throughout our land the functions of managing and administering are overrated and professionally rewarded, whereas real teaching and its essential correlative, personal and progressive scholarship, are often reduced to the status of Cinderella. Meanwhile, too, towns and cities seem not merely to be under a curious competitive strain of costly architectural display, but to suffer from the itch to expand the high schools into little municipal universities, where a great many "subjects" may be briefly touched and superficially fingered over, and soon forgotten. The surface of all these "courses" is indeed wide: *superficies* is the Latin for surface; these "courses" are indeed veritable "floods," but so shallow that a mouse could not drown in them.

The next in order of this survey is my biography of Cicero. This too was first presented as a series of lectures to graduate students, at intervals of three to four years. Of course, in the case of the Arpinate, a great many graduate courses had preceded this biographical comprehension: his rhetorical writings, the orations, some sixty-five in number—not counting the fragments of those lost—his correspondence, and the philosophical treatises of his last years. All these, separately grouped, had engaged my closest attention for decades. Asconius, and further the splendid Onomasticon by Orelli, and also the wonderful Concordances by Merguet cited in my last chapter—these particularly had been utilized to the utmost. For strictly biographical purpose and for a closer vision of the Arpinate's ingenium, his correspondence is a veritable gold-mine.

Academic friends, especially certain ones at Yale, had urged me to add a biography of Cicero to that of Caesar. When I surveyed the huge mass of "literature" and controversy clustering about the name of Cicero, the first and foremost name in Roman letters, I realized that, unless I were willing to be swamped, and my readers with me, I must now, if ever, adhere to the utilization of primary and contemporary utterance preserved so largely by his own pen or by the services of his own freedman and secretary, Tullius Tiro.[10] I was aware also, that I was entering upon a well-beaten path, trodden by many biographers before me, such as Boissier in France, in England by Middleton (1683–1750), Forsyth (1862), Strachan-Davidson (1906). Of Drumann I have spoken.

Much more than to all these collectively I owed to the life-work of Robert Yelverton Tyrrell of Dublin and his colleague and successor, L. Purser: *The Correspondence of M. Tullius Cicero arranged in chronological order*, 6 volumes, from 1886 onward, now in second edition—a work of cyclopaedic learning, but distinguished also by the most delicate sympathy with the smallest detail. In the course of the years, I traversed these volumes three times. As I gradually and systematically made myself familiar with the best Ciceronian learning, let me say, of the half-century

[10] Whom Cicero called *Tiro*, because this young amanuensis was, in a way, in following and serving a veteran, a *recruit*.

preceding my own biography, I became deeply convinced that Tyrrell was the most eminent Ciceronian then living when finally my stout volume began to go through the Yale University Press, March, 1914. But even before this, when I had completed my MS. in August, 1913, before the place or mode of publication was at all definite, I asked permission of Dr. Tyrrell to dedicate this work to him. I received the following acceptance:

East House, Greystone, County Wicklow, Ireland.
Friday, Aug. 22, 1913.
My dear Dr. Sihler:

Many thanks for your kind letter and enclosures. I hasten to assure you of my keen sense of the kindness which prompts you to offer to me the dedication of your forthcoming book on Cicero, which I am sure will be an epoch-making work and a decided counter-blast to Mommsen and Drumann. The honor conferred on me by the dedication will be regarded by me as the very highest distinction and the words of approval which you accord to the work of Purser and myself are most welcome to us. Before we had any personal communication with you we had learned to appreciate the immense value of your *arbeit* on Cicero as well as the literary finish of your style, and it was a great pleasure to come a little nearer to you through the medium of correspondence. I had the privilege of making the acquaintance of that admirable scholar Dr. Gildersleeve in Baltimore, in 1893. You characterize him justly in praising his rare delicacy of perception and interpretation . . . I remain with very many thanks,

Very sincerely yours,
R. Y. TYRRELL

It was tragic: the Great War having begun, Dr. Tyrrell died in a private hospital in London, September 19, 1914, when the first copy, the one addressed to him personally, was on the Atlantic.

How utterly different the conception of Cicero held by Niebuhr, and that held by Mommsen: both were natives of Schleswig-Holstein. But there is one mighty aid in the study of the Roman Republic, which in this survey I must not pass over: Fischer's *Römische Zeittafeln* (from the founding of Rome to the death of Augustus, 14 A. D.), a wonderful guide and repertory. I have little doubt but that it was always on the working-table of Mommsen and Madvig. It was issued in 1846, but is still indispensable and unrivalled: chronology, legislation, offices, elections, conquests, war and peace; and then also the most delicate determination of the history of letters and authorship, with the print so set back that this may be traced separately. In a way, it is the very skeleton of the history of the Eternal City. On a single chronological determination, Fischer sometimes brings in Livy, Sallust, Plutarch, Velleius, Orosius, Florus, Eusebius, Jerome. Cicero was born January 3, 106 B. C., and perished in December, 43 B. C.; these sixty-three years are spread before the student on pages 158–332; thirty-one percent of the vast total was compassed by the life of Cicero. Now there is no life of the ancient world that we know so intimately as that of Cicero. More: as I said in my Preface: "During the last twenty years I have tried to gain a close vision of Cicero's life and the movement thereof in all its aspects; a life curiously interwoven with, and reflected by, the letters of the Arpinate. If all the works of his pen were to be extinguished forever, works intensely personal in the main, but marvelously comprehensive and indeed cyclopaedic in their range of interest and concern, what an Egyptian darkness would enshroud much of the ancient world! . . . One may here learn to know Cicero's faults and weaknesses, no less than become familiar with his lofty ideals and his quite wonderful industry, and further on one may perceive how that critical period of political disintegration and social decadence was mirrored in the lively mind and recorded by the masterful pen of one who was indeed the most gifted son of ancient Italy."

The correspondence of Cicero contains more than seven

hundred letters *from him*—not counting a goodly number of letters addressed *to him*. He had no idea that his letters to his bosom friend and dearest confidant, "Atticus"—long self-expatriated from Rome—would ever see the light. They cover a quarter-century, from 68 to 43 B. C., and we are under great obligations to his amanuensis Tiro.

I must say a word of Ferrero, the Italian journalist-historian, a great and clever journalist among historians, a unique historian among journalists, his real and original guild. If one were to ask me to-day for an historian of the Roman Republic ranking closely to the unique Mommsen, I should point with positive, nay, exclusive, preference to W. E. Heitland of St. John's College, Cambridge, England. Also I have no hesitation in demanding that the man who writes that much-written story must hold as an intimate and familiar friend Polybius of Megalopolis, the noblest, most searching, and most estimable historian of the Ancient World. But to return to the Ferreresque type of Roman historiography with its catching trick of clothing ancient life and political figures in the modern garb of to-day and yesterday, I beg here to quote from my critique of the son-in-law of Lombroso: "If only we could garb Cicero in a frock-coat and put a *pince-nez* on his nose: if only we could put a telephone-receiver into the hand of the 'old banker,' Crassus, or have the waiter bring in some Veuve Clicquot for Cleopatra and a box of Havanas for the towering Julius while he is studying the pattern of the mosaic floor and is on the point of citing an appropriate sentiment from Sappho or Anacreon—if this only could be done, then the whole would be even a little more Ferreresque, a little more modern than it is now, a *little* more, but not indeed much more. We must then positively decline to follow Ferrero into his shop filled with social labels of to-day or yesterday, which he spreads so calmly over the world of Italy and its Mediterranean Empire as the housemaid spreads the counterpane when she makes up the beds."[11]

I now return to my *Cicero, an Appreciation*, in Gildersleeve's *American Journal of Philology*[12]: "He felt as one surrounded by a cloud of witnesses, the shades of the past, the choir invisible of Roman worthies, who, as in the Dream of Scipio, were translated from this narrow and treacherous earth to live by themselves in bliss, in a heaven of civic immortality. In Cicero there was a conflict of two voices which never chimed in harmony; that of the scholar and idealist on the one hand, and that of the practical man of the world, husband of Terentia, father-in-law of Piso, Crassipes, and Dolabella. The latter needed and sought material success. The fond and voracious reader, working in the garden-library of his Tusculanum, the student of noble thoughts and lofty principles—this is the one of the two Ciceros, the one whom we justly cherish and honor, and consider it not unimportant to transmit to future generations. But we must not overlook the other one. This is the young aspirant for fame and distinction, son of a quiet and retired gentleman of moderate wealth, born in the highlands of upper Liris amid a simple and unspoiled folk of yeomen. The aristocracy had splendid mansions, especially on the Palatine, where their luxury held high revels and where a silly anecdote would have the Arpinate susceptible to the beaming beauty of a Clodia. Cicero's purchase of a mansion, a mansion once belonging to rich Crassus himself, and his relations—however temporary—to Antonius in the latter's Macedonian exploitation, and to P. Sulla, are not pleasing reading for those who would like to believe him flawless.

"Few personages of all time—no one personality of Classic antiquity—are so well known to us as he. Few men

---

[11] *American Journal of Philology*, 1914, p. 389.
[12] *Ibid.*, pp. 1–11.

have left so large a body of extremely private correspondence to the tender mercies of a curious and dissecting world. Every chambered cell of his growing life lies revealed. Every foible, every passing mood lies before us as though we observed his heartbeat through a casement of glass. His infinite sensitiveness, no less than his swift and sure intelligence, his fears and prejudices, his faculty of fathomless hatred, are turned to our gaze, no less than his noble aspirations for justice, equity, and righteousness. His was a warmly beating heart; few men in all history have been so resolutely grateful as Marcus Tullius Cicero. On the other hand, his cast of temperament and will compels us to rate him somewhat lower than Caesar in the domain of forgetting and forgiving. The volcanic passion of his vindictiveness even now may cause our souls to shudder and tremble with a positive horror.

"The deep intellectuality of the man himself is revealed in his last years, especially after the death of the only one of his children who seemed to deserve his strongest affection. He had lost his Tullia—he was himself desolate and bared of joy and hope, like a tree in December. He had heard the knell of almost all of his ideals; the world in which he went on living was dreary to him, for it was vicious, frivolous, shallow, decadent. 'It was within the power of Themistocles to live a life of leisure, it was within the choice of Epaminondas, it was—that I may not go into ancient or foreign spheres—it was permitted to *me:* but somehow there is deeply rooted in the mind a certain presentiment of future ages, and this is quickened to life most in the greatest intellects and in the loftiest souls, and it is also readily revealed in them. If this were cancelled who would be so imbecile as always to live in toil and danger?' "[13]

Some years before my *Cicero of Arpinum* went to press,

---

[13] *Tuscul. Disput.*, I, 33.

FROM HOMER TO AUGUSTINE

beginning in the summer of 1911, I resumed Greek work on a wide scale. Professor G. W. Botsford[14] of Columbia had assumed the task of composing a large work on *Hellenic Civilization* in the series projected by James T. Shotwell of the same University. Dr. Botsford, like myself a resident of Mt. Vernon, requested my coöperation probably because I had written *Testimonium Animae*. As time went on, he formally intrusted me with fully half of the proposed labor. When the volume finally appeared, in 1915, it was one of 719 pages. Now poor Botsford had for years overworked himself and was really half an invalid, and of course his impaired health reacted on many things; whereas I enjoyed robust and unvarying health: a contrast thus appeared in the pace which each of us pursued, which I sometimes forgot. I may transcribe here from a letter that he wrote me after the appearance of the volume, from Cornwall-on-the-Hudson, September 15, 1915: "It seems to me to be a magnificent book in appearance and contents and that we have a right to congratulate ourselves and each other on the results of our long task." Important contributions also were made by W. L. Westermann of the University of Wisconsin (Ph.D., Berlin, 1902) who had studied under Eduard Meyer. Our work carried the story of Hellenic Civilization from Homer and Hesiod, nay from the Minoan Age, down to Alexander and the dynasties established by his generals, nay to the physician Galen. Of course Hellenic Civilization without some survey of Greek philosophy from Thales down was a somewhat defective exposition, but I was outvoted: the volume would have become too bulky. As for material compensation, the *work* that I did was then my chief reward, and remains so: and this, to speak candidly, is almost a canon for the scholar's pen. Whether I did a little more than half, or a little less, is not important. It was all a joy to me, a late joy it is

[14] He suddenly died in his study in Kent Hall, Columbia, in December, 1917.

true, for I had turned fifty-eight when my collaboration began and was nearer sixty-three when the volume appeared with the imprint of the Columbia University Press. There was one important point in which Botsford and I were in complete and cordial agreement:[15] we were determined *not* to make a compilation from the manuals of modern scholars, but to resort, as far as possible, to the self-attestation of the Hellenic world itself; the task of choosing the best meant to choose the most significant, the most characteristic, the most self-revealing in a given epoch, the leaders, if possible. This choosing and selecting clearly is the chief task of the historian of a given civilization. We of course ransacked Herodotus, Thucydides, Xenophon, Polybius, Arrian, Diodorus, Strabo, Athenaeus, Plutarch, Pausanias, Oxyrhynchus Papyri, the "Fragments" in Müller's famous collection, Aristotle's *Constitutional History of the Athenians*, his *Politics*, Plato's *Republic*, Attic inscriptions, the Attic orators, and the comedy-writers down to Menander.

Of course we used some translations, i.e., of those of approved excellence, with full credit. But almost throughout I compared them with the original texts, and sometimes made a slight revision. In many cases we made our own translations, as Botsford did of Aristotle's *Constitutional History of Athens*. Of my own I may mention Tyrtaeus—neither blank verse nor an exotic attempt to reproduce the ancient metres—Alkman, Archilochus, Semonides of Amorgos, Mimnermos, Anacreon, Theognis, Simonides, the Laws of Gortyn in their Cretan dialect—the most laborious of all my tasks—selections from Hippocrates, the inscriptions dealing with the construction of the Erechtheum, and many other original texts. The organization, the architectural design of the whole, was entirely the work of

---

[15] Although "bibliography," the bogey of my life, was superabundantly provided for in our volume, Pauly-Wissowa, as far as it then went, in this aspect of positive utility greatly exceeded our own work.

the Columbia professor. The Index was my own: a toilsome task. What gave me the keenest satisfaction was the occasional drawing or characterization of a literary personality, as of Aristophanes, the intimate friend of my Berlin and Baltimore days, or of Hesiod, the famous poet of Askra under Helikon. May I here insert a specimen of these belated labors—my sketch of the first-named?

It was long the custom, as in the heavy and ultra-serious essay by Ferdinand Ranke, to assign to the author of the *Knights, Clouds, Peace, Birds,* and *Frogs* a niche among the thoughtful patriots, deep political thinkers, and even moral reformers, who gave lasting distinction to Athens. On this subject, however, there is room for difference of opinion. It is always a question how far our poet should be taken seriously. Thucydides and his great work afford a curious foil to the political comedy of the Peloponesian war-period; they illumine one another in the most felicitous manner. The faculty of symbolical caricature and a drastic power of allegory and invective, intermingled with lofty lyrics and harlequinade, language sometimes running on the even keel of current Attic dialogue, but often interlarded with sudden and incalculable spurts of slang and vulgarity, an abandon of obscenity and semi-intoxication of demeanor—all in close harmony with the essential character of the vintage festivals; sudden attacks on some familiar minor figures, with sustained persecution of some greater personage in public life—these and many other ingredients may be found in the plays of Aristophanes. Besides the eleven preserved plays, he wrote about twenty-nine others. Was the political influence of an Aristophanes comparable to that of the orators who addressed the Ecclesia directly, when all were sober and in a deliberate frame of mind? Plato has borne witness that the caricature of Socrates in the *Clouds* had a lasting and an evil effect on the reputation of that philosopher. The typical humanist who would duly revere both the philosopher and his reckless traducer, finds himself in a somewhat difficult plight. That Aristophanes pleaded for peace and that, with his brilliant and piercing intellect, he discovered the evils of the developed Attic democracy, cannot be denied; but it seems equally true that sheer love of fun interfered with the serious pursuit of any serious object.

On Hesiod (p. 8 *et seq.*) :

The poet, a shepherd and farmer, suffered from scoundrelly litigation at the hands of his brother Perses. Out of such experiences the *Works and*

FROM MAUMEE TO THAMES AND TIBER

Days came forth. The seasons of the year and all the tasks and toil which they bring in their train are here set forth. In his personality there are reflected thoughtfulness and meditation rather than imagination and enthusiasm. His *Theogony* was the first effort of the Hellenic world to construct, through a system of genealogies and pedigrees, a unity of Heaven and Earth and their history. The epic of the *Heroines* continued that constructive process and dovetailed it into the ancestral legends of the chief families associated with the principal communities or states of Greece. The fact that but one elaborate simile occurs in Hesiod is significant of his prosaic character, while the deliberate and didactic trend of his manner and mind is equally manifest in both epics. There are two sides in him: he is gifted in presenting actual, even minor and petty things with remarkable precision. On the other hand, he is indeed a man of deep reflection. From this vein, especially in *Theogony*, a world of abstractions arises, which the poet of Ascra knows how to clothe with dazzling nomenclature. Common to both epics, specifically speaking, is the conception of Woman, a gift of Zeus which he bestowed upon mankind in his wrath. The Pandora-myth in both poems is episodical, but favorite themes and favorite plaints are apt to crop out, or to steal in, as episodes, particularly in didactic poetry. If anything, the Pandora-myth of the *Works* (94, *et seq.*) is more malicious, because the woman is made responsible for the diffusion of evils through the world, evils tempered only by the retention of Hope. Hesiod's ethics are those of Cato the Censor and Franklin's *Poor Richard*: they are largely based on the virtues clustering around *Frugalitas*.

With my lifelong preference for the Greek language and literature, it is needless to observe that my work on this volume of the Columbia Press was done *con amore*. I had found that actual life and its vicissitudes had denied me the ideals and glowing hopes of youth and early manhood. Here, however, I must insert a personal, biographical item. In the last years of the academic service (1898 *et seq.*) of Dr. Baird, he asked me to assume, in his stead, the graduate work in Greek. I was happy and gave in order the following courses: "Gods in Homer," "The Wasps of Aristophanes," and "History of Greek Literature to 404 B. C." The most eminent of my students in the last-named course proved to be T. Leslie Shear, who, in the autumn of 1901, entered Dr. Gildersleeve's seminar in Baltimore, took his Ph.D. in 1904, and ultimately became one of the leading archaeologists of our time.

It is true, in May, 1902, on the retirement of Dr. Baird (whose service extended from 1859 to 1902, forty-three years), Chancellor MacCracken offered me the choice of assuming the Greek chair or keeping my own. But I was sadly aware, all around me, of the waning of Greek in America, a consumptive process that no devotion of any individual enthusiast in the academic world could arrest or reverse.

The last and, I believe, the maturest of my greater works was begun through a curious first cause and a curious concatenation of circumstances. The last work was not, at first and for some time after, conceived or designed as a whole; and still, in the end, its clear unity will, I believe, satisfy the most exacting critic or scholar in this particular field. In April, 1916, Professor L. M. Sweet of the Bible Seminary of New York, called on me to make enquiries about Ph.D. work.[16] After becoming acquainted with my *Testimonium Animae*, he urged me to become a contributor to the *Biblical Review*, a quarterly of New York. The results: after a summary of my *Testimonium Animae*, which I called "The Spiritual Failure of Classic Civilization," October, 1916, urged as I was to continue, I entered upon a series of eleven further monographs, on each of which as a rule I spent half a year, the last one appearing in July, 1922. These essays and studies, averaging twenty-five pages each, deal in chronological order with the contact and conflict of classic paganism and Christianity. Their titles are: "Stoicism and Christianity," "Under the Antonines," "Clement of Alexandria," "Tertullian of Carthage," "Neoplatonism and Christianity," "In the Era of

---

[16] His valuable dissertation, *Roman Emperor Worship*, a work of 153 pages, was published in 1919.

Diocletian," "The Emperor Julian and His Religion," "The Old Believers in Rome and the Dusk of the Gods," "The Earlier Stages of Augustine," "The Two Sons of Theodosius and Aleric the Goth," all ending with Augustine's "City of God" (*de Civitate Dei*).

I was sixty-three when this series of monographs was begun, and sixty-nine when the last one went through the press. I kept in touch of course with Gibbon and Gregorovius, and, on the side of ecclesiastical history, with Neander and many others of that guild; our Lagarde Library was very helpful. Never in all my long life of first-hand classical study and authorship did I more rigidly and successfully adhere to the principles and methods that I had so deeply and so firmly made my own in my prentice-years in Berlin, Leipzig, and Baltimore. This was my practice: let the contemporary authors tell the story, revealing themselves and their day as they write. No prejudice on *my* part, no itch for a novel or "original" presentation or character-drawing, must disturb my vision or guide my pen. Many of the sources were old friends, such as Seneca, Lucian, Pausanias, Eusebius, Minucius Felix, the Acts of the Apostles, Augustine's *Confessions* and *De Civitate Dei*, Orosius, Servius, Macrobius, Justin Martyr, Symmachus of Rome, the *Chronicon* of Eusebius-Jerome, the Apostolic Fathers.

Still the greater and the more substantial part of my material was for me, if not *terra incognita*, at least not familiar as yet, not truly acquired. Among these, e.g., were Irenaeus of Lyons, the pupil of Polycarp, and Clement of Alexandria. May I speak of the latter? I excerpted and abstracted the twelve hundred pages of the Oxford edition of 1869 with scrupulous care. "Clement taught and preached, too, in one of the greatest—we may confidently say in the greatest—centre of Greek culture then existing within the Roman Empire. The enormous range of his classic citation has tempted some scholars to suggest that he resorted to anthologies, and, in the domain of philosophy and general erudition, to certain current collections called doxographies. It is quite undeniable that, in his surveys of the data of learning and letters, Clement often reminds us of Diogenes Laertius and Athenaeus." The historical problems of the Gnostics and Gnosticism commanded my close attention for rather more than a year. And, over against his speculative semi-Christianism, we meet the worship of Antinous,[17] the veritable apex and ultimate point of classic paganism. Clement indeed is more of a speculative compromiser than a fearless confessor, supremely academic and more of a "Greek" than a "Father": "that deeper experience of the essential impotence of the soul, which turns to God in Christ as the hart pants after the waterbrooks—this, I say, is an experience, which, as an experience, unless I am mistaken, is unrecorded in Clement's extant works." I utterly refused to follow the Presbyter of Alexandria in his efforts to find some elements of Christianity in some great classics of Greece, as in Plato. I was not at all impressed by his efforts to graft Christianity on Platonism, or Platonism on Christianity—as Philo of Alexandria claimed that Plato derived his philosophy from Moses.

The fearless and heroic character of Tertullian and the superb positiveness of his asseveration of Christ were vastly more sympathetic to me. This was in no wise tinctured, hampered, or diluted by that same *saecularis sapientia* as was the case with the Presbyter of Alexandria. "Long before the *Dies irae, dies illa* of mediaeval times began to ring out its majestic peal to Christian consciousness" (p. 116), "the glowing pen of Tertullian elaborated that theme in his own way and for his own world, the pagan

[17] Hadrian's concubine who perished in the Nile. Some inscriptions at Rome tell us of the brotherhoods who worshipped the imperial Ganymede.

world. If the Tiber floods the city, if the Nile fails to inundate the fields—if there is an earthquake, if a famine, if a plague—at once the cry is: 'To the lions with the Christians!' an impressive confirmation of our Lord's own prediction (Matt., 24, 9): 'And ye shall be hated of all nations for my name's sake.'"

When I wrote my chapter on "Neoplatonism and Christianity," dealing first with Plotinus the founder of that cult, I did not know that Dean Inge of St. Paul's had written two volumes on Plotinus, an ignorance which I regretted when it was too late. I used the text edited by the honored teacher of my prentice-time at Berlin, Adolph Kirchhoff, helped also not a little by Steinhart of Schulpforta. With all his apparent theism and monotheism, Plotinus had a place also for the mundane and the sublunar "gods." Plotinus' editor, biographer, and favorite disciple, Porphyry of Tyre (*circa* 234–304 A.D.), died a half-century before Augustine was born. His fifteen books *Against the Christians* were much noted, and drew a reply from Eusebius. Porphyry defended the cult figures very positively, and even claimed that the decline of the worship of Aesculapius caused the prevalence of epidemics; the gods withdrew when men ceased to sacrifice to them: "Since Jesus was honored, no one became aware of any public benefaction on the part of the gods." Iamblichus was the third of the three Neoplatonic prophets of expiring paganism. In him the grossness of the Pagan cult quite settled back on conformity with the traditional idolatry, except that he resorted to the "blending and fusion of the gods," leaping over the ancient bars of ethnical separateness. He sought and found data for his Theokrasia[18] in many other nations of the pagan world. His writings and his defense of idol-worship were a veritable gospel to the

---

[18] Liddell and Scott's rendering of ϑεοκρασία as "mingling with God" is absolutely faulty.

FROM HOMER TO AUGUSTINE

Emperor Julian. I closed this important chapter in my general theme with a sober analysis of Plato's Ideas or "Forms." I relied there in part on the report of his great pupil Aristotle, who did not remain a pupil; I drew heavily on the great Concordance of Aristotle of my Berlin teacher, Hermann Bonitz. In concluding this excursus I wrote (p. 162): "Nothing, I dare say, has ever been gained for Christianity by any support of any philosophical speculation or sect; and this is the deeper reason why its mundane appearance must ever be that of an *ecclesia militans*. St. John's Gospel is particularly that in which its own higher spiritual significance is curiously blended with the glowing words of actual concrete reminiscence of that disciple whom Jesus loved and who, although he was a nephew of Mary, declined to place his own name in juxtaposition to that of the Incarnate Word. The single parable of the Prodigal Son, if only man's eyes are opened to his spiritual self, is both a surpassing revelation and a consolation compared with which all the dithyrambic flights in Plato's myths are what to a famishing wanderer is some baronial hall hung with arras, figures to look at, nothing more."

For the Era of Diocletian, I relied largely not on Gibbon with whom I was intimately familiar, but on Arnobius of Sicca (Africa), and even more on Lactantius the classical scholar, brilliant rhetor, and earnest Christian and Christian thinker. His facing and confronting of Paganism and its pre-Christian philosophy—apart from the high dignity of his Latin style—gave him a lasting distinction in my study of that eventide of the Classical World. Eusebius, contemporary of Diocletian's era, furnished an admirable foil to the Latin rhetor. Now Gibbon makes a charge against the Bishop of Caesarea, saying "that he has related what might redound to the glory and that he has suppressed all that could tend to the disgrace, of religion." But I showed, in the conclusion of the chapter, that this sweeping judgment was untrue. Eusebius (VIII, 1) viewed the entire Persecution as a "divine judgment" (θεία κρίσις) on the worldliness which had crept into the Christian churches before the Edict of Nicomedia (303 A.D.) : "Gibbon therefore wrote of the ecclesiastic historian not merely what was unfair, but what was simply much worse, namely untrue." I had read and reread Gibbon very much from 1875 to 1920, and gradually emancipated myself from him. Few do, because they shrink most naturally from examining the bristling multitude of sources. Leslie Stephen (in the *Dictionary of National Biography*) calls him a Voltairian.

In my study of Julian I had the rare satisfaction of referring to an essay of the earlier manhood of Dr. Gildersleeve. I realized of course that church historians, like Socrates, could hardly be quite fair to the Apostate; therefore my chief material was sought in the essays, letters, decrees of Julian, and the writings of his guide, ideal, and oracle, Libanius, the pompous publicist of Antioch; then Eunapius; and finally Ammian who crossed the Euphrates on that ill-fated expedition against the Parthians, 363 A.D. In taking leave of this meteoric figure, I have great pleasure in citing from Gildersleeve's essay the following passage: "Opposition to Christianity as such, no matter in what form, has its source deep in the human heart; and the deeper the heart, the more earnest the nature, the farther down we must sink the shaft of our investigation. Julian was a thorough Greek in his pride; and the doctrine of the cross could never have been other than foolishness to him."

In *The Old Believers in Rome and the Dusk of the Gods*, I returned from the Euphrates to the Capital of the Mediterranean world and studied the last struggles of Symmachus and his associates. It was, on the Christian side, the era of Damasus, bishop of Rome, of Jerome of Stridon, of Ambrose of Milan; the struggles against the official ending of Jupiter Optimus Maximus on the Capitol and against the further worship of the Dei Consentes and against the financial disestablishment of the Vestal Virgins. Here too we have the pagan conventicle of Macrobius' *Saturnalia* and its members, the very background of expiring Roman paganism. Prominent in that conventicle of the Christmas season is Servius, the young professor and Vergilian commentator. To him I had devoted much labor long before, when I prepared an index to his Vergil-commentary and discovered also that he was a consistent and fervid Neoplatonist. Some presentation also of the Mithras-cult was necessary. The tenacity of the pre-Christian cult among the aristocracy was striking. We see then that, even so long after Constantine, Serapis and Isis were very much resorted to, and that some Senators still attended the chariot of turret-crowned Kybele, on the days of the Megalensian games in the earlier part of April when the castrated Attis was proclaimed to be the same as the Sun. The letters of the would-be Ciceronian, Symmachus, are supremely rich in historical matter. I will transcribe but a single utterance which clearly iterates Porphyry: "For the Kindliness of a Higher Being, unless it is held by worship, is lost." His demand addressed to Valentinian II that the statue of Victoria be replaced in the *curia*, the senate-house at Rome, and the rejoinder by Ambrose of Milan, are historical documents of uncommon importance. Zosimus, a Byzantine official of high rank, whom one may call the last of the pagan or pro-pagan historians, traced the fall of the Western Empire to the abandonment of the old ritual. His bitterness in dealing with Constantine is extreme.

The *Earlier Stages of Augustine* reveals the spiritual history of that extraordinary man, his career as a brilliant rhetor and finally municipal professor at Milan until he was baptized by Bishop Ambrose, in 387 A.D. His restless pen thereafter was engaged on his two great problems: God and the Soul. His struggles with Neoplatonism extended well into the period of his Christian conversion. His *Retractationes* are a survey of his own previous works, in which he modifies or cancels many of his former positions. In and after the great crisis of his life (386 A.D.), he still often appears with Cicero and Plato on one side and St. Paul on the other. His memorial to his mother Monica is the pearl in his self-review. It is often very difficult to distinguish between the philosopher and the theologian. But he found rest at last "because Thou didst make us for Thee and restless is our heart until it repose in Thee" (inquietum est cor nostrum donec requiescat in Te).[19]

The Sack of Rome (August, 410 A.D.) by Alaric the Goth, in a way meant the end of the Western Empire or the beginning of the end. The enemies of Christianity made that religion responsible for the catastrophe. For this Epoch, Claudian, the poet and publicist of Stilicho's fame, Prudentius the Spanish pilgrim to Rome, Synesius of Cyrene, but especially Zosimus the Byzantine furnished me ample material, the latter, as I have already said, a stubborn defender of moribund paganism. Orosius the Spanish cleric and protégé of Augustine even then called Rome a community infected with "proud wantonness" and a "blasphema civitas" (VII, 59). Rome experienced what once she had inflicted on Carthage, 146 B.C.

In his *City of God*, Augustine, now bishop of Hippo, disputed the charge of the old believers that the Gothic catastrophe was due to the rise and spread of the Christian religion. This then (*de Civitate Dei*), the greatest of the greater treatises of Augustine, surveys the ancient world, its culture, its religion—with heavy drafts on Varro—down to his own time; and sets over against it the Bible. He surveys the great Empire and condemns Imperialism with burning stricture: "that lust for holding sway keeps in unrest and grinds to pieces the human race with great evils"

[19] *Confessions*, I, 1.

FROM HOMER TO AUGUSTINE

("Libido ista dominandi magnis malis agitat et conterit genus humanum. III, 14). It is preëminently a book for classicists surveying the eventide of things classical; but, at the same time, it is the greatest document explaining and justifying the consummation and termination of that civilization.

My satisfaction was complete when, in late summer, 1922, the Cambridge University Press in England arranged to publish these twelve essays under the title *From Augustus to Augustine*. It is my pleasant duty at this point to record the fact that I owe much to the friendly mediation of Dr. T. R. Glover of St. John's, Cambridge, Public Orator, and in that function successor to Sir John E. Sandys, whom I had the pleasure to entertain, both in my seminar-room and also at Mrs. Sihler's table in Harlem, in April, 1905. This then, the last of my books, was received by English and Scottish reviewers almost throughout with a kindliness and a degree of warm appreciation such as I had not experienced with any of my former works. I will here take the liberty of adding that among these reviews was a brief but very flattering one in the London *Times*, of August 8th, 1923, written by Dean R. W. Inge of St. Paul's. The first copies were exposed for sale in the windows of Paternoster Row close by St. Paul's, that famous lane through which I had first wandered with silent awe in April, 1875, at twenty-two. Now I was seventy.

I must not close this chapter of my life-story without making full avowal of the great debt which, in this last and maturest of my greater things, I owed to British scholars. I refer here particularly to the *Dictionary of Christian Biography*, four massive volumes, 1877–1888, edited by Smith and Wace, a masterful work and an honor to British scholarship, done by some one hundred and thirty contributors, of whom some thirty-five were of Oxford, thirty-three from Cambridge: also there were among the authors

FROM MAUMEE TO THAMES AND TIBER

of the monographs archbishops, bishops, canons, rectors, vicars, nay curates also. Of the greater names were those of Lightfoot, Westcott, Bryce. Often I would ask myself in my seminar-room while elaborating my successive themes: "Have we in America any men comparable to these, or to men like Tregelles, Hort, Alford, Scrivener, Venables, Mozley, Plumptre, Salmon, and many others, *all classically trained?* If not, why not?" Often, up there in my beloved cabinet, my questioning mind would sweep over our broad land teeming with "institutions of learning."

In absorbing myself in these studies from 1916 to 1922, I was dominated and sustained by an additional motive: to forget, in some measure, the daily agonies of the European War.

XVI
DE SENECTUTE

OLD AGE, to most souls and minds, is an odious term. It ends in the grave, we all know that; but where precisely does it begin? That depends on the individual, and is a very relative matter: it depends on certain reserves of health and strength, physical and mental, to sustain work. Mere reflection is a vain and sad thing. "Three score years and ten," says the psalmist.

Cicero's essay is deservedly famous. He wrote it in 44 B.C., after the Ides of March and Caesar's assassination, from which he had vainly hoped a restoration of the old order. He had then completed sixty-two and his friend Atticus sixty-five. Few old or aging men have such an *alter ego* as Atticus was to him. After all, it depends on the survey backward which an old man takes, and which he cannot take too often. "The Truth shall make you free" said the Greatest of the Great to all who will hear Him (John, 8, 32). Of all His great sayings this is one of the greatest. What "Truth"? When He stood before Pilate he repeated this: "To this end was I born and for this cause came I into the world, that I should bear witness unto the Truth," (John, 18, 37). Pilate said unto Him: "What is Truth?" And forsooth the world is full of Pilates. What they aim at is Pleasure, Power, Profit. Now the professional scholar, if true to his vocation, must pursue Truth. The world of men scorns this pursuit, even if it be but academic truth in some of the many lines in which academic lives are spent.

President Gilman at Johns Hopkins hesitated long before he chose a motto for the new University; but in the end it was a scriptural one, the one recorded from the mouth of Christ, above, John 8, 32: *"Veritas vos liberabit."* Jerome rendered it in a slightly different order: "veritas liberabit vos," following the Greek text scrupulously as he generally does. And while I humbly and freely admit that a scholar's quest for Truth deals largely with secular things, still even here there is something spiritual, and a worldly reward is but rarely won by the scholar. His work, if carefully and thoroughly done, must generally be its own reward.

In surveying my own long life, I find a gloomy series of wars and a consistent disregard of the Prince of Peace. The very earliest memories of my childhood fall in with the years following the Crimean War. The very first political picture that I recall was a portrait of Alexander II of Russia (murdered in 1881). Then came our own Civil War: often I heard then the lines: "Hang Jeff Davis on the sour-apple tree," or "Tramp, tramp, tramp, the boys are marching," or "When this cruel war is over." Then came the three wars by which Bismarck united the German people and brought what was German into the Empire: the war of 1864, that of 1866, and that of 1870–71 with Napoleon III. Why enumerate the others? Most of them were determined by the never-satisfied leech of Imperialism. It is a gloomy and sad survey, and it makes the sober thinker question the automatic operation of what men call Progress.

To return to Cicero, to whom I have devoted so many years of my own life. We observe that he would not like to return to infancy once more and lie in the cradle, a wailing babe. On the other hand, he craves immortality of the soul and exhibits his familiarity with Plato's *Phaedo*. Curious: in November, 1916, Sir Robert Allison, of Scaleby Hall, Carlisle, England, sent me his blank-verse version of Cicero's essay *On Old Age;* he sent this because, as he wrote me, he had been gratified by my *Cicero of Arpinum*. I quote

DE SENECTUTE

from his letter: "I asked my bookseller to get me a copy when it was first issued, but I suppose *on account of the war* it has only now come." Everywhere the ogre of that catastrophe: "The Suicide of Old Europe," as many call it, and this is the title of a book by General Birdwood Thomson (1922). "Yes, Europe committed hari-kari," a German industrialist said to me in July, 1927, when I once more was revisiting Berlin and Leipzig, the cradle-spots of my academic life.

Here I find myself driven to go back to the very beginning of the great conflagration, which, in the end, drew almost all mankind into its tragic orbit. Sailing for Italy with my dear wife, I landed at Naples on June 29, 1914, a day after the assassination at Serajevo on St. Vitus Day, when a St. Vitus dance began, on the Danube, and by and by spread gradually over our planet. On July 26th, I went with my wife from Basle to Paris. On Saturday evening, August 1, 1914, about 6.30 P.M., I translated for her—just as we came out of a tea-restaurant near the Pantheon—the universal call to arms signed by the two heads of the French Government, Poincarè and Viviani, and then and there foretold to her the general aims and motives of the impending war with a definite precision absolutely verified by the history of the coming four years. In the general meeting of Americans, many of whom found themselves financially stranded, a meeting held in the largest hall of the Grand Hotel, under the presidency of Elbert H. Gary, I said to my compatriots that this war would extend from the Thames to the Black Sea. Actually it spread much farther.

Never did I cherish a home-coming so intensely, as when, returning from Havre by the *Chicago* on August 23, 1914, we espied the Ambrose light-ship once more. As for the term "propaganda," in the fourteen years that have gone by since that Sunday afternoon, that term and its moral and political associations have become malodorous all over the world and are fairly avoided in the current vocabulary of political discussion. "Truth is the first casualty in any war."[1]

So much for the beginning of the *cataclysm*. It was prophetically called *cataclysm* by Colonel House, a full month before the murder at Serajevo.[2] My aging years of which I am now writing, were doubly embittered by this long-drawn-out agony of civilization—and even now I am often reminded of the "fires (or glowing coals) hidden under the treacherous ashes" (Horace, Odes, II, 1).

In September, 1918, when on our campus at University Heights Mars seemed to have driven out Minerva and the Muses, and when all classical study seemed to be near extinction or hanging by a futile thread, I offered to the authorities of our University to retire under the rules of the Carnegie Foundation. I was then, in terms most honorable to me, urged to stay on, and soon after, on November 11, Kleio turned over a new leaf in the history of our poor Earth. Minerva returned to my seminar and to my lecture-room, where I cultivated her graces more than ever, the more so as the administration of Chancellor Brown by five successive annual resolutions asked me to continue in service. Thus, then, my academic service ended on September 1, 1923, when I had completed eight months of my seventy-first year.

I went to New Haven a few days before completing my seventieth year, in the last days of 1922, to attend once more the annual meeting of our American Philological Association, which I had joined in 1876. The sessions were held in Osborn Hall, December 27–29, 1922. I presented an essay on Strabo: of course it was too long to be presented in full. The President that year was Francis Greenleaf Al-

---

[1] As said by the Rt. Hon. Arthur Ponsonby of England in 1927.
[2] *Intimate Papers of Colonel House*, 1926, I, p. 249.

DE SENECTUTE

linson of Brown, once a younger comrade of mine at Johns Hopkins, in the long ago. For me these were rare meetings, largely through the social opportunity of chatting with old fellow-classicists, from Dartmouth to the Golden Gate. It was one of the best-attended meetings that I remembered in the forty-six years since 1876. Now on the last day of the sessions, December 29, I experienced what I may fairly call the greatest and most gratifying surprise of my life, only four days before my seventieth birthday. It was indeed, as young women are wont to say of a proposal of marriage, "so sudden." Professor J. A. Scott, a former President of the Association, interrupted the readings to present a Resolution; and my indulgent readers will pardon me for copying it here, I being as innocent as a new-born babe: "Resolved: that the American Philological Association felicitate Professor E. G. Sihler on the completion of seventy years, so many of which have been devoted with singular fidelity to the highest ideals of scholarship, and join with its congratulations the hope that he may still live many happy years and that he may often be present in future meetings of our Association to encourage and inspire our members."[3] Unprepared as I was, I begged leave to say a few words of deep-felt thanks, chiefly this: that even if I had not been the *Alpha* in any single field of our professional studies, I was content, like Eratosthenes of Alexandria, to have been a *Beta* in several.[4]

My seventieth birthday brought me a veritable basket of flowers, chiefly academic flowers, felicitations from the Chancellor of our University and many of my colleagues, nor were the students behindhand. A letter from the President of the Carnegie Foundation added not a little to my joy on that occasion.

At the end of my last academic year, my career was

[3] *Proceedings*, vol. 53, p. xv.
[4] Cf. Suidas s. v. Eratosthenes.

rounded out by a diploma or parchment which I cannot copy here, presented by the Graduate Faculty. It meant much more to me than the Ph.D. degree given by Daniel Coit Gilman in June, 1878, almost exactly forty-five years before.

Meanwhile, musing as I am on the theme of retiring for age, and the aging of a scholar, I will take the liberty of inserting here a few utterances, dealing with age—letters from the foremost classical scholar of America, touching this very theme. I mean of course Dr. B. L. Gildersleeve. He actually lectured at Johns Hopkins from 1876 to 1915, that is to say from his forty-fifth almost to the completion of his eighty-fourth year. I have reason to believe that this letter dealing with *senectus* and written a few days only after his retirement (Baltimore June 29, 1915) will be welcomed by many readers and especially by all those who are interested in American scholarship:

Dear Professor Sihler:

A few years before his death, Vahlen, a fellow-student of mine, wrote to me somewhat slightingly of the "Suessigkeiten" that had been showered upon him on the home-stretch, and every old man as he nears the end sees the vanity of human praise. It was well for me not to have had "ces commencements d'enfant gaté." The commendation such as I really prized was withheld until I became what you Romans call a "senex," so that I was not tempted to think more of myself than of my work. Of course I am gratified by your estimate of the work of my life, as it shows that even so discriminating a judge as you have shown yourself to be in your characterization of Caesar and Cicero, may be swayed by personal association and personal affection. For myself I only say ἱκόμην ἵν' ἱκόμην[5] words that answer as well for those who regard life as a tragedy as those who look upon it as a comedy. I have retired from my work as a teacher in good time—at the end of a pleasant and successful session—the Trustees have granted me the use of my old quarters . . . there is to be no diminution in my income, no change in my mode of living. I have work laid out for many more years than I shall live to see. I am in good health

---

[5] "I've reached the point I've reached."

DE SENECTUTE

and live in an atmosphere of good will of which you have just given me evidence. With many thanks,

Yours faithfully,
B. L. Gildersleeve.

I will add but one letter more, written in the last June of Dr. Gildersleeve's life:

1002. N. Calvert Street, (dictated)[6]
Baltimore, Md. June 17, 1923.

Many thanks for your highly interesting letter of the 14th, dealing as it does with a career familiar to me for well nigh fifty years, with its aspirations, its trials, its achievements, its rewards.

My best wishes follow you into your retirement from which the world will hope to receive additions to the erudition which have given you a place all your own in the annals of classical scholarship.

Yours faithfully,
B. L. Gildersleeve.

To stop for a moment at the summer of 1923: the question for me arose, What shall I do? I plunged with enthusiastic concentration into a task long conceived. It was a study and characterization of Polybius of Megalopolis, my long-cherished ideal in the domain of historiography. It is now the longest, most comprehensive, perhaps the most successful of all my monographs—actually published some three and a half years after completion, in the *American Journal of Philology*, 1927. One of the most gratifying and, since the death of Mommsen (1903), most competent appreciations came to me from an eminent historian of Republican Rome, long connected with St. John's College, Cambridge.

On March 15, 1924, with my dear wife, my oldest son, and his spouse, I sailed for Naples, a full decade after I had visited the classic peninsula—the long interval being due to the Great War. Even on the Italian steamer, I began to plan a new series of monographs centering around the most important Greek book, the New Testament,

---

[6] His eyesight had failed for several years before that.

studies designed to bring into greater clarity the spiritual condition of the Mediterranean World at the beginning of the Christian era. Of course, I was gratefully alive to the exquisite charms of an Italian spring. Here I must set down an incident connecting the vernal loveliness of that gulf of paradise, the Bay of Naples, with Nero, St. Paul, and an ultra-modern historian of Rome, himself a native of Italy. It was on March 31st. I had gone out from Naples through the tunnel to the neighboring Pozzuoli (Puteoli). Both Cicero and Seneca once had villas near by. The ancient harbor-basin is still distinctly before us, where in Seneca's time huge granaries received the grain-fleets coming from Alexandria. Behind and above the modern town lies the amphitheatre where once Nero entertained Tiridates, King of Armenia. I seemed to be absolutely alone there, mightily stirred by memories sweeping backward by more than eighteen centuries, examining with much interest the grates in the arena, grates through which it seems the wild beasts were brought up from their cages below to pursue and to rend their human victims—Roman civilization at its apex indeed! I *thought* that I was alone in that historical spot—when from the *cavea* or spectator's section there came towards me, not a Roman legionary or a wild beast, but a young English gentleman, a Mr. C. hailing from Trinity College, Cambridge, then engaged in an archaeological excursion during the spring vacation. Of course we soon drifted into a theme suggested then and there, the Italian historian of Rome's "Greatness and Decadence," Ferrero. The Cambridge student told me that Dr. James Smith Reid, Professor of Ancient History at Cambridge, had told his students that the most searching critique of Ferrero had been published by an American scholar in the *American Journal of Philology:* it was E. G. S.; and so here in the Neronian amphitheatre of Puteoli—where there was nothing but ruins and memories

DE SENECTUTE

—I plucked a rare and unexpected flower: Curtain! my indulgent reader.

Soon after, we went to the Cocumella near Sorrento for a full month's stay. In a few days, all the roses began to exhale their perfume through the garden and orange grove, with the sapphire sea far below, the stern ridges of the Apennine above Vico Equense in the East, and also the brown cone of Vesuvius, and the bold contours of Ischia in the West.

In Rome I frequently visited that noble edifice in the suburban district west of the Tiber, the American Academy, an exquisite spot ideally fitted to study ancient history and especially the annals of Rome, pre-Christian and Christian as well. More than in former visits, I deeply felt that Italy is very poor and is indeed largely living on the glories of the past and to-day claiming a place as a Great Power not justified by her own resources. No more can she exact tribute from the Euphrates to the Atlas, and from the Nile to the southern edge of Caledonia. Much of my time I spent standing up, copying inscriptions—for myself—no matter what had been done by Mommsen, Henzen, de Rossi, and their successors. There is always (to me) a charm in reading the voice of the past from the stone directly as in the cloisters contiguous to St. Paul's outside the walls where pagan and Christian tombs speak to the visitor in curious juxtaposition. Our further stations were the common ones: Florence, Venice, Lake Garda, Como, St. Gotthardt, Lucerne, Interlaken, Montreux, Geneva, Milan, Genoa, home.

In the spring of 1925, I went as far as St. Paul—my first visit—lecturing first at Ann Arbor, and especially at Northwestern University, under the auspices of my generous friend John A. Scott; revisiting also Milwaukee, where I had taught thirty-four years before. Finally I made some stay in my native city of Fort Wayne, now a flourishing and beautiful place of one hundred thousand inhabitants. But most of the dear old landmarks are gone, such as St. Paul's parsonage where I was born, while the church is now a beautiful Gothic edifice. In the country around, all the forests are gone, gone almost everything that could recall my happy childhood days, all but the well near the parsonage; above all, gone were all the "old familiar faces," while the cemeteries, east and west, alone recalled the names with which my childhood was familiar, tombstones alone speaking of the past.

In May, 1927, once more I sailed for Bremerhaven, the first time by that route since September, 1872—then a youth of enthusiastic expectations, now an old man nursing a world of memories. I was to speak on certain political trends antedating and leading up to the Great War. I saw far more of Germany than in all my former visits: and my visions and judgment of the catastrophe were improved and corrected in numberless points. The universities clearly were making a new start and seemed well attended. I lectured at the Universities of Halle, Munich, Marburg, and Cologne, being favored with the close attention and cordial approbation of my hearers; and I was happy in realizing that German universities had in no wise been reduced to the place of a Cinderella in the intellectual life of Europe. Never did I enjoy so much the noble pines of the Black Forest or the Cathedrals, or, as at Goslar, the memorials of the mediaeval empire. I saw very much of the Ruhr, but declined to descend into the coal-mines. Who will find fault with the pleasure of an old scholar born on the Maumee when he discovered three or four of his own works not only at Berlin and Leipzig, ever dear to him from those prentice-years, but also in the university libraries of Göttingen, Marburg, Halle, and Breslau? At Berlin I was a guest at a lecture of one of the foremost classical scholars of Europe, by permission granted in advance. It was fifty-five

DE SENECTUTE

years before, that I first sat there as a recruit—now clearly a veteran. May I be pardoned for recalling from my Diary the words of honor and greeting with which I was then and there introduced? "Ladies and gentlemen: We have the honor of having with us to-day the Nestor of American Classicists, whose works on Caesar and Cicero are well known and esteemed in Germany, who has combined historical with philological study, who many years ago here did listen to Moritz Haupt; few are now living who once heard him." An intrusive tear would well in my eyes, as those far-away years, more than a half-century before, seemed to come before me once more, those important semesters which I have endeavored to sketch in the fifth chapter of these memories. A little later, in August, a guest in a fine manor-house in eastern Silesia, not far from the new Polish frontier, I stood by the grave of my grandsire. On Sundays, I gladly listened to the peal of deep bells newly cast to replace those melted up to serve the exigencies of cruel Mars; and gladly I sat in the churches and joined in the chorals familiar to me and cherished since my childhood days on the Maumee. But I must close these notes of travel with some jottings that I made after hearing Johann Sebastian Bach sung four times in the church made world-famous through his work, St. Thomas's at Leipzig, jottings dated August 26, 1927: "I do wish I had the power to describe Bach's glorious work. This time it was *Jesu meine Freude*. After each stanza of the beautiful choral there was a fugue or terzett on some verses of St. Paul, Romans, 8. One might suggest, *a priori*, that the great Cantor did not himself compose the sweet melody of that exquisite hymn. True, but he did much more: he endowed each stanza with an original expression that fitted the deepest spiritual meaning of the words, of every sentence or sentiment, with a glorious felicity—and the hearer who followed the text could not but realize, that in a way, he (the hearer) had never dreamed of the power, the melting sweetness, defiant force, calm consolation, and, withal, the *majesty* which the greatest of religious composers evoked from the text, nay from every sentence in that hymn. Yes, the greatest painters and sculptors have vied with each other to glorify the Son of God from Giotto onward, ever essaying the greatest of subjects; but all of these, collectively, can never stir the reverent love and admiration for the Only One as Bach did and still does."

But I must come to the end of these memories. In January, 1928, a sudden and treacherous malady carried out of my home and out of my life the sweetest and the best in it, my dear Wife, who had been at my side in sunshine and also in stormy weather with even devotion and service for more than forty-six years. I was happy in one particular thing. In January, 1923, when pondering to whom to inscribe the last and most notable of my works, the one published by the Cambridge University Press, I had written:

To

Emily B. Sihler

whose splendid support and self-denial during four decades have made possible the execution of the greater tasks of the author's life, this, the last volume of his production, is with all gratitude and sincerity inscribed by   the Author.

So, on January 23, 1928, five years later, we bore her out of the home whose crown and pillar she had so long been. As the casket was being slowly lowered to its last resting-place in Woodlawn, I cast a rose upon it and turned away in great sadness.

Cede Deo.

—We are such stuff
As dreams are made on, and our little life
Is rounded with a sleep.

INDEX

INDEX

Achenbach, Conrector, 35
Adams, Henry Carter, 110
Adams, Herbert B., 98
Aeschylus, 68
Alaric, 246
Allen County, Ind., 18
Allen, Prof. Frederick D., 90
Allen, Prof. Jerome, 152
American Academy at Rome, 213, 257
American Consciousness, 66
American Journal of Philology, 130 et seq., 233 et seq.
American Philological Association, 90, 92; session at Baltimore, 107; at Philadelphia, 127; at Yale, 136; at University Heights, 163; at Yale, 252
Ancient History, 120
André, Major, 81
Andrews, Wm. Loring, 154
Anthon, Prof., 88
Apostolic Fathers, 45
Apparatus, Classical, 211 et seq.
Aristophanes, 59, 60, 79, 90, 103; characterization of, 237
Aristotle, 67, 69, 143, 198
Arnold, Major, 74
Athenaeus, 79
Athletics, College, 163
Attic orators, 108
Augustine, 245 et seq.
Augustus, 190
Augustus Princeps, monograph on, 209
Avantageur, 6
Azores, 184

Bach, Johann Sebastian, 259
Baird, Prof. Henry Martyn, 88, 148
Baltimore, 95 et seq.
B. & O. Railway, 108
Bancroft, Geo., 111
Banks, David, 154
Baseball, 31
Bennett, Prof. Charles E., of Cornell, 207
Bennett Law of Wisconsin, 141
Berlin, University of, 6; author's study and residence at, 55 et seq; the city of, in 1872, 63 et seq.; Museum, 71; revisited, 199, 258
Bevier, Louis, 114
Biblical Review of New York, 239
Bismarck, 70
Bleke, farmer, 40
Bloomfield, Maurice, 99
Böckh, 132
Bonaparte, Jerome, 4
Bonaparte, Mrs. Patterson, 112
Bonitz, Hermann, 69, 243
Borghese, Villa, 191
Boston, visit to, 39
Boström, Eric, 178
Botsford, Prof. G. W., 235 et seq.
Bowerfind, Lily Sihler, 23
Brandt, Prof. H. C. G., 104
Brauer, Prof., at St. Louis, 45
Bremen, voyage to, 54
Brown, Chancellor E. E., 166
Bryce, Viscount, 70
Büchsel, Dr., at Berlin, 66
Butler, B. F., 154
Butler, Charles, 151

Butler, William Allen, 147

Caesar, Annals of, 223 *et seq.*; British reviewers of, 228; German version of, 226
Caesar, Julius, monographs concerning, 136; bust of, 193
Caesar's Gallic War, A Complete Lexicon of the Latinity of, 135
Centennial Year 1876, 91
Chambers, Rev. Dr. Talbot W., 122
Cicero, 77, 169, 179, 192; *de Officiis,* 170; *Second Philippic,* 170; correspondence of, 231; on Old Age, 249
Cicero of Arpinum, 228 *et seq.*
Civil War, paper money in, 38; Soldier's Home, 142
Clark, Charles Upson, 212
Clement of Alexandria, 240 *et seq.*
Cleveland, Grover, 133
Cocumella, 187, 257
Coliseum, 191
Collegium Poetarum at Rome, 214
Concordia College at Milwaukee, 139 *et seq.*, 144
Concordia Gymnasium at Fort Wayne, 29 *et seq.*; graduation from, 39
Concordia Theological Seminary at St. Louis, 44 *et seq.*; social pleasure at, 48
Cooper, Prof. Lane, 212
Crämer, Prof. August, 47
Craig, Thomas, 110
Crosby, Rev. Dr. Howard, 92, 122, 133, 134, 137, 155; death of, 137
Crystal Palace, 80
Curtius, Prof. Ernst, 71

Dante, 184
Deinarchos, 136
DeKalb County, Ind., 38
Delamarre, Dr. Louis, 178

Demosthenes, 109
Dictionary of Christian Biography, 247
Diocletian, 243
Divinity School at St. Louis, 43 *et seq.*
Döllinger, Ignatius, 219
Douglas, Stephen A., "the Little Giant," 26
Draper, Prof. J. W., 149
Dresden, 7, 55
Drisler, Prof., 88, 122, 135, 156, 223
Droysen, Prof. Johann Gustav, 59
Drumann, 223

Eckman, Dr. George P., 175
Edinburgh, 82
Education, real meaning of, 152; grave faults in modern methods of, 153, 154
Election, national, of 1860, 26–27
Elegy, a German, 197
Elgin Marbles, 200
Eliot, President Charles A., 100
Elliott, Prof. A. M., 104
Ellis, Robinson, 191; the author's host at Oxford, 201
Elmer, Prof. H. C., of Cornell, 96
Engel, Prof. Robert, at Fort Wayne, 34
Environment, 13
Eratosthenes, 253
Erie Canal, 37
Etruscan League, 196
Eusebius, 244

Fay, Prof. E. A., 104
Fellows, the first twenty of Johns Hopkins, 98; their Academic Club, 100
Ferrero, 232, 256
Ficinus of Florence, 70
Fischer's *Römische Zeittafeln,* 231
Florence, 195
Fort Wayne, beginnings of, 14;

INDEX

Franco-German War of 1870, 51
Franklin, Fabian, 99, 101
Free tuition, policy of, 155
French settlers, 14; history of, 15; growth, 16; first families, 17; Concordia Gymnasium at, 29; election of 1884, 133; to-day, 257
Freshmen, Latin for, 169
Froude, A., on Caesar, 225

Games, 28
German immigrants, 17
German literature, 21
Gildersleeve, B. L., 73, 76, 90, 92, 95, 96, 99, 101; as author, 104, 111, 130, 135, 164, 175, 184, 209, 222; on old age, 254; last letter from, 255
Gillett, Prof. William K., 155
Gilman, President Daniel C., 91, 96, 97, 99, 111, 115, 249
Glover, Dr. T. R., 247
Gneisenau, 7
Godkin, 97
Goethe, 188
Goodwin, Prof. W. W., 92, 107, 123, 129, 136
Gould, Miss Helen Miller, 162; donor of Memorial Library, 162, 203, *et seq.*
Graduate Courses, 156; in Latin, 174 *et seq.*
Graebner, A., 34
Greece, lectures on history of, in fifth century B. C., 113
Greek, rehabilitation of, in American colleges, 179 *et seq.*
Greek Club of New York, 122 *et seq.*
Greek courses at Concordia, Fort Wayne, 33
Greek letters, preëminence of, over Roman, 85, 171
Gregory, Dr. Casper René, 78

Hall, Isaac, 124
Hall of Fame, 162, 164
Hall, Rev. John, 137, 154
Hall, Prof. R. W., chemist, 150
Harms, Pastor Louis, 47
Harpers, 128
Harvard entrance examinations, 119; Greek exercises for, 137
Harz Mountains, 68
Hattstaedt, W., 34
Haupt, Moritz, 59, 259
Havemeyer, Wm. F., laboratory, 154
Heitland, W. E., 232
Hendrickson, Prof. G. L., 213
Hering, Prof. Daniel W., 150
Hermann, Gottfried, 67
Hermes (Classical Quarterly), 131
Herodotus, 61
Hesiod, 86; characterization of, 237
High Schools, American, 153; teachers in, 228; scattering of "studies" in, 228
History, source-work in the study of, 60; teaching of, 119; philosophy of, 218
Home farm, idyl of the, 11
Hoover, Rev. Jesse, 15
Horace, 95, 171, 193, 207, 212
House, Colonel, 252
Hübner, Prof. Emil, 62 *et seq.*
Hülsen, Prof., 189
Humanists, 220
Humphreys, Prof. Milton W., 58, 59
Huxley, 97

Idealization of classical antiquity, 71
Inge, Dean R. W., of St. Paul's, 242

Johns Hopkins University, 72, 90, 91, 96; Fellows of, 98 *et seq.*; public lectures at, 102; Philolog-

ical Society, 105; first examination for Ph.D. degree, 109 et seq.; first bestowal of, 110; motto of, 249
Julian, Emperor, 244
July, Fourth of, celebration of, 40
Jungfrau, The, Bernese Alps, 197 et seq.

Kant, 67, 76
Kastanienwäldchen, 64
Kelsey, Prof. Francis W., 186
Kendallville, Ind., 1875–6, 87 et seq.
Kennedy, Mr. John S., benefactor of N.Y.U., 164
Kern, Susanna, 10 et seq.
Kiepert, the geographer, 68
Kirchhoff, Prof. Adolph, 61
Know-Nothing Party, 26

Lachmann, Carl, 59
Lagarde Oriental Collection, 151
Lambros, Spyridon, the Grecian, 60
Lange, Prof. Ludwig, at Leipzig, 77
Lange, Prof. Rudolph, at Fort Wayne, 34
Lanier, Sidney, 106
Lanman, Charles R., the Sanscrit scholar, 101, 114
Latin, the author's first lesson in, 30; courses at Concordia, 32; prose at N. Y. U., 167; themes, 168; prize, 109; upperclass courses, 173; speaking in, 173; lectures in, 174
Latin authors in high school, 181
Latin verse of Dr. San Giovanni, 176–178
Leipzig, battle of, 4; visit to battlefields of, 78
Leipzig, University of, Southerners studying at, 73

Leonard, William Ellery, translator of Lucretius, 213
Lewis, Charlton T., in Greek Club, 122
Lewis, Tayler, the Grecian, 148
Library, Royal, at Berlin, 67
Lincoln, Abraham, in 1860, 26, 27
Livy, 32, 170
Lodge, Gonzalez, 105, 212
Loeb, James, 120; series of classics in translation, 213
Löhe, Rev. W., 9
London, 80; revisited, 200
Lucerne, 196
Lucretius, 174 et seq., 213
Luther, 22, 24, 66, 71
Luther College, Decorah, Iowa, 86
Lutherans in America, 29 et seq.; in Milwaukee, 139

MacCracken, Chancellor H. M., 137, 155, 156, 164, 204
MacCracken, John Henry M., 165
McCulloch, Hon. Hugh, 17
McHenry, Fort, at Baltimore, 95
Macrobius, 245
Madvig, 33, 210
Magoffin, Prof. R. V. D., 213
Mahaffy, 217
March, Prof. Francis A., of Lafayette College, 92
Marquand, Allan, 114
Martin, Prof. H. N., the biologist, 97
Marysville, O., 11
Mau, the archaeologist, 186
Maumee River, 13, 25, 35, 61
Mayflower, Minerva, 89, 91
Merrill, Prof. Elmer T., 212
Merrill, Prof. William A., 213
Miller, Prof. C. W. E., 105
Milwaukee, Public Library, 144; See Concordia College
Moltke, 6
Mommsen, Prof. Theodor, 57, 69, 115, 189, 192, 210, 223

INDEX

Monte Cairo, 188
Morris, Prof. Charles D'Urban, 101
Mother, the author's, 85, 86
Mount Vernon, N. Y., 165
Murray, Prof. Daniel A., 150

Naples, 185; University of, 185
Neopaganism, 220
New Testament, in Greek, 46
New York, 9, 53; in 1879, 117
New York University, 92; Uptown Movement, 137, 155; rebirth of, 155; Greek chair offered to author, 239; Graduate lectures on Greek literature by the author, 238
Northwestern University, 257
Norwegians, 47

Odium theologicum, 44
Ohio Field, 161
Old Believers in Rome and the Dusk of the Gods, The, 244
Oldfather, Prof. W. A., 213
Overbeck, 77
Oxford, Martyrs' Monument at, 201

Page, Walter Hines, 98
Palaestra Ciceroniana, 79
Palisades, 205
Parsonage of St. Paul's, 13 *et seq.*; domestic economies at, 18–19; Christmas, 22; hard times, 38
Paton, Prof. J. P., of Nottingham, 82
Peabody Institute in Baltimore, 106
Pedagogy, School of, 151
Perrin, Bernadotte, of Yale, 213, 228
Ph.D. degree at N.Y.U., 175; printing of thesis, 175
Philosophy, 75
Pia Desideria, 179
Pilate, Pontius, 75, 249
Pitt, William, 81

Plato, 69, 75, 86, 113, 126, 144
Plautus, 63, 75, 178
Pliny's Letters, 172
Plotinus, 242
Plutarch, 168
Pochhammer, 6, 73
Pole-raising, 27
Polybius, 171, 255
Pompeii, 186 *et seq.*
"Ponies" *(Pons asinorum)*, how to deal with, 168
Ponsonby, Rt. Hon. Arthur, 252
Porphyry, 242
Posilipo, 186
Pozzuoli (Puteoli), amphitheatre at, 256
Prentice, Prof. William K., 214
Prentice, Col. William P., 123
Preuss, Dr. E., 45
Price, Prof. Thomas R., 133
Prince, Prof. J. D., the linguist, 151
Protagoras of Plato, 113, 128
Prussia, patriotic verse of (1813–15), 22
Purser, L. *See* Tyrrell

Quintilian, 34, 152, 154, 167, 174, 180

Ranke, Leopold von, 58
Rauch, the sculptor, 64
Reinke, steward at Concordia, 40
Religion, Greek, 221
Remsen, the chemist, 96, 99
Renaissance, 177, 195
'*Res angusta domi*,' 134, 159
Reviewing, 131
Rhine, 69
Riga, 8
Ritschl, Friedrich, 73, 74, 79, 132
Robinson, Prof. David M., 213
Roman civil law, 179
Roman letters dependent on Greek, 171
Roman Republic, lecture on, 77

Roman spirit and character, 221
Royce, Josiah, 100, 111
Rudelbach, Dr., 9

Sachs, Dr. Julius, 115, 118, 119, 124
Sage, Mrs. Russell, 162
St. Paul's, Fort Wayne, 14, 22; chimes of, 23
St. Peter's at Rome, 192
San Giovanni, Dr. E., his Latin verse, 176-178
Saxer, Director, at Fort Wayne, 33
Saxon Lutheran emigrants, 29, 43; churches, 44
Scanning Latin verse, 170, 171
Schick, Rector, 34, 86, 91
Schumann, Clara W., 68
Schweidnitz, 4; gymnasium at, 5
Scott, Prof. John A., 105, 213, 253, 257
Scott, Sir Walter, 83
Seminar, Classical, at Berlin, 62; Greek, at Baltimore, 101 et seq., 108; Latin, at University Heights, 203 et seq.
Settlers and settlements, near Fort Wayne, 16, 40; in Wisconsin, 141
Seyffarth, Dr. Gustavus, 128
Seymour, Prof. Thomas D., of Yale, 213
Shear, Dr. Theodore Leslie, 213
Sihl, a Swiss river, 3
Sihler, Christian, M.D., the author's brother, studies in Berlin, 56; fellow of Johns Hopkins, 99
Sihler, Christian George, the author's grandsire, 3
Sihler, Elizabeth, 53
Sihler, Emily B., the author's wife, 121 et seq., 159; death of, 260
Sihler, Ernest G., 13; spelling-lessons and early schooling, 19 et seq.; secretary of Greek seminar at Johns Hopkins, 103; Ph.D.,

there, 111; assists Dr. Drisler, 126; marriage, 128; first son, 132
Sihler, Frederick, 3
Sihler, Gotthold, 4
Sihler, Robert von, 79
Sihler, Rev. Dr. William, the author's father, 4 et seq.; Ph.D., 7; one of the founders of Lutheranism in the Middle West, 10; his marriage, 11; founder of theological seminary in Fort Wayne, 16; his study, 24; mode of education, 39; his death, 135; book-fund in his memory, 146
Silesia, 67, 79
Skating, 37
Smith, Dr. Charles Forster, 76, 78
Socrates, 75
Sorrento, 187 et seq.
Sparta, State socialism of, 142; Aristotle on Spartan constitution, 144
Spurgeon, Rev. Charles, 82
Stoddard, Prof. Francis Hovey, 150
Stover at Yale, 163
Strabo, 68, 252
Stub, Hans Gerhard, 47
Sweet, Prof. L. M., 239
Swimming, 35 et seq.; in Mississippi, 50; Rhine, 69; Tiber, 193
Sylvester, Prof., 99, 112
Symmachus, 245

Tacitus, 85, 169, 178
Taft, Lorado, 95
Teaching, requisites for, 118; tact in, 158, 167 et seq.
Terence, 172
Tertullian, 241
Testimonium Animae, 221
Thucydides, 60, 90, 102, 126
Tieck, 8
Tischendorf, 78
Trier, farmer, 40

INDEX

Tyrrell, R. Y., 209; and Purser, 229; letter from, 230

Überweg, 75
Uhler, Philip R., 106
Ulster, 83
University Heights, 158, 160, 161
University Place Church, 157

Values, spiritual and aesthetic, 219
Vergil, graduate study of, 181
Vermont, 39
Via Appia, 195
Via Latina, 188
Victoria, Crown Princess, 56, 63
Voigt, Prof., 77

Wackernagel, 20 *et seq.*
Walther, Dr. C. F. W., 44, 48
Warren, Prof. Minton, 191
Wars, 250; beginning of the World War, 251

Washington's Birthday, 36
Washington Square, courses at, before the removal to University Heights, 157 *et seq.*
Wayne, Anthony, 13
"Weltgeist," Hegel's, 218
Westminster Abbey, 81
Wheeler, John H., 103
White, Horace, 125
Whitehouse, Frederick Cope, 123
Whitney, William Dwight, 92
Wiese, Dr. Ludwig, 73, 78
Wight, Dr. Carol, 188
Wilamowitz, 131
William I at corner window, 64; birthday, 65, 78
Wilson, Woodrow, 153
Wyneken, Pastor, 10

Zeittafeln, Fischer's *Römische*, 231
Zeller, Eduard, 69
Zosimus, 245